# *James* FLETCHER-WATSON

## A CELEBRATION OF THE ARTIST'S LIFE AND WORK

GILL FLETCHER-WATSON

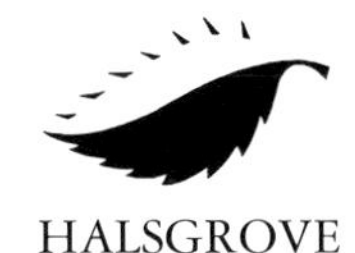

HALSGROVE

*For all James's painting friends*

## ACKNOWLEDGEMENTS

My thanks to Simon Butler for asking me to compile this book,
and to Josephine Neil and Bishop Peter Nott for their input.

First published in Great Britain 2007



British Library Cataloguing-in-Publication Data
**A CIP record for this title is available from the British Library**

ISBN 978 1 84114 615 7

**HALSGROVE**
Halsgrove House, Ryelands Industrial Estate
Bagley Road, Wellington, Somerset TA21 9PZ
Tel: 01823 653777  Fax: 01823 216796
email: sales@halsgrove.com  website: www.halsgrove.com

Printed and bound by D'Auria Industrie Grafiche Spa, Italy

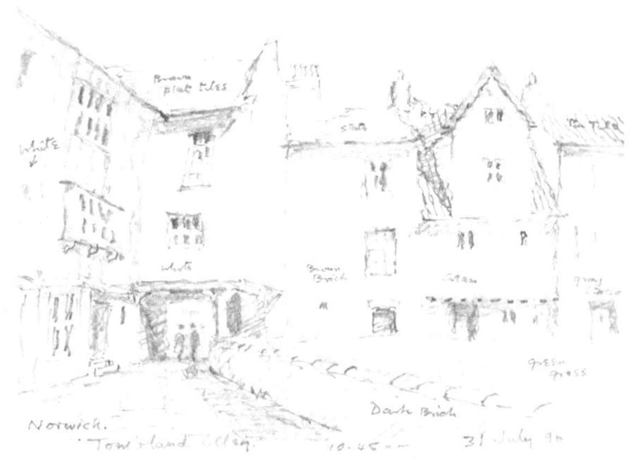

# CONTENTS

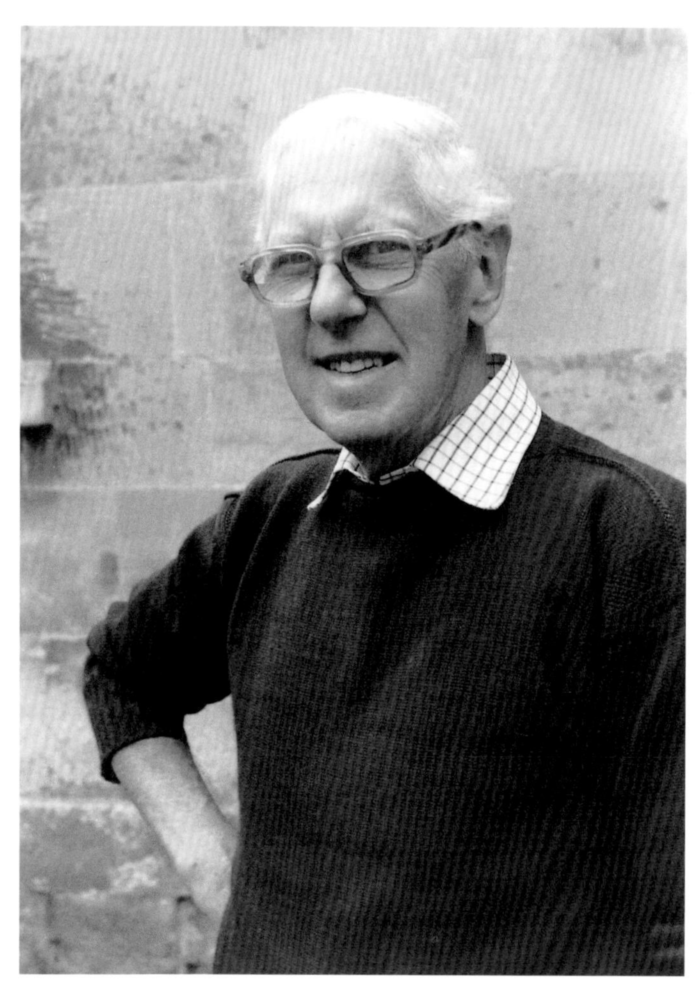

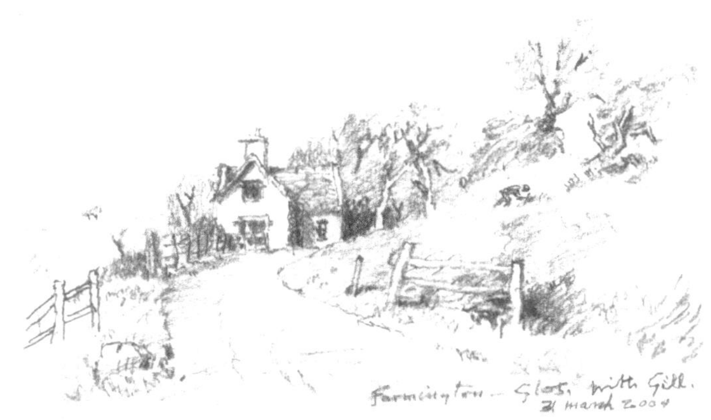

# FOREWORD

I have been asked to write a Foreword to this lovely book of James's paintings, but that is not easy – as a modern American painter said in another context, 'If you could say it in words there would be no need to paint'.

James was wonderful – a truly great man – and his watercolours reflect that greatness as a painter, as well as his appreciation of the beautiful world in which we live. I am sure the paintings and sketches will bring back happy memories of times spent with him, or of places he painted, or an enjoyment of the great gift he shared with so many.

His enthusiasm was infectious – he wanted to carry on the tradition and skill of painting in pure watercolours, and to share with many people the challenge and enjoyment of doing this. He is still, through his paintings, a very real presence.

*Gill Fletcher-Watson*

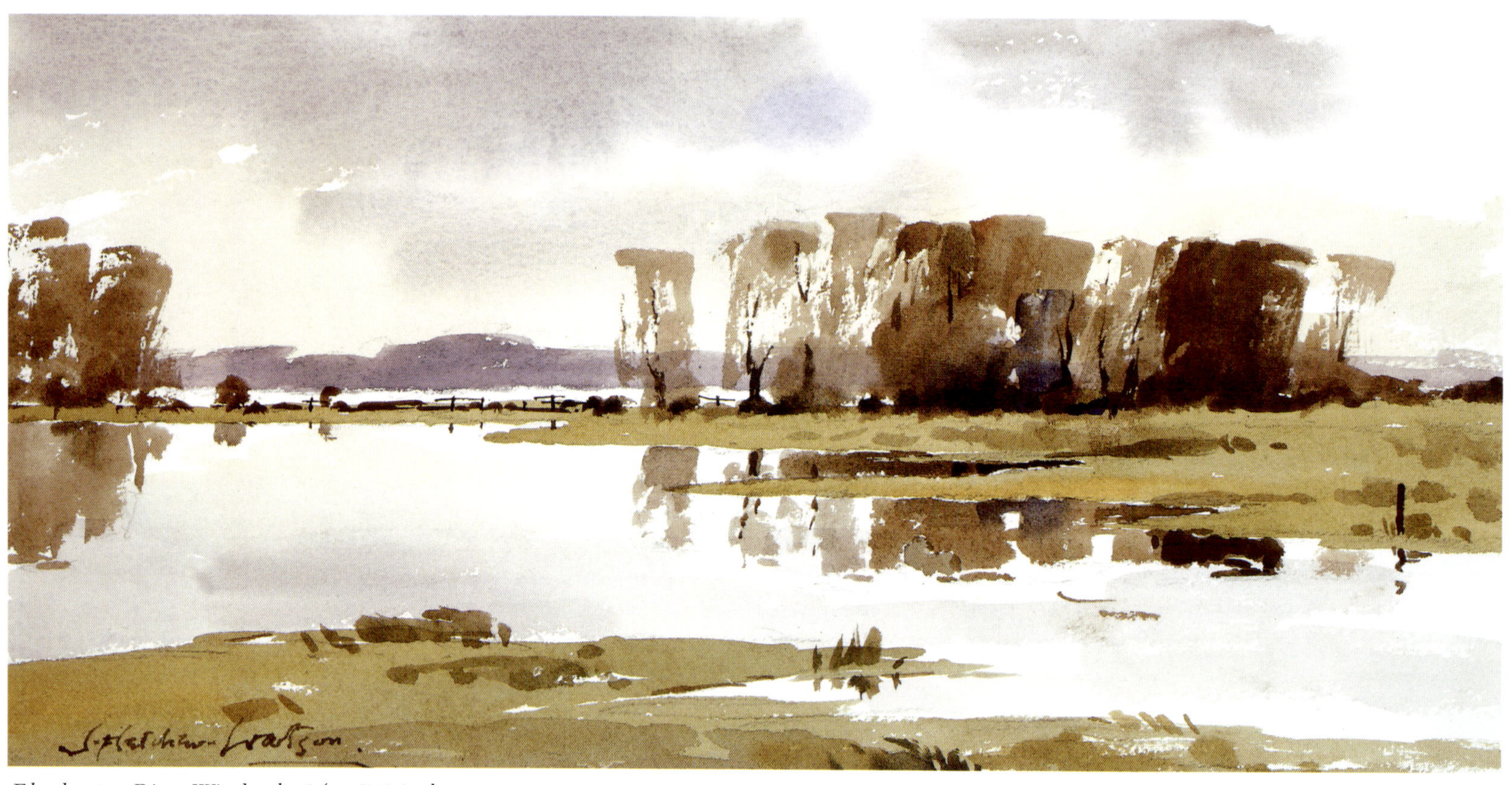

*Floodwater, River Windrush  14 x 9.5 inches*

# INTRODUCTION

James's passion for painting was apparent from an early age, in fact it could be said that artistic ability was in his genes.  His grandfather, Pilfold Fletcher-Watson RBA, was also a professional painter.  In 1888, following the gold rush, he joined other watercolour artists from Europe to form an art society and became the first President of the Australian Academy of Art.  He painted in Australia for fourteen years, and a number of his pictures are in the permanent collection at the Russell Library, Sydney.

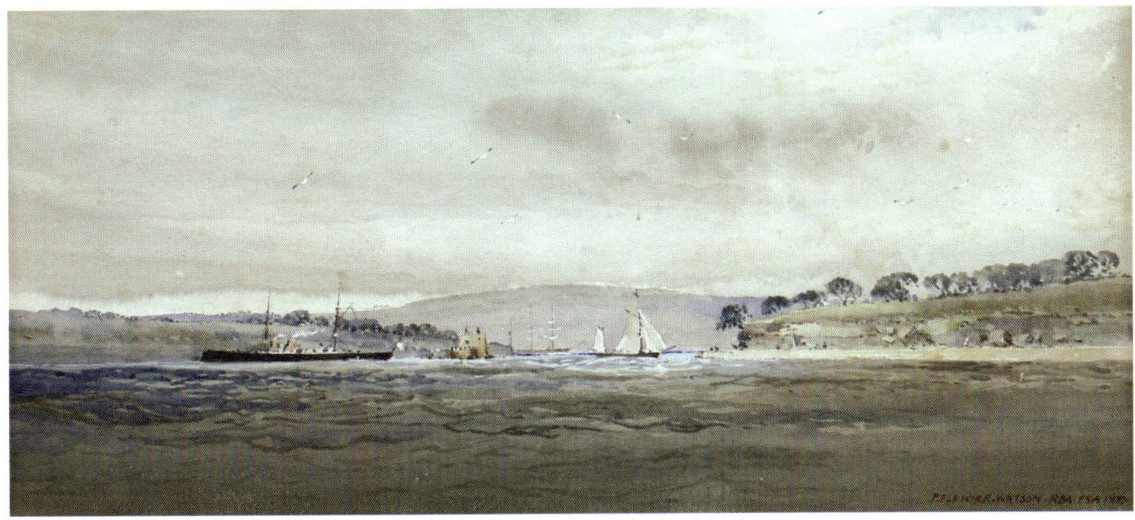

*Sydney Harbour 1889, by Pilfold Fletcher-Watson RBA*

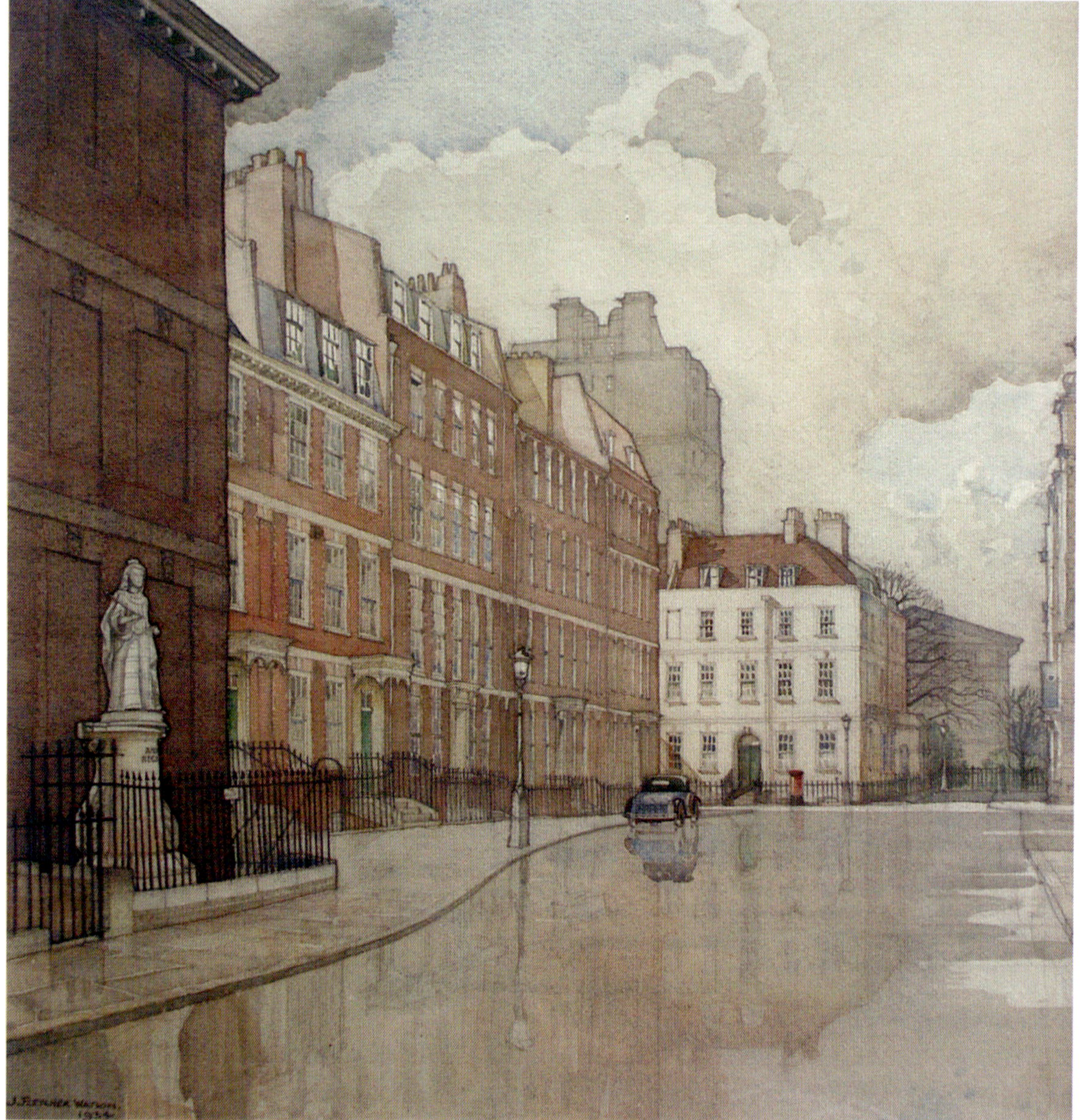

*Queen Anne's Gate – James's first painting to be exhibited in the Royal Academy.*

James spent much of his early years in Norfolk, where he was influenced by the Norwich school of painters, who rejoiced in capturing the light and drama of the East Anglian skies.  He was an architect by profession, having trained under Edwin Lutyens and Albert Richardson, then joined Maurice Webb and Partners in London where he was offered a partnership.  Painting, however, remained close to his heart and he had his first picture accepted by the Royal Academy at the age of twenty-one (see above).  He was also awarded an Honourable Mention for his picture of Norwich in the Paris Salon.

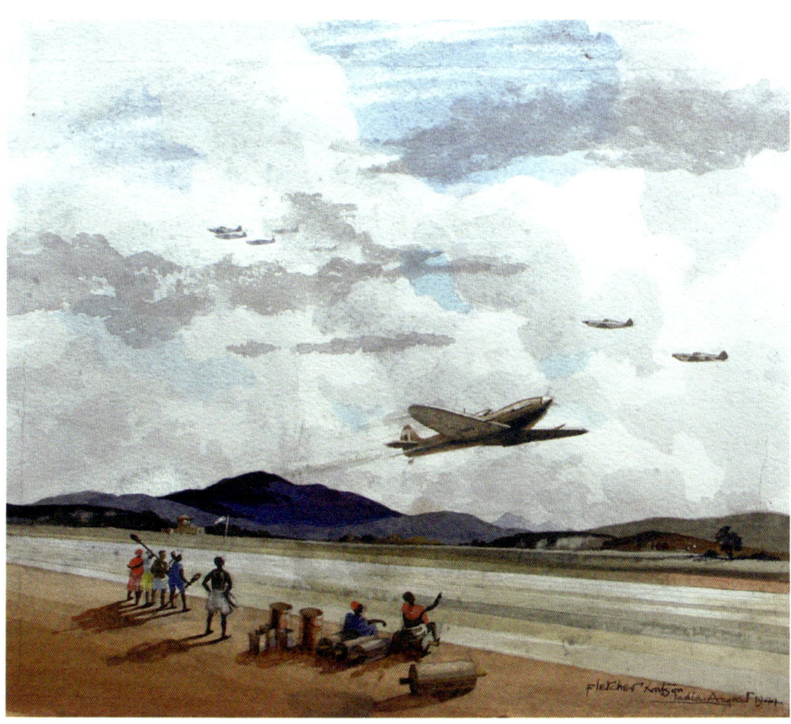

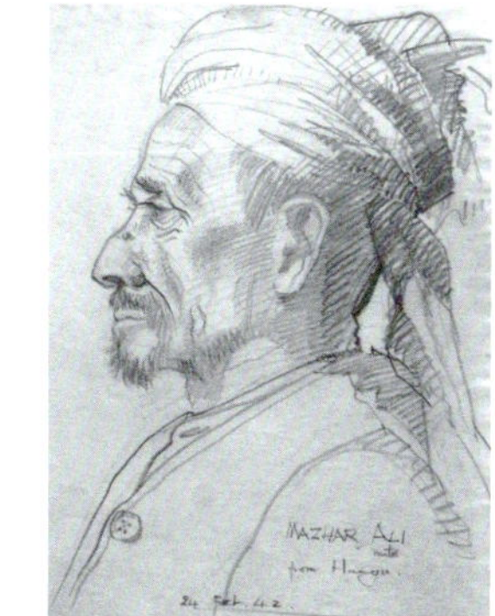

His skills as an architect played what proved to be a critical role during the Second World War, when James was despatched to India as one of the first emergency commissioned officers of the Royal Engineers, to oversee defences and camouflage. He was chosen by General Slim to design forward runways into Burma with the 14th Army, and the strategically vital Imphal aerodrome. He sketched and painted wherever he went and wrote an account of his experiences before he returned home in 1945, which were reproduced in his book, *Soldier Artist in Wartime India*, published in 2002.

After the war he became well known for his architectural work in Norfolk – Bawdeswell Church is already a Listed Building, (the first post-war church building to be listed Grade I), and others are under consideration, the Bishop's House in Norwich being one of the most exceptional. He began his own architectural practice in London in 1959, where his commissions included designs for Coutts Bank, Dashwood village and Nottingham University, where his famous library ceiling was described in a review as 'a triumph of geometry' – it was a tribute to his design genius that it was, in fact, designed by eye!

Throughout his architectural career James remained passionate about maintaining the tradition of pure watercolour painting. He was a disciple of the old masters of the medium, such as John Constable, J.M.W. Turner, De Wint and Thomas Girtin. 'They have shown us the way,' he used to say and so he continued the tradition of these great painters he admired, not slavishly copying their work but 'absorbing a lot of their enthusiasm and the way they set about finding a subject and painting it'. Like these early masters, James would always carry a sketch book to record a quick impression of a view if time was limited, making notes about colour and light, then creating a beautiful painting from his sketch in the studio at home. However, he was a firm believer in painting 'live'. To quote from his book, *The Magic of Watercolour,* 'I advocate plenty of painting on the spot as well as from sketches, so that we may learn all about nature's moods and acquire knowledge of how to paint shadows, cloudy skies, rocky foregrounds, distant woods and mountains and all the thousand and one items that make a landscape.'

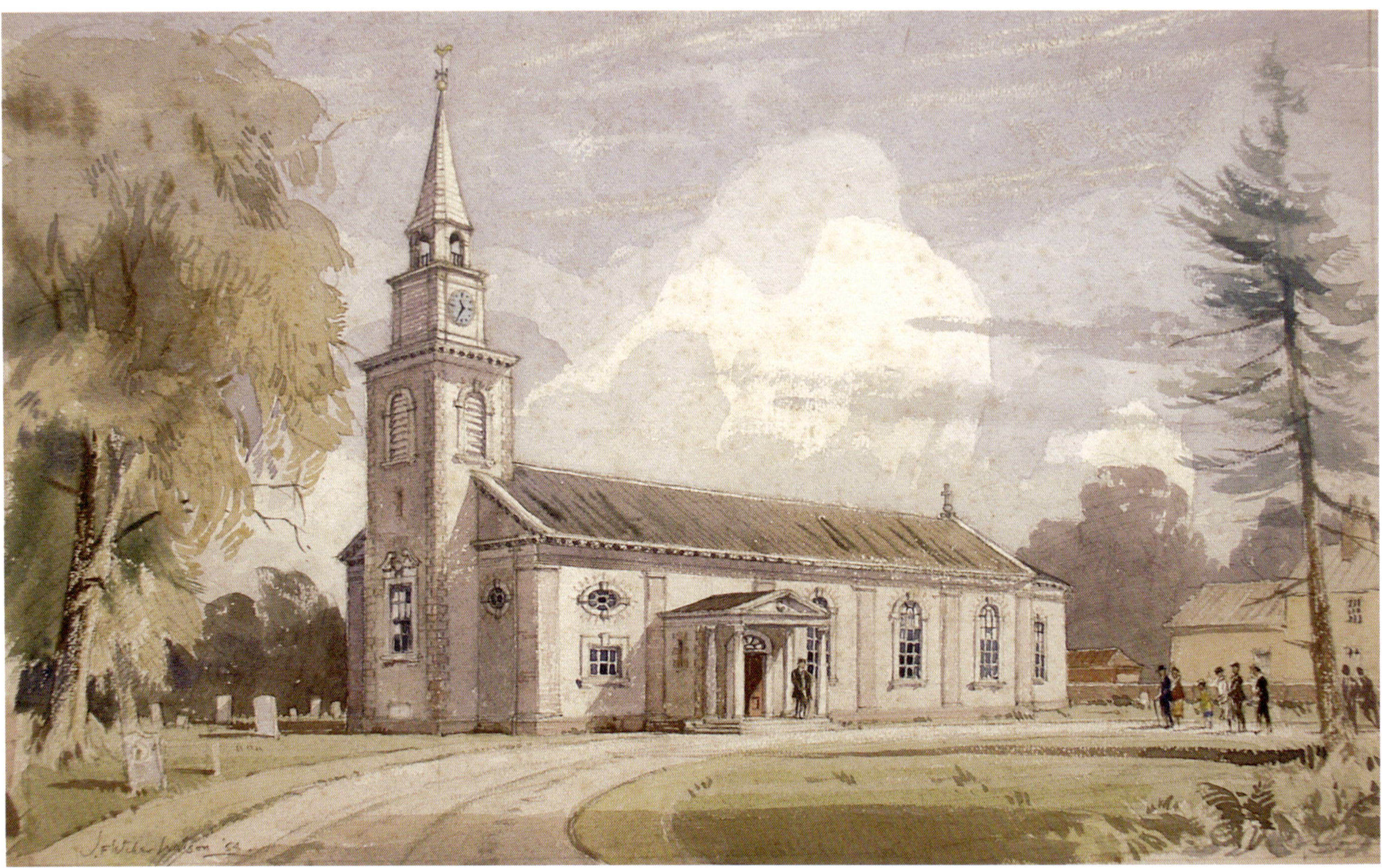

*Bawdeswell Church, Norfolk – James designed the church at Bawdeswell in the 1950s. This picture is his visualisation of the finished project, painted while building was still in progress.  The church was dedicated in 1957 and was listed Grade I during his lifetime.*

Throughout his life, James enjoyed the company of fellow artists who shared his passion.  He met Edward Seago soon after leaving school and spent a happy time with Alfred Munnings in his early years.

He was a friend of Rowland Hilder and shared a warm friendship with Edward Wesson from the time they were both elected to the Royal Institute of Painters in Watercolour in 1952, and subsequently to The Royal Society of British Artists, as well as serving together for many years on the R.I. Council.  It was Edward who was the chief influence in persuading him about the importance of his teaching role, and as James recorded in his Foreword to the Edward Wesson book (by Peter Slade, 2001): 'Edward asked to see me when he was in Guildford Hospital following a stroke and begged me to take over his courses at Philipps House, Dinton.'

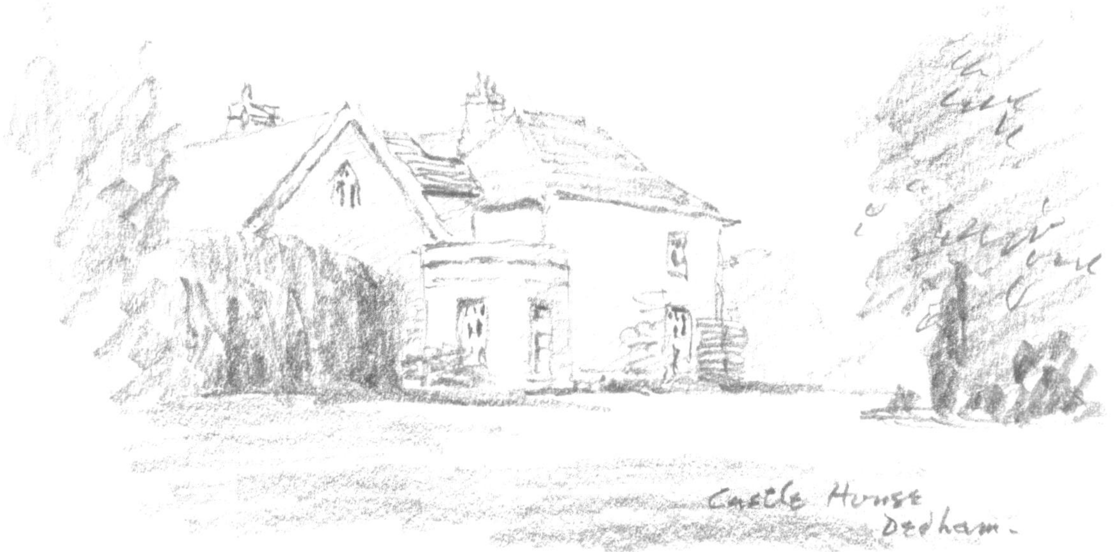



*Alfred Munnings's House*
*As a promising young artist, James was invited to spend a day at Dedham with Alfred Munnings. Having knocked on the door of Castle House, he was surprised to have it flung open by the great man saying, 'Be a good fellow and take these letters to the post for me.' Things got better after his return, and they drove off together in an open car, visiting various pubs, sketching, and finally Munnings shaking his fist from the car at the modern painters who had recently taken up residence in the village. James enjoyed revisiting the house when teaching in Dedham.*

James had many pupils, though he never used the term, referring to them always as his 'painting friends'. The thrill of attending one of James's courses is described by one of these painting friends: 'There is inspiration in reading his books, excitement in watching his videos, but the real magic was to sit beside him and watch him paint. Those of us fortunate enough to witness this know that it was like listening to a live performance from a great musician.'

James may not have been a trained teacher, but he was definitely a natural and very gifted one. He imparted his knowledge generously and withheld nothing if he felt that it would help his fellow painters. That generosity in sharing both personal insights and hard-won professional techniques was noted and appreciated by many people. It is perhaps no coincidence that one of his best loved books is entitled *Watercolour Secrets*.

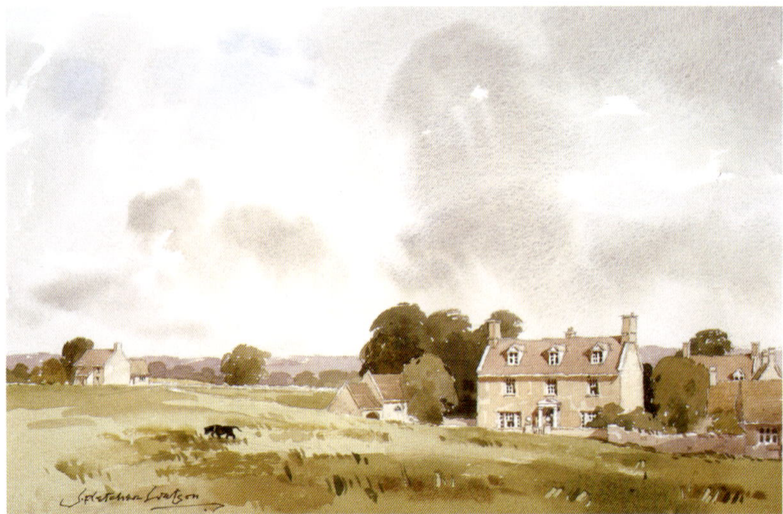

*Windrush House, 14 x 10 inches*

In 1964, James and his wife Gill moved to Gloucestershire where they established his Windrush Gallery in their home. Together they organised annual exhibitions in the gallery, and ran courses from Windrush, as well as in Wiltshire, Suffolk and abroad. The mountainous landscapes of Scotland and the Lake District were amongst his favourite subjects, but he was equally at home painting the grand East Anglian skies he knew from his youth, as well as the Cotswold cottages, barns and rivers near his home.

But he enjoyed painting many other parts of the world, holding one-man shows in Australia and America, and also in London. He was, of course, particularly fond of Venice where his architect's drawing skills made the most complex townscapes look effortless. In fact, it was a Venetian scene that featured in the last moments of his life. 'Help me to the bottom of the bed,' he said to Gill on the morning he died, 'so I can see that wonderful view of Venice.' Was it memory, imagination or a vision? No doubt a combination of all three, because he was a visionary, someone who saw beyond the reality that others perceived: he looked through and beyond the landscapes that he painted. It was not long after that beautiful moment that James died peacefully.

A large congregation celebrated his life in Windrush Church, during which his old friend Bishop Peter Nott said, 'James's passion was not just to paint: it was to communicate what he saw. He had a vocation to share his vision, to try by any means possible to tell others of the beauty he perceived in landscape and in buildings.

'James often spoke of the influence of Girtin and Bonington – two eighteenth century painters who died in their twenties. Because he learned

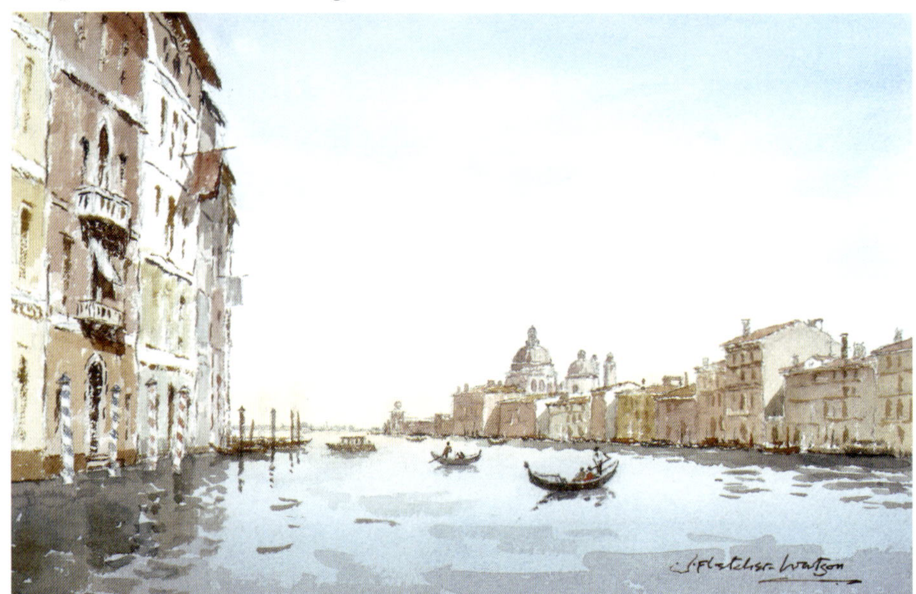

*The Grand Canal, Venice 18.5 x 12.5 inches*

from such gifted but very young men, I have wondered if that is one reason why he always communicated so well with the young.  Another reason is, of course, his simplicity: his unselfconscious enthusiasm.  The first time I painted with James, we went to Morston Quay in North Norfolk.  We sat beside each other and he gently guided me; we spent some time finding the right viewpoint, and then he sat in silence and looked long and hard.  While he painted he paused often, and he looked and looked, and muttered, and told me what he saw and how to tackle the problem.  It was as if, like me, he had never seen this landscape before.  Of course, he had painted it many times, and I realised then that every painting, every sketch, was a new beginning, a new adventure for him: fresh excitement; new every morning.

'He always spent a long time looking, and thinking about what he saw.  Painting with him was an exercise in meditation as well as in techniques of drawing and painting.  He was really a contemplative, who looked and strove towards a vision that lay beyond the landscape that was in front of him.  Through that careful looking he taught others to look.  Even if we never learned to paint well, at least we learned to look, which is amongst the most precious gifts to us.  Like all true contemplatives he was always on a journey, always seeking, always learning, always asking questions.'

James Fletcher-Watson touched so many people's lives and his loss is felt by all of those who knew him and learned from him.  But he has left behind a rich and beautiful legacy that will be inherited by future generations.  Many examples of his most inspiring paintings and sketches have been reproduced in this commemorative book which celebrates a remarkable lifetime of work.

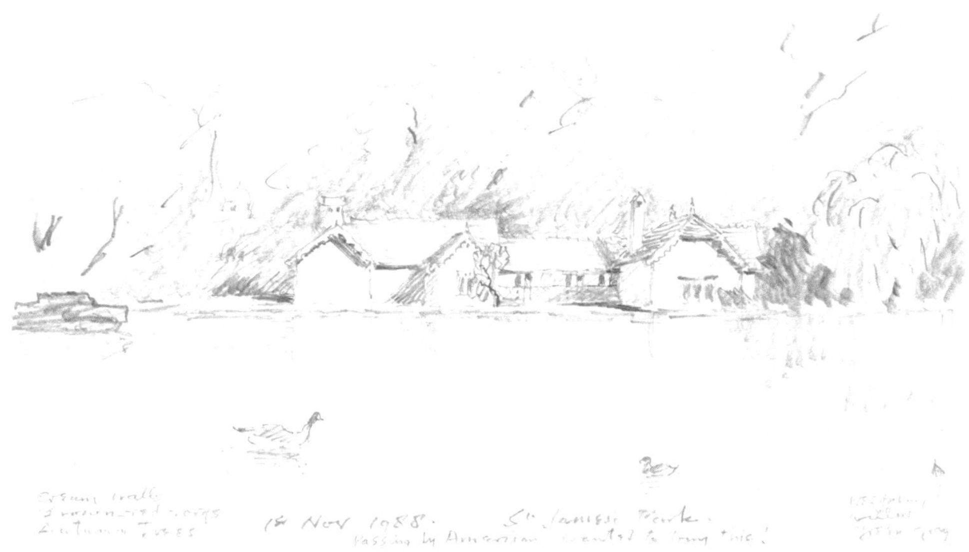

*Duck Cottage, St James's Park, London, designed by John Burgess Watson, James's uncle.*

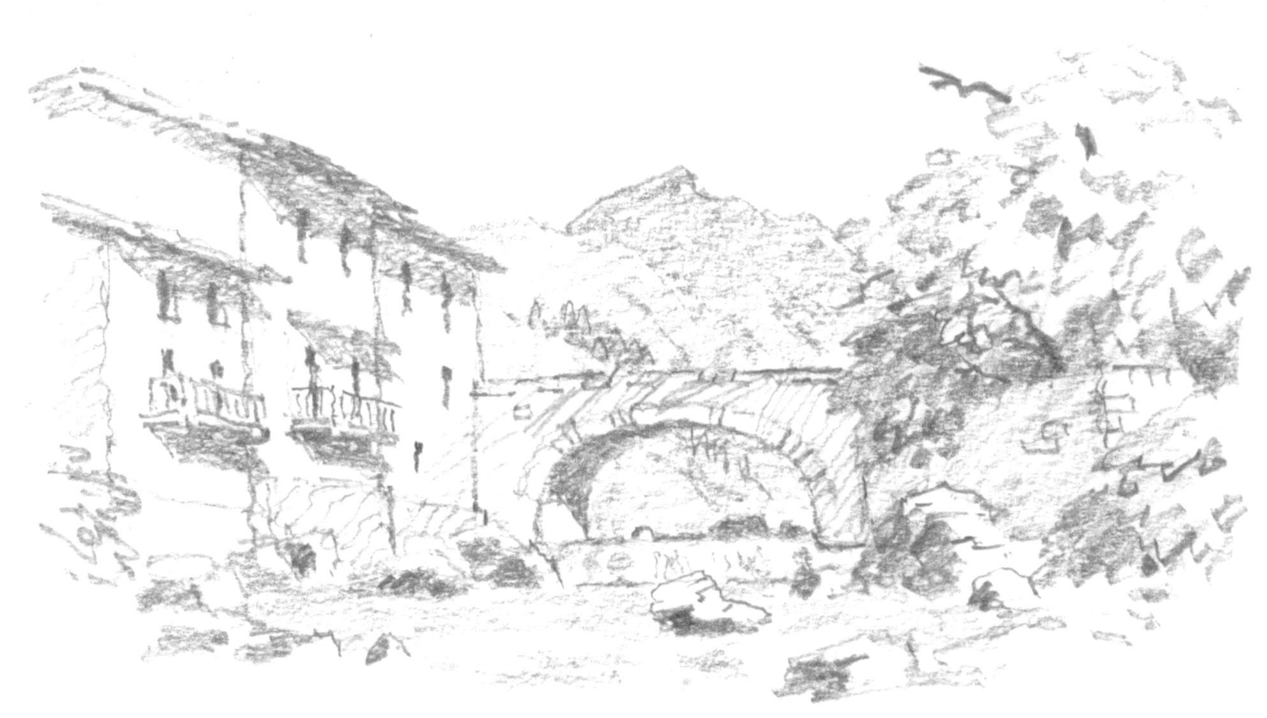

*James once said, 'When I paint landscapes
from nature I am always observing something
fresh every time I go out to paint.  It may be a
beautiful new effect of light and shadow, or I stumble
across a new way of painting a sky.  It is always
absorbing and always something to enjoy.'*

# EARLY PAINTINGS

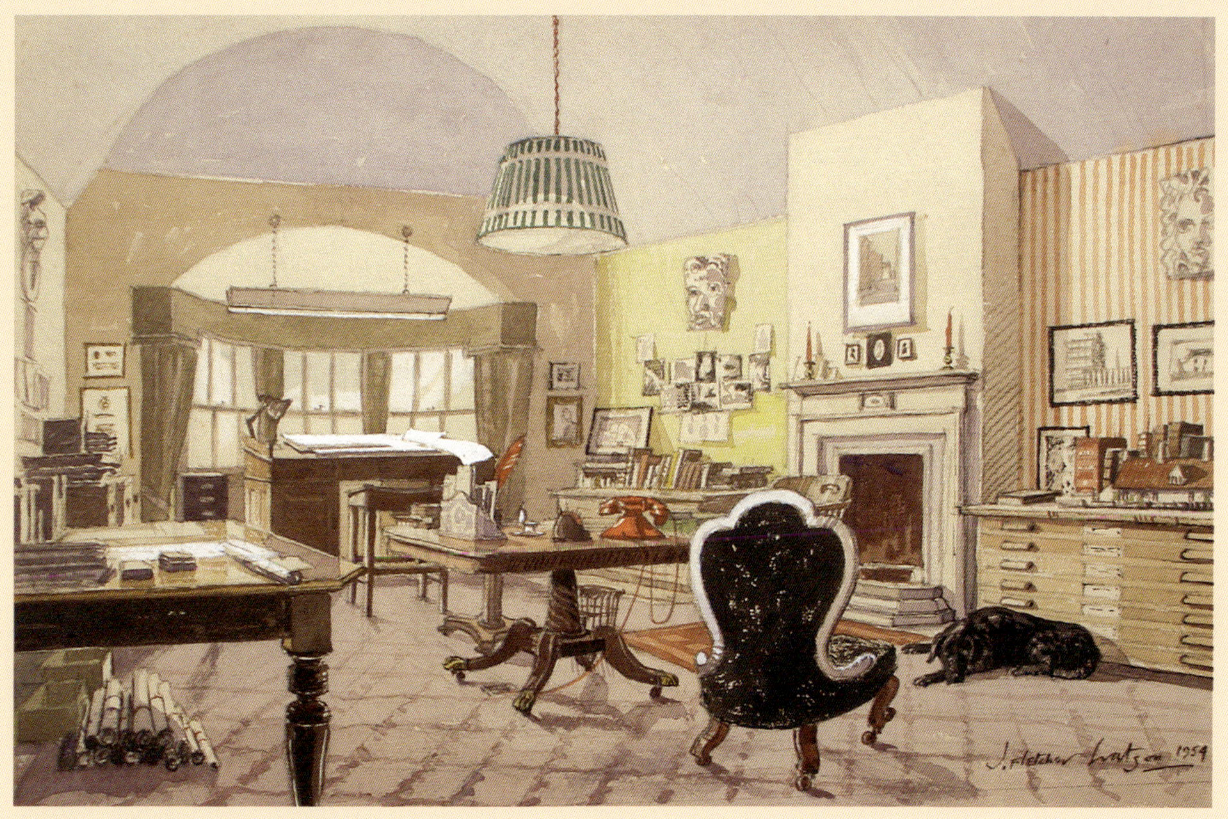

*James's architect's office at Pulls Ferry, Norwich*

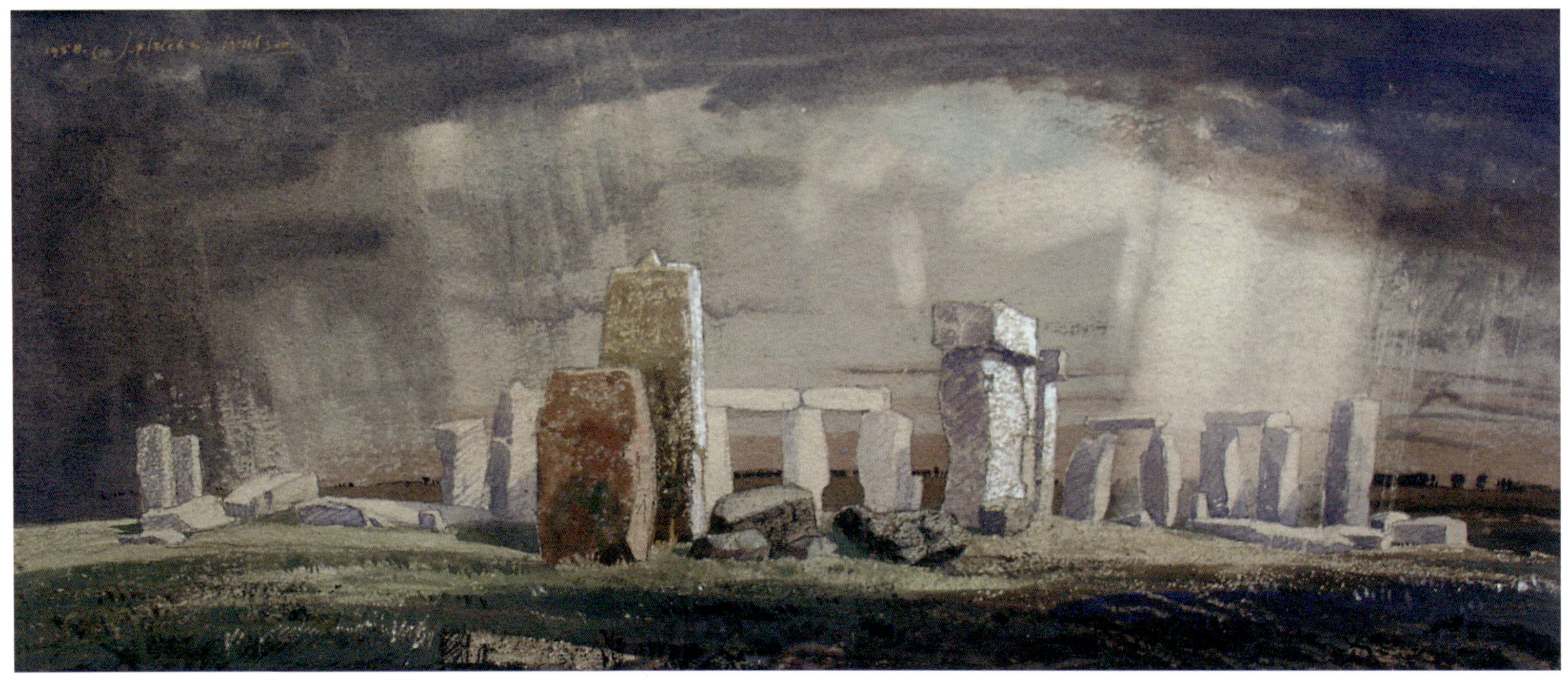

*Stonehenge  14 x 11 inches*
*Painted in the early 1960s when it was possible to picnic amongst the stones and sense solitude and mystery*

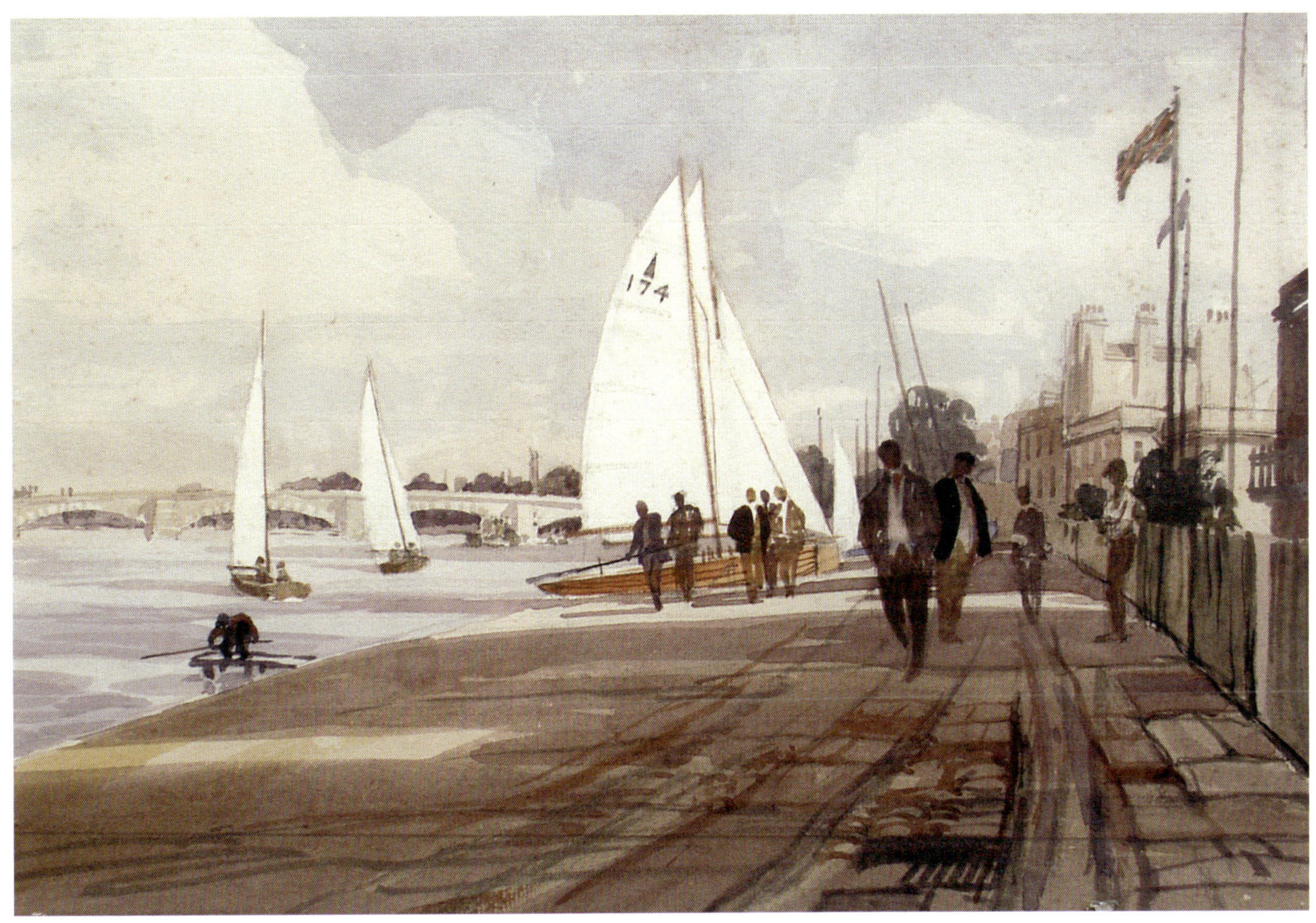

*Sailing Boats, Putney  16 x 12 inches*

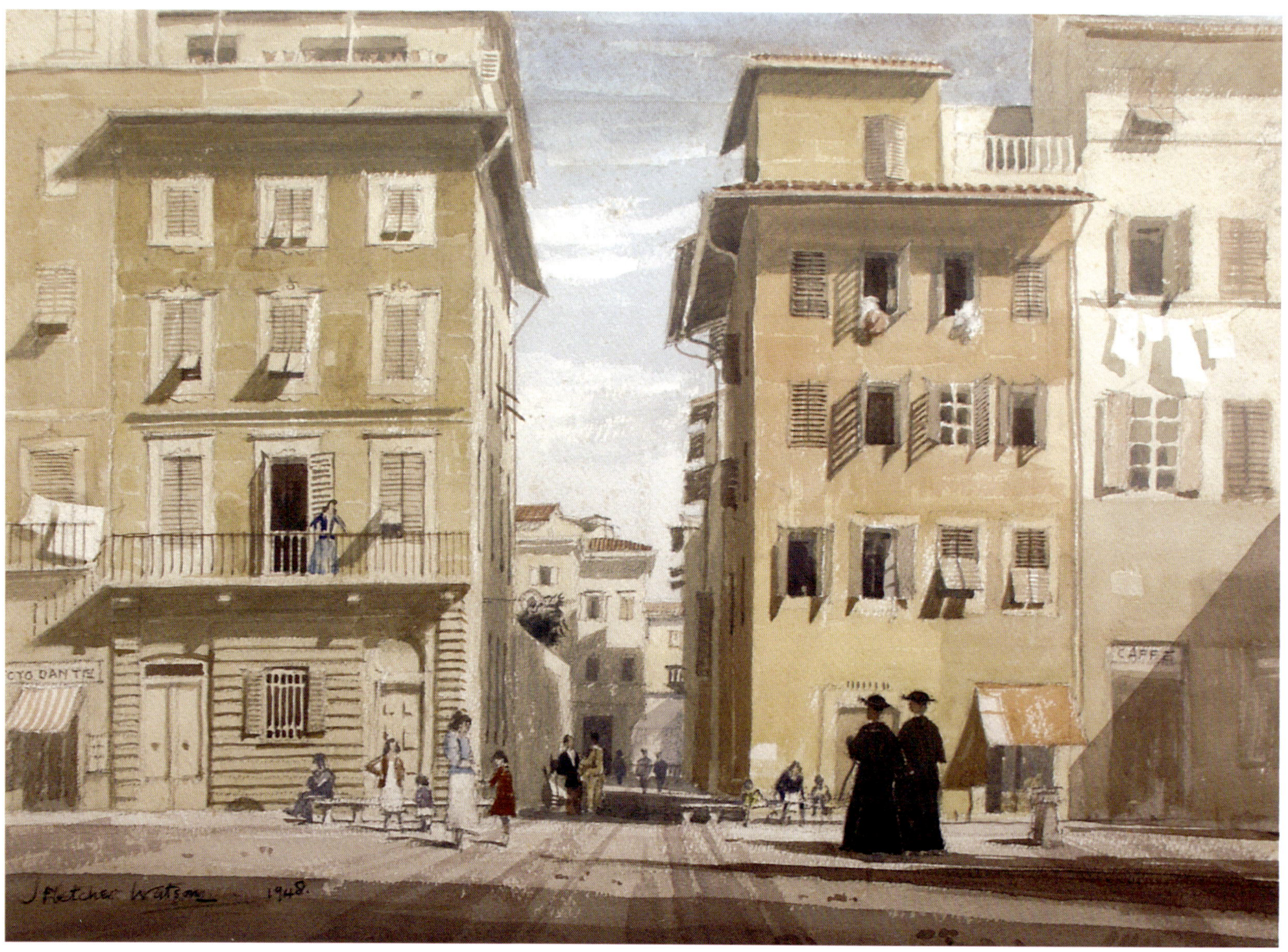

*Florence, 1950s  18.5 x 13 inches*

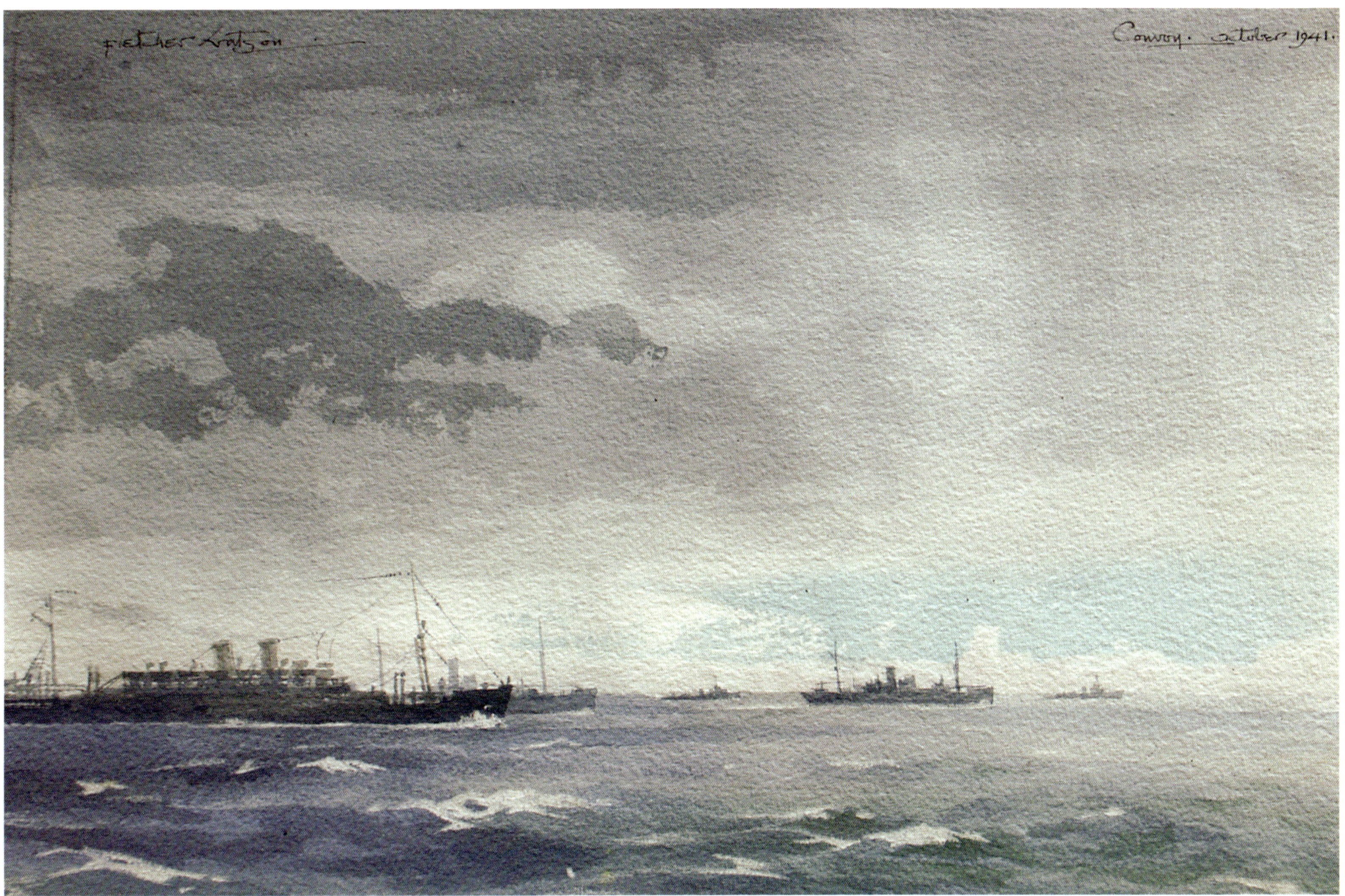


*The convoy in which James sailed to India, 1941   16 x 10 inches*

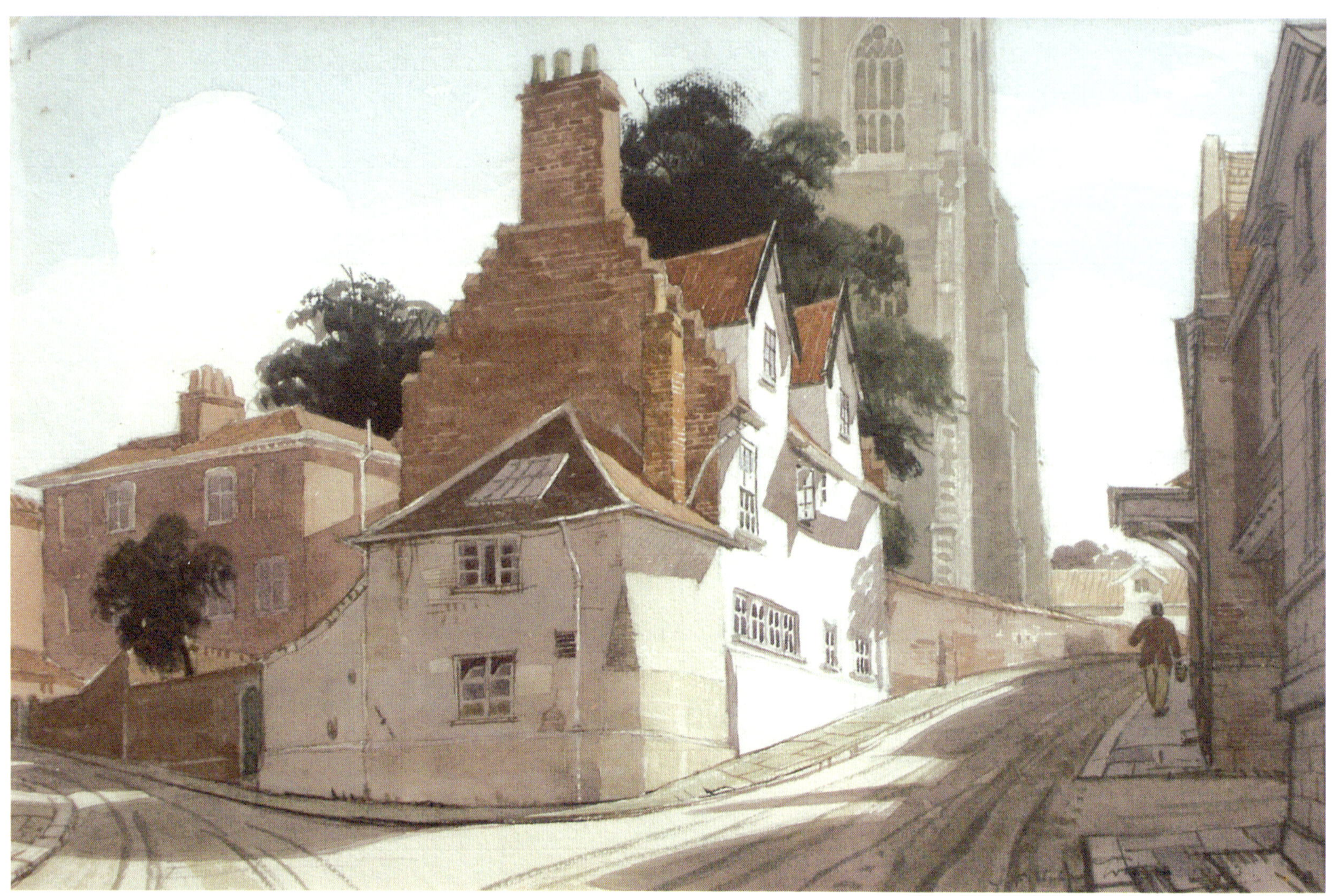

*Cow Hill, Norwich  14 x 10 inches*

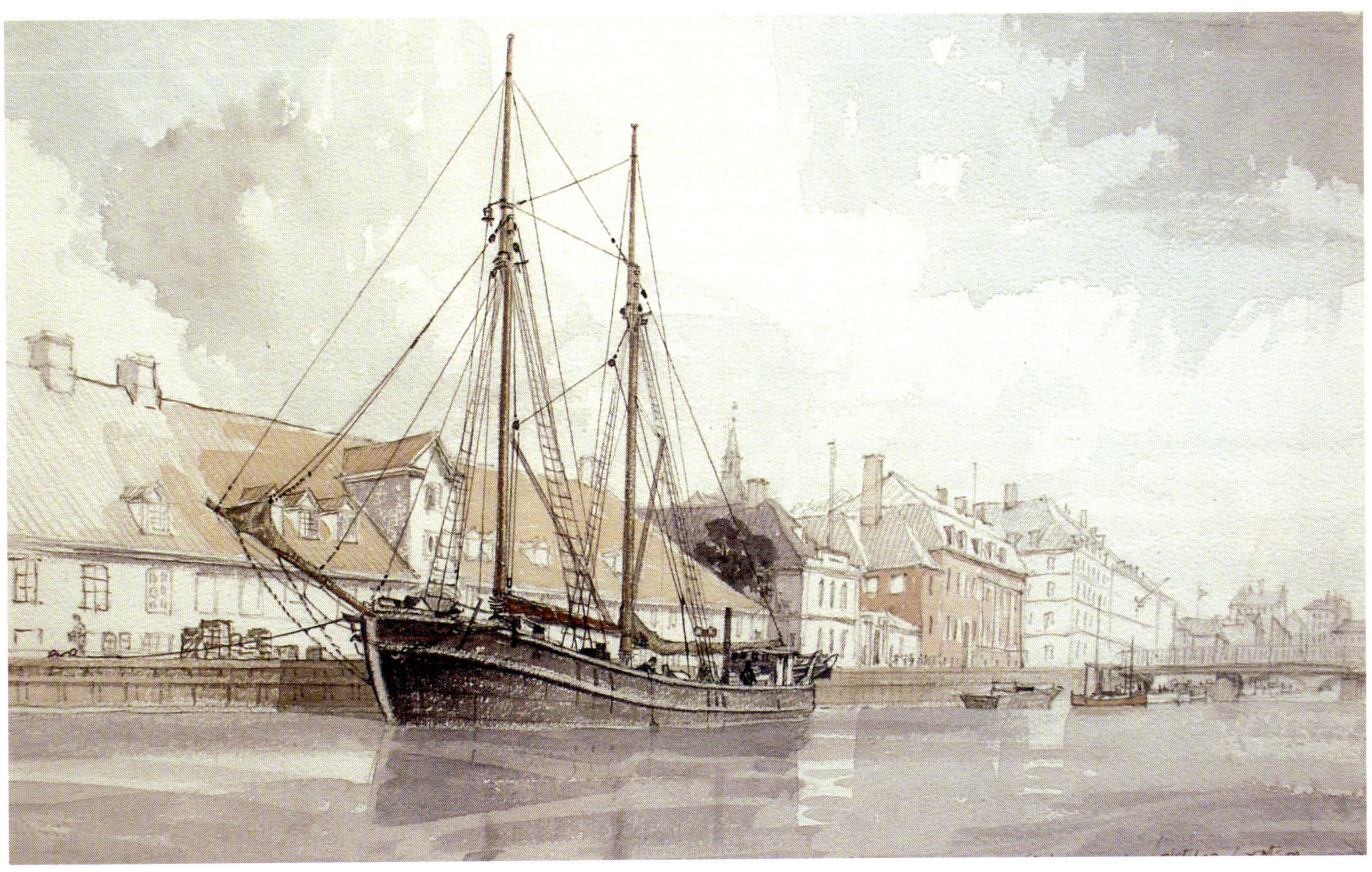

*Copenhagen (unfinished)  18.5 x 12.5 inches*

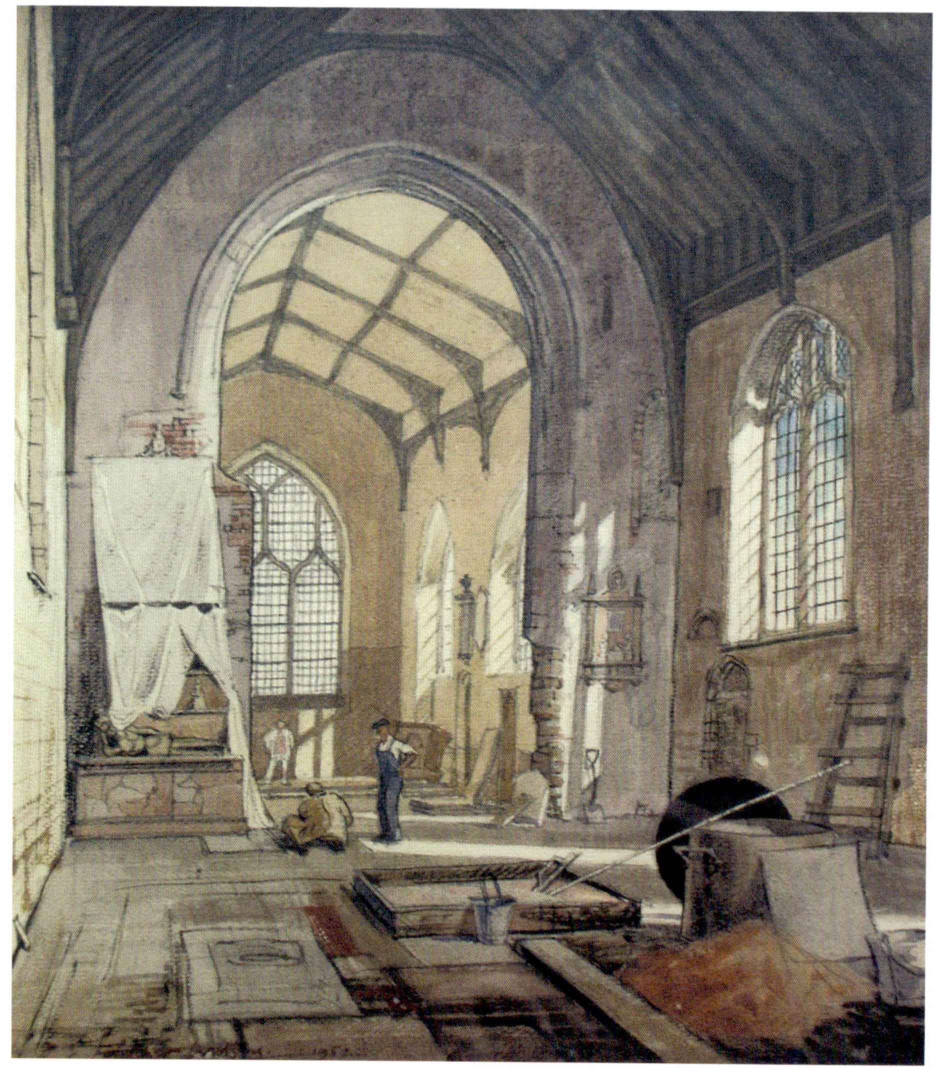

*St Simon and St Jude's Church, Norwich  12 x 14.5 inches*

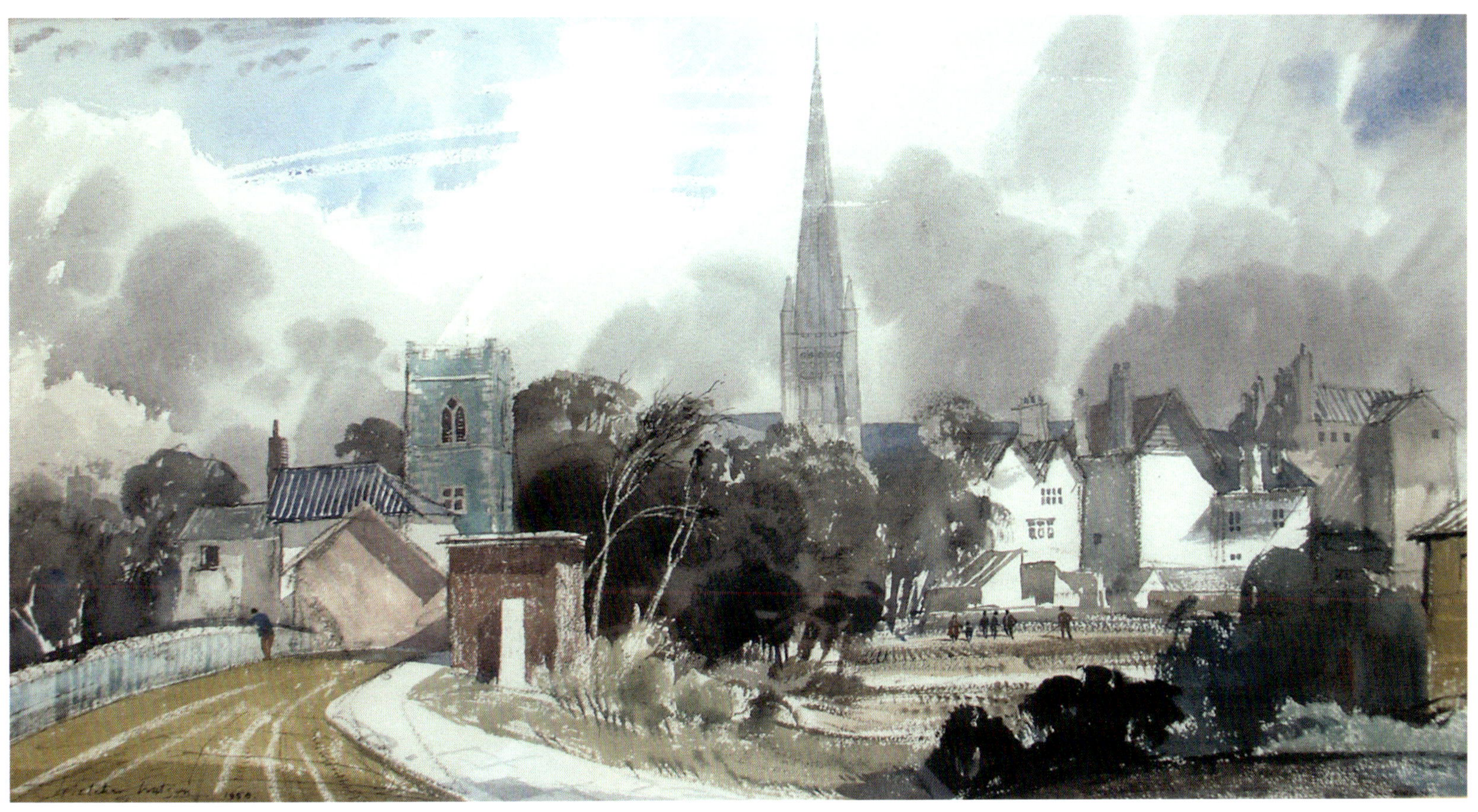

*Norwich, 1958   27 x 15 inches*
*This painting received a Special Award at the Paris Salon*

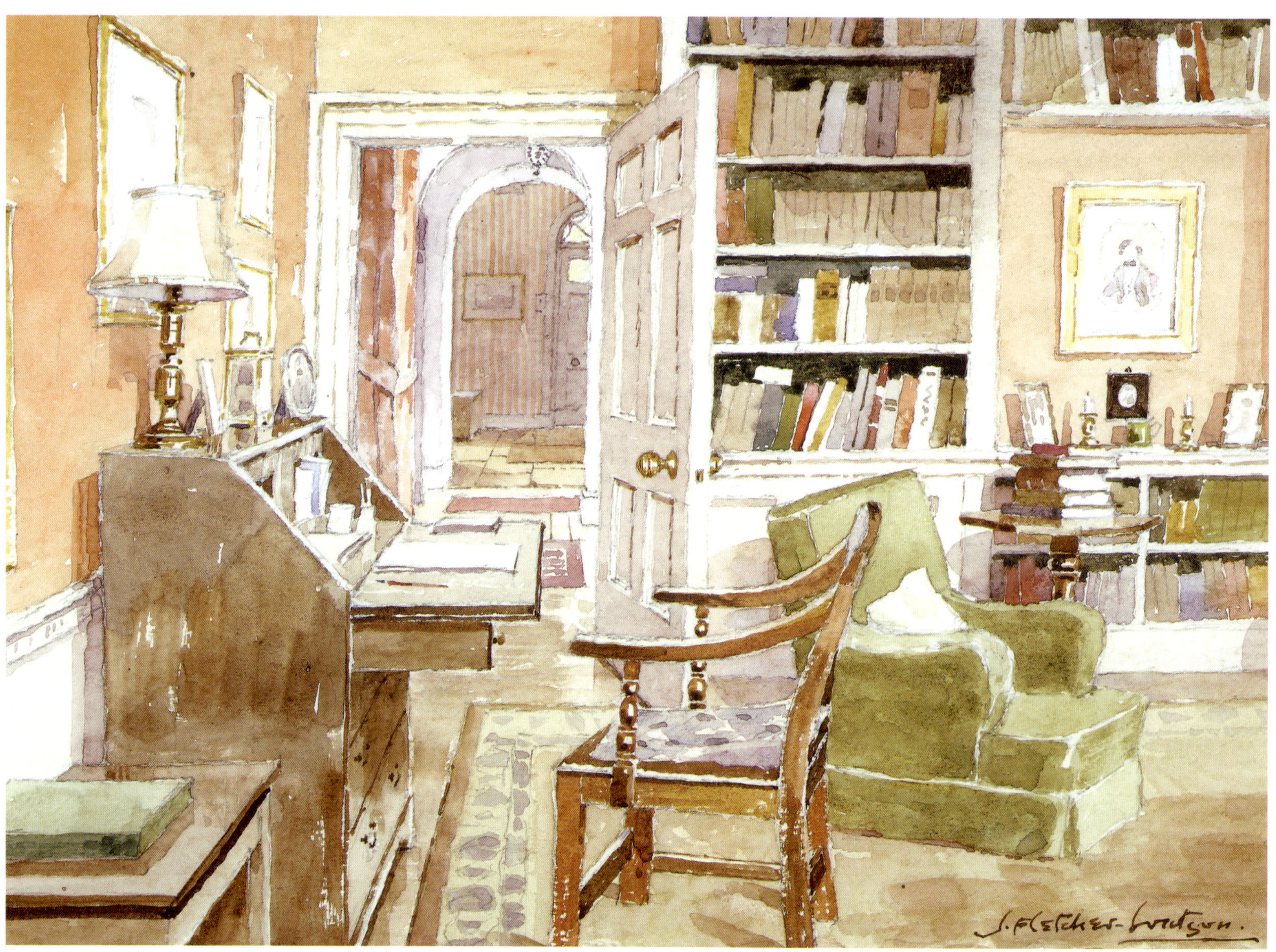

*Interior, Windrush House   18.5 x 12.5 inches*

# PAINTING IN BRITAIN

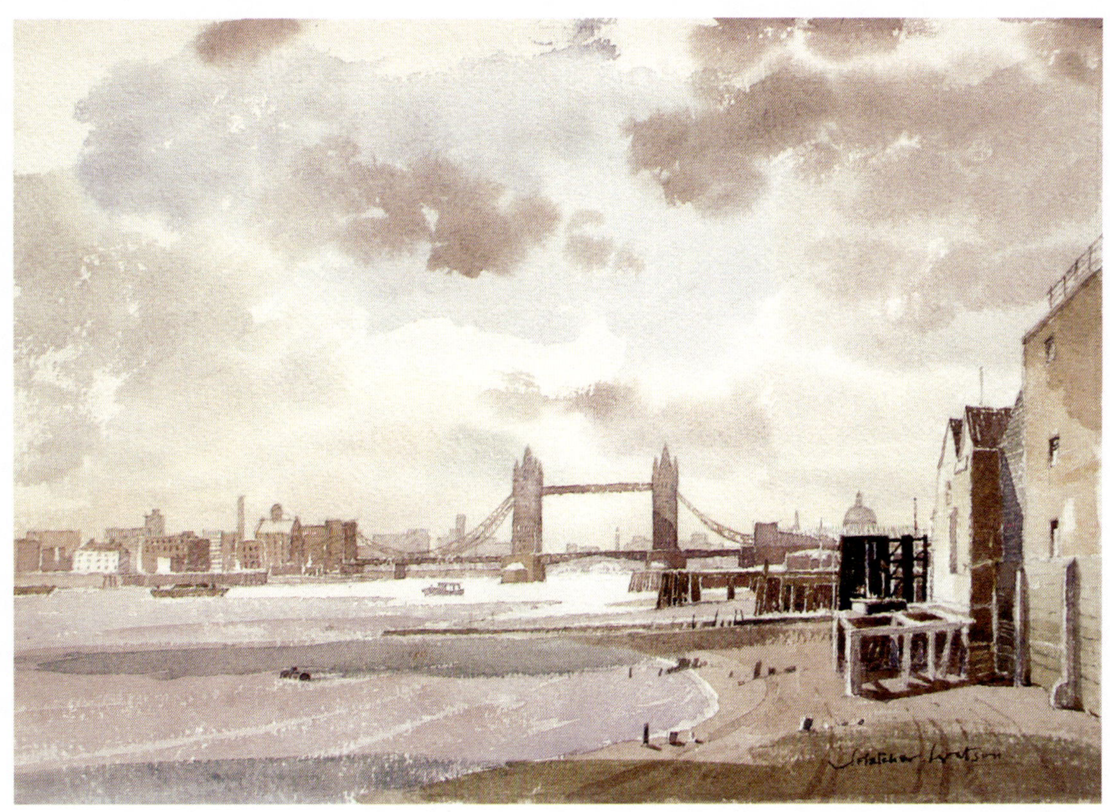

*Tower Bridge, London   15.5 x 12.5 inches*

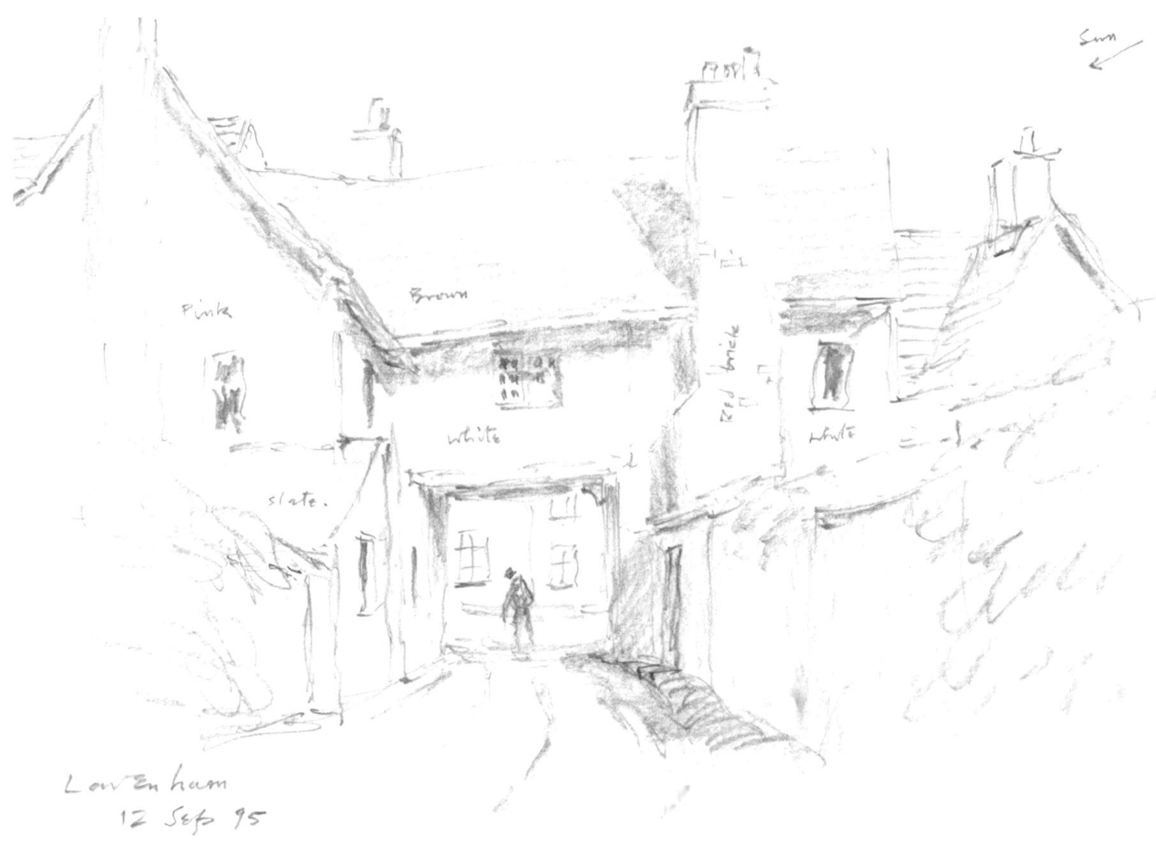
Pink
Brown
Red brick
Sun
slate.
white
white
white
Lavenham
12 Sep 95

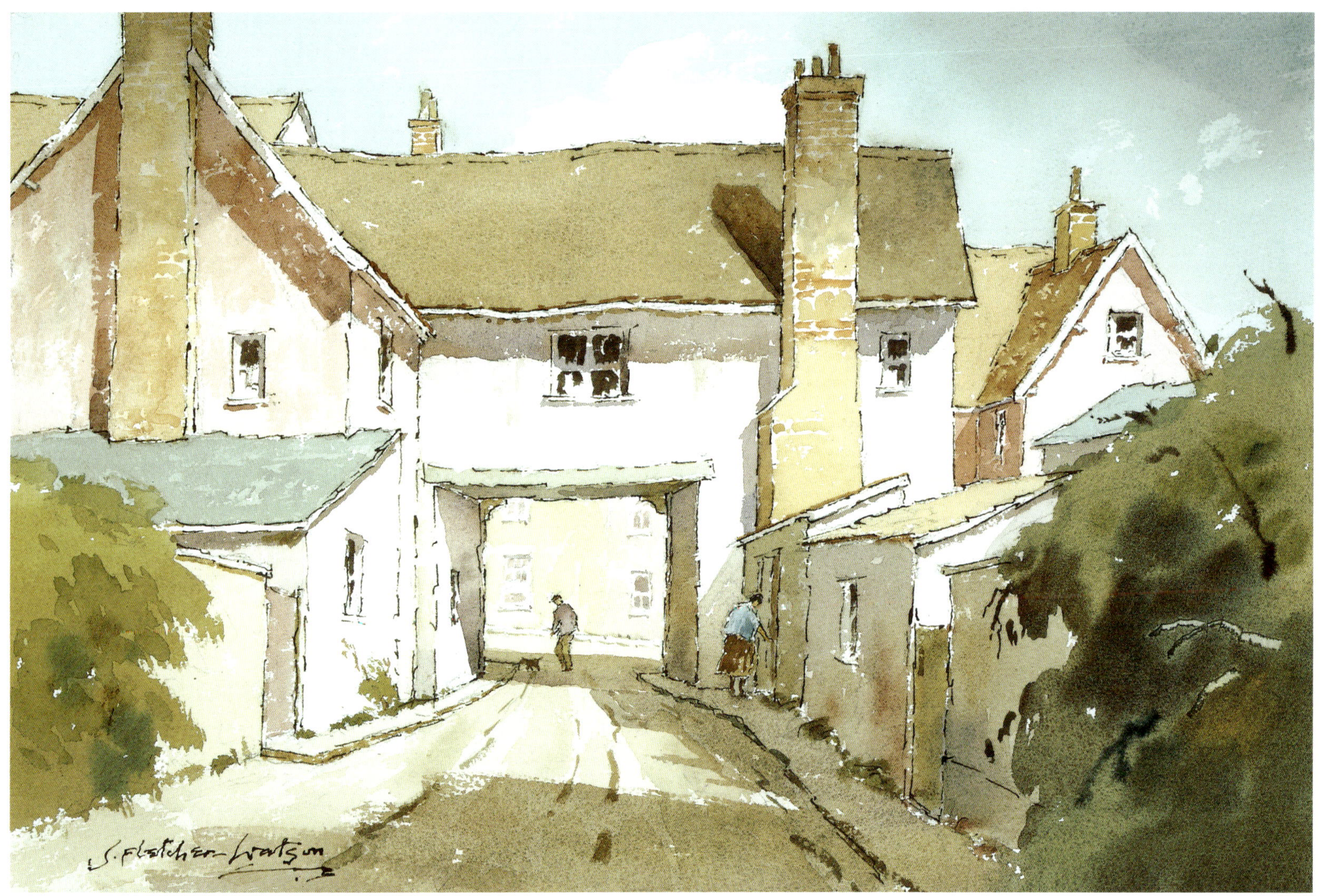

*Backyard, Lavenham  9.5 x 6 inches*
*James loved exploring the unaltered backs of buildings*

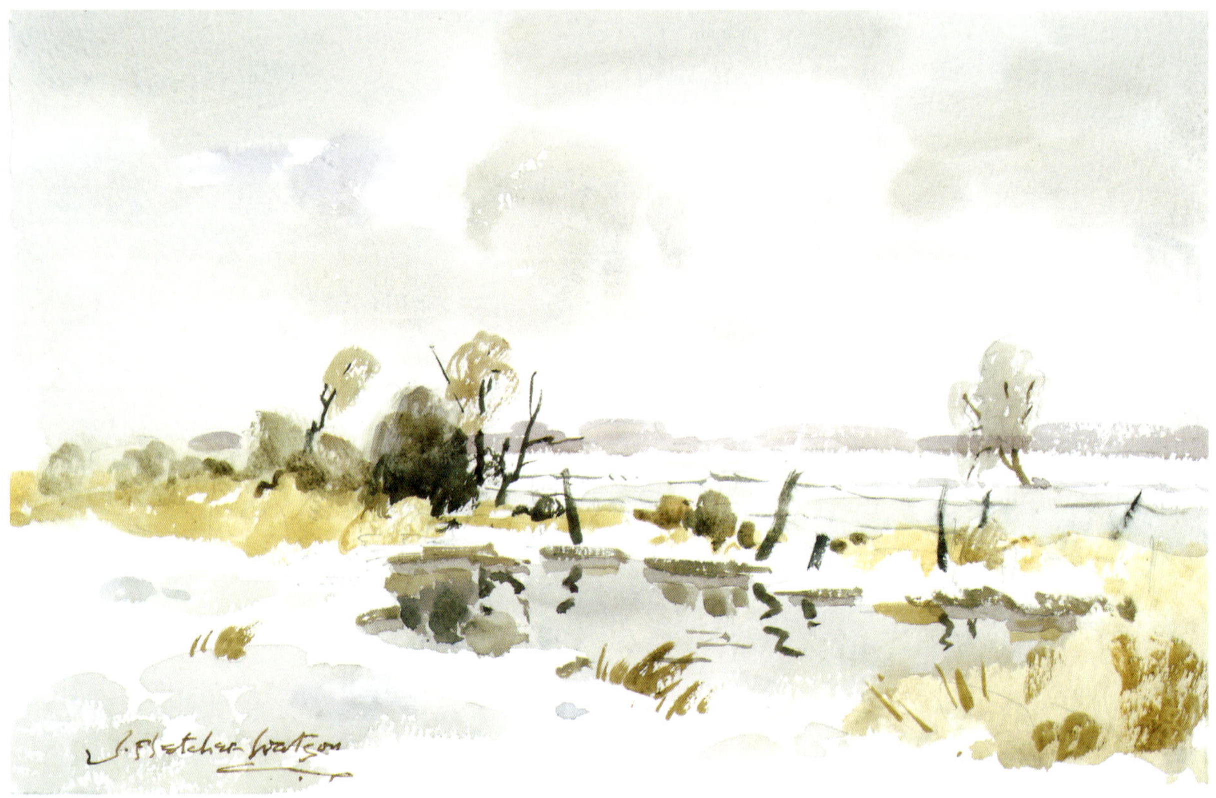

*Snow, Windrush Valley   14 x 10 inches*

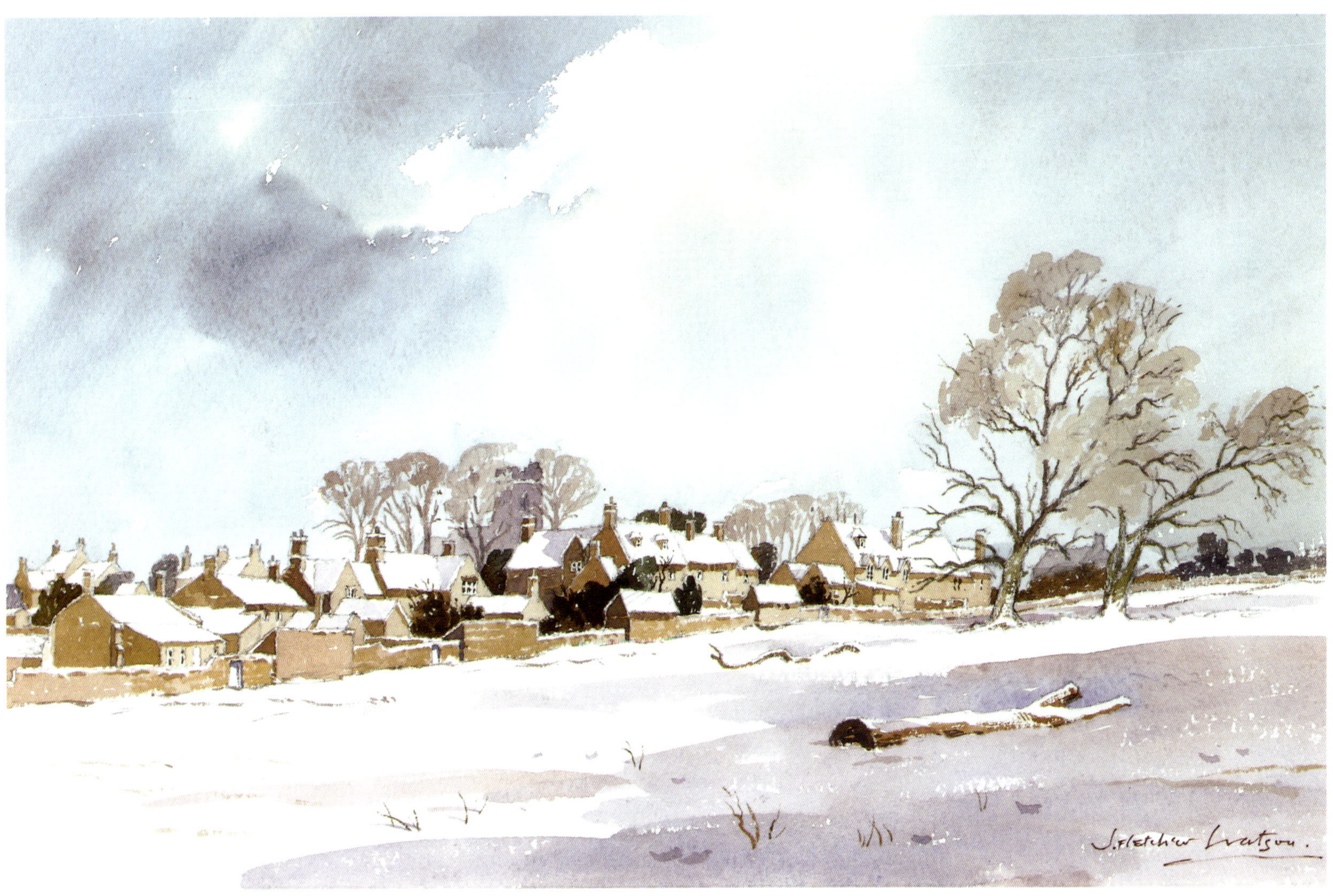

*Windrush Village in Snow   18.5 x 12.5 inches*

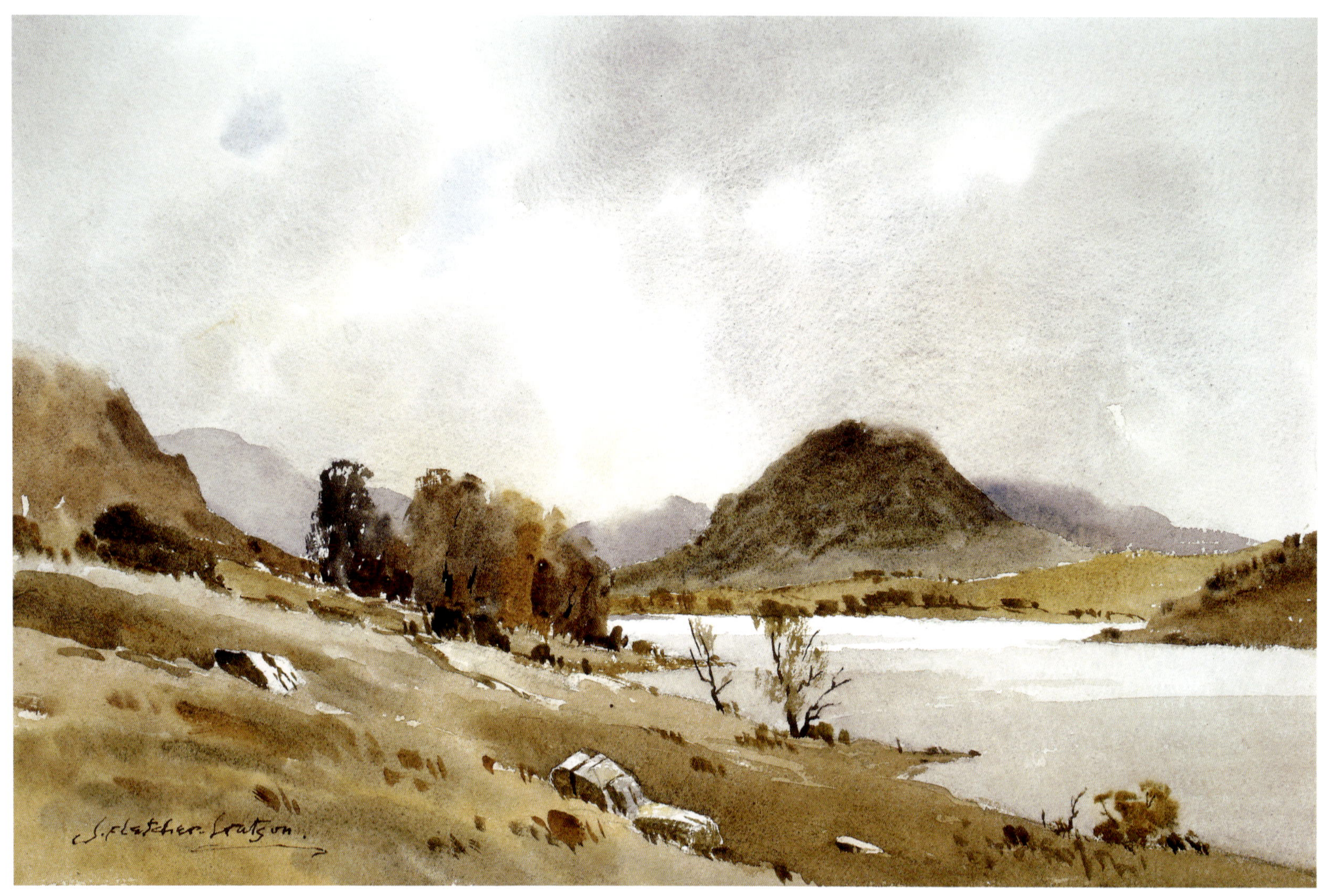

*Loweswater, Cumbria  18.5 x 12.5 inches*

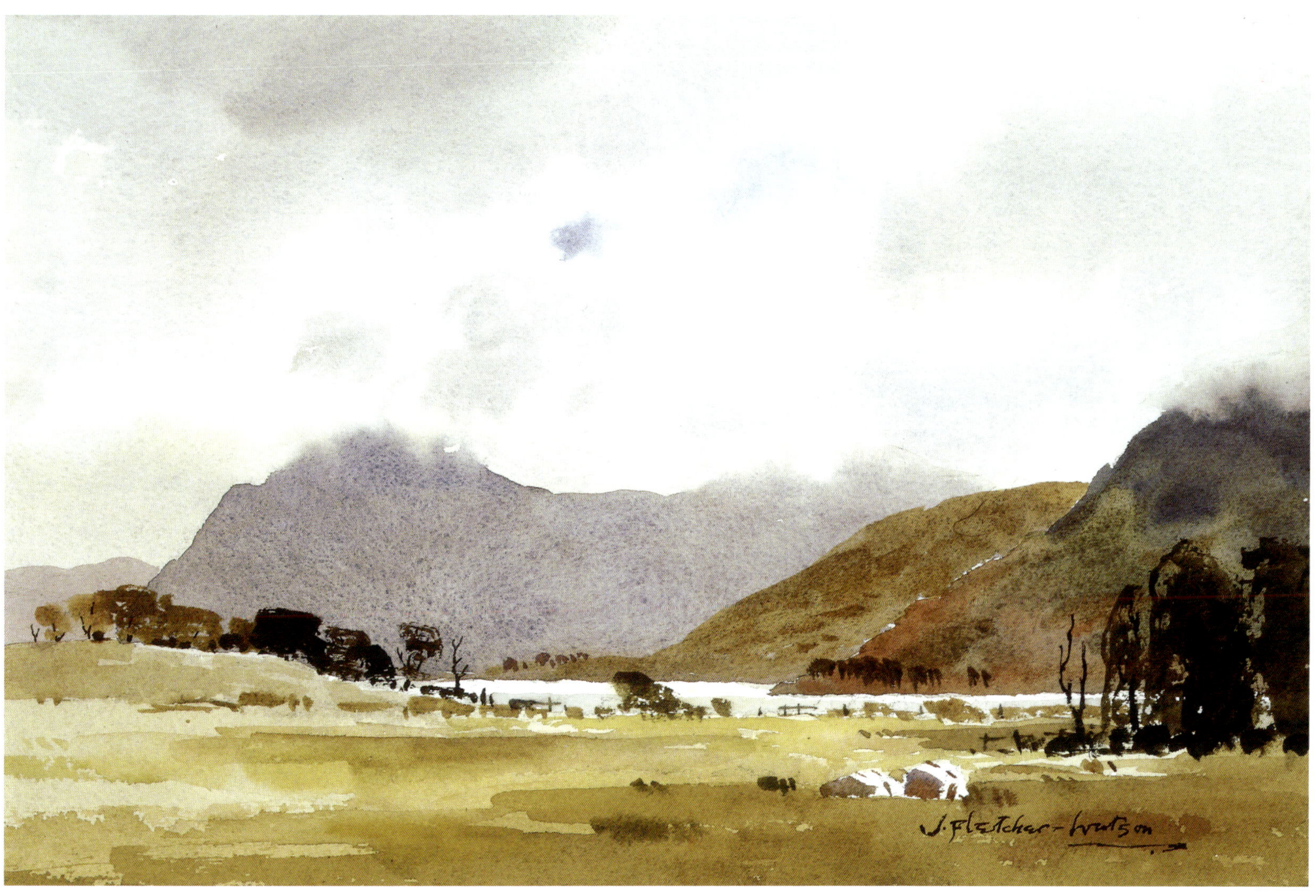

*Buttermere, Cumbria 18.5 x 12.5 inches*

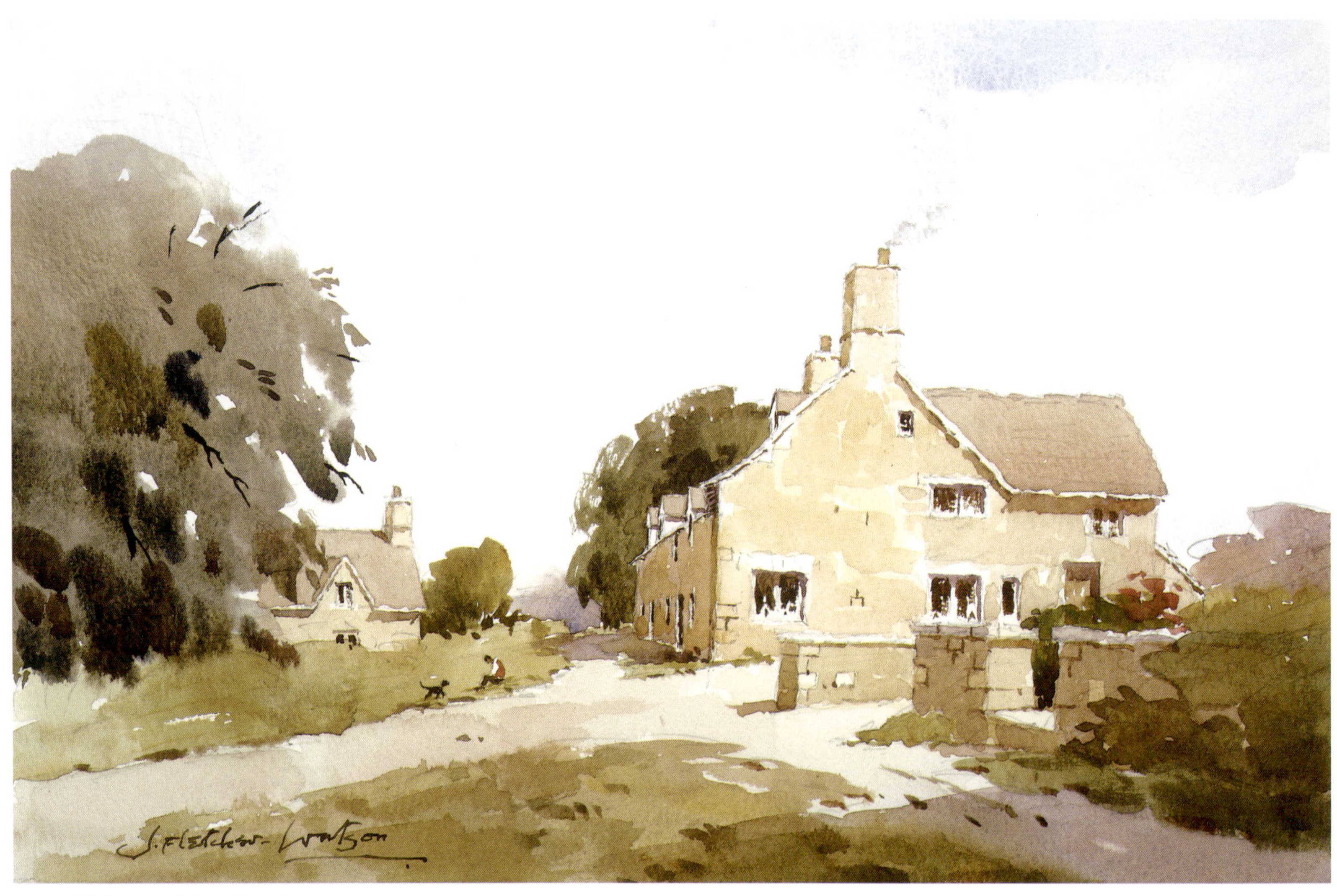

*Cotswold Cottages 10 x 14 inches*

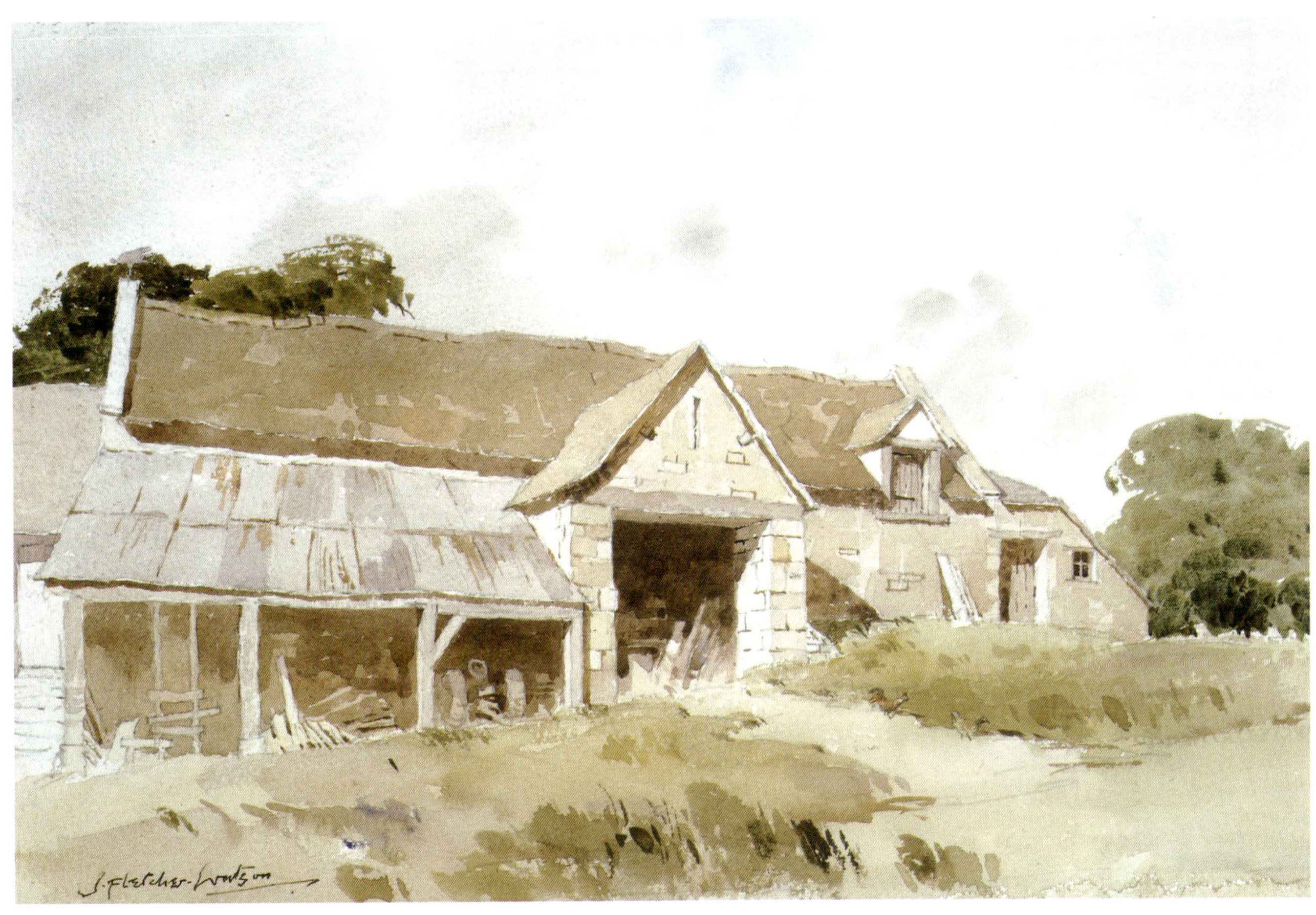

*Cotswold Barn   18.5 x 12.5 inches*

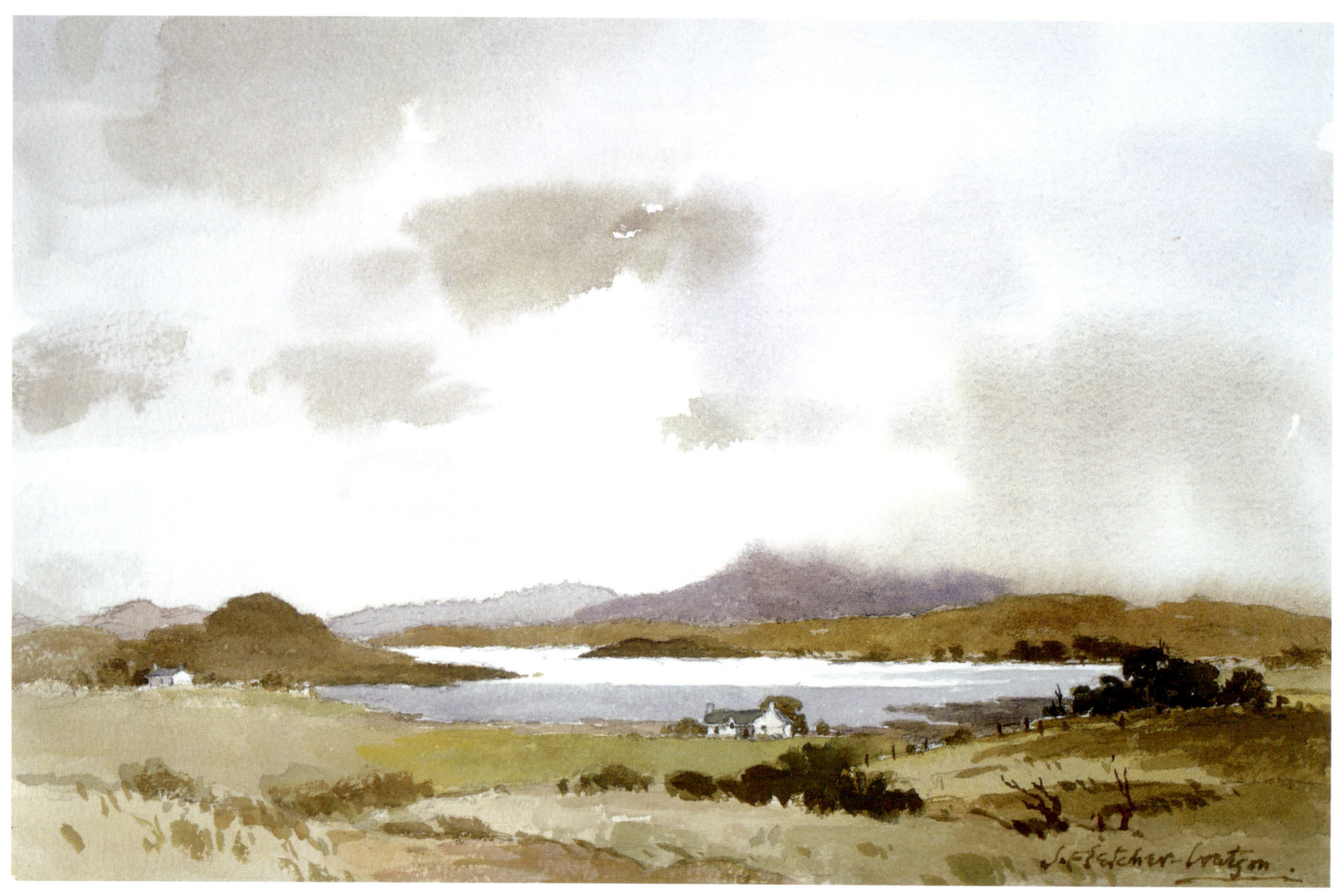

*Loch Snizort, Northern Skye  14 x 9 inches*

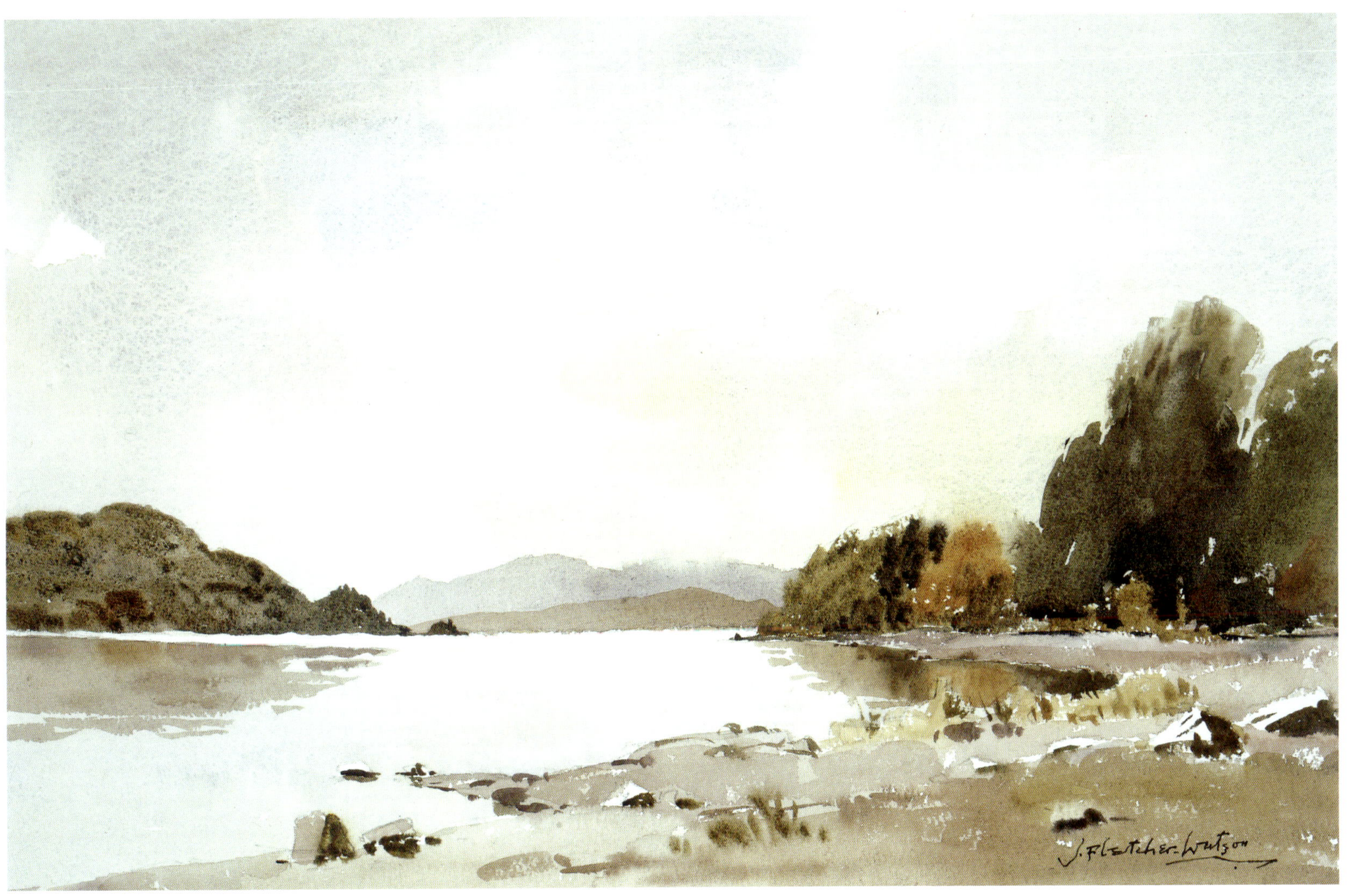

*Loch Awe, Scotland  18.5 x 12.5 inches*

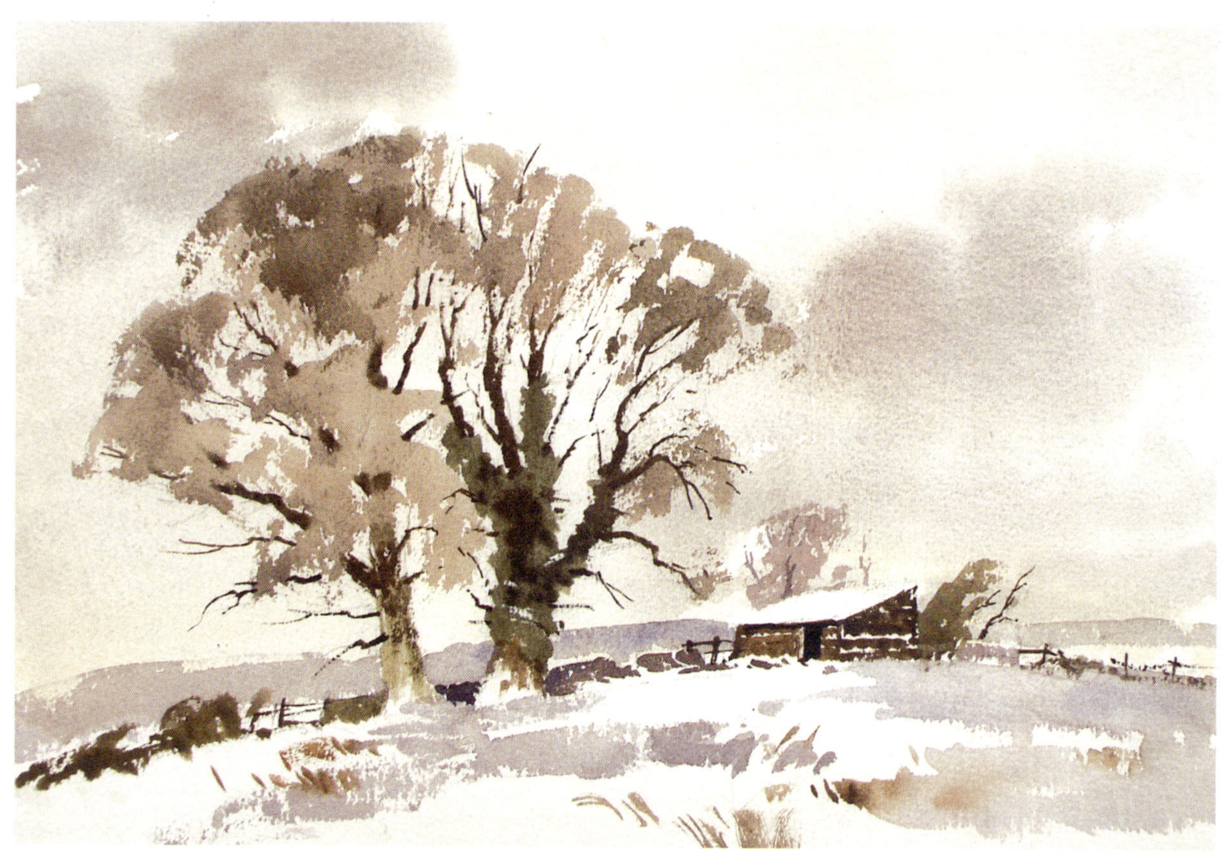

*Winter Trees  14 x 10 inches*

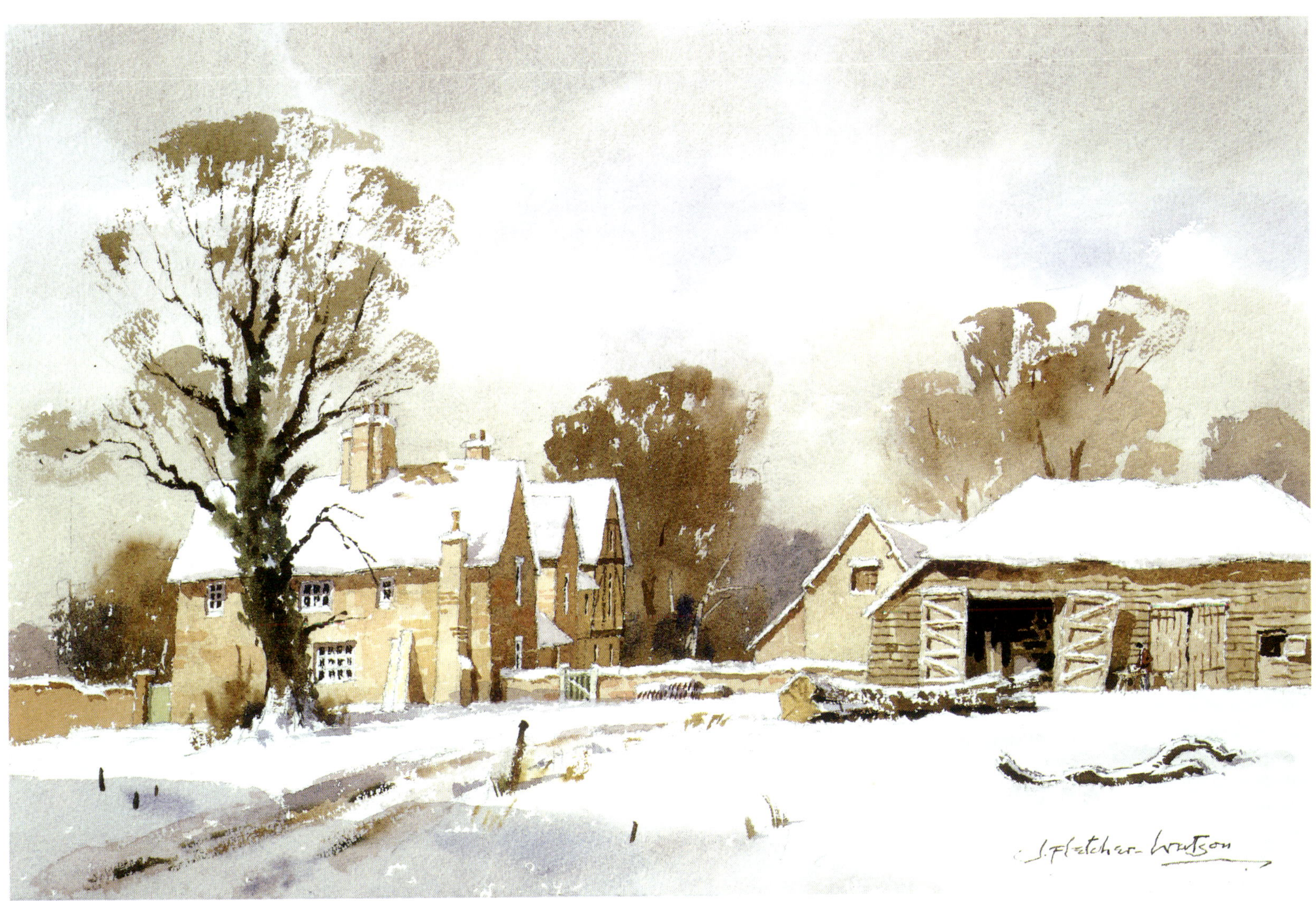

*Barns in Snow, Buckinghamshire  18.5 x 12.5 inches*

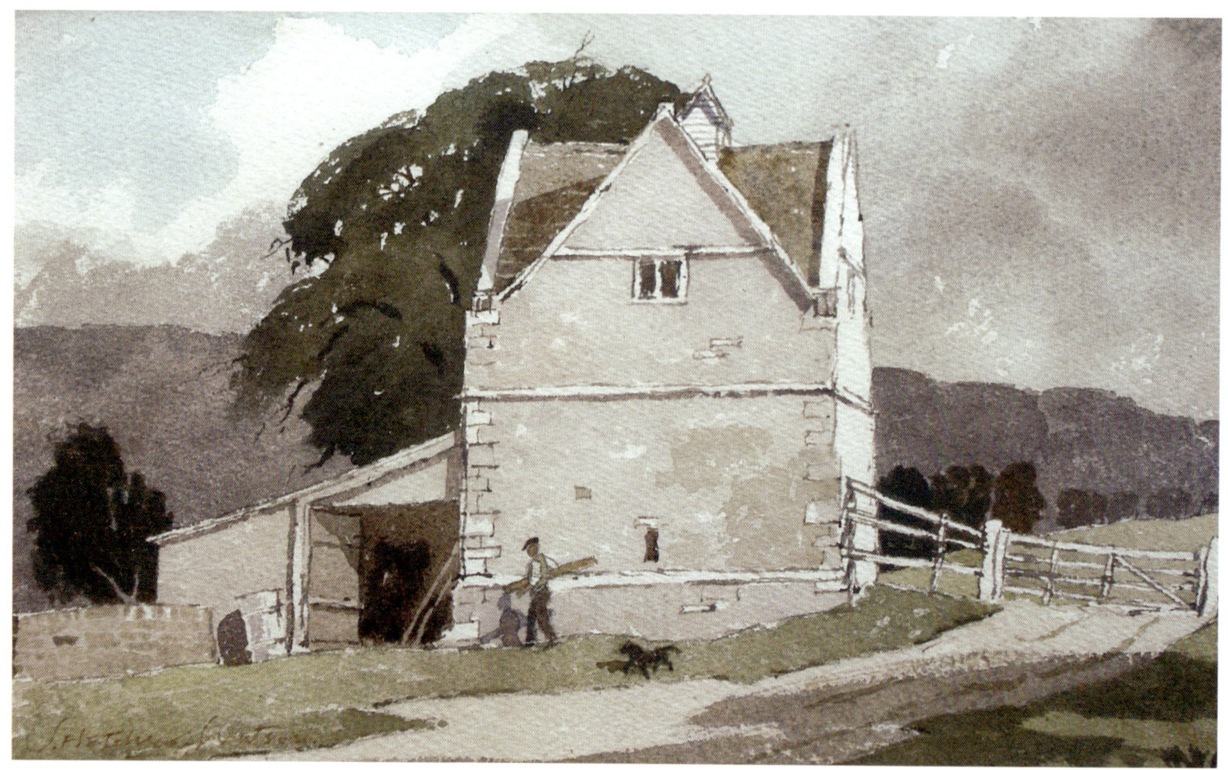

*Dovecote, Naunton, Gloucestershire  12.5 x 8.5 inches*

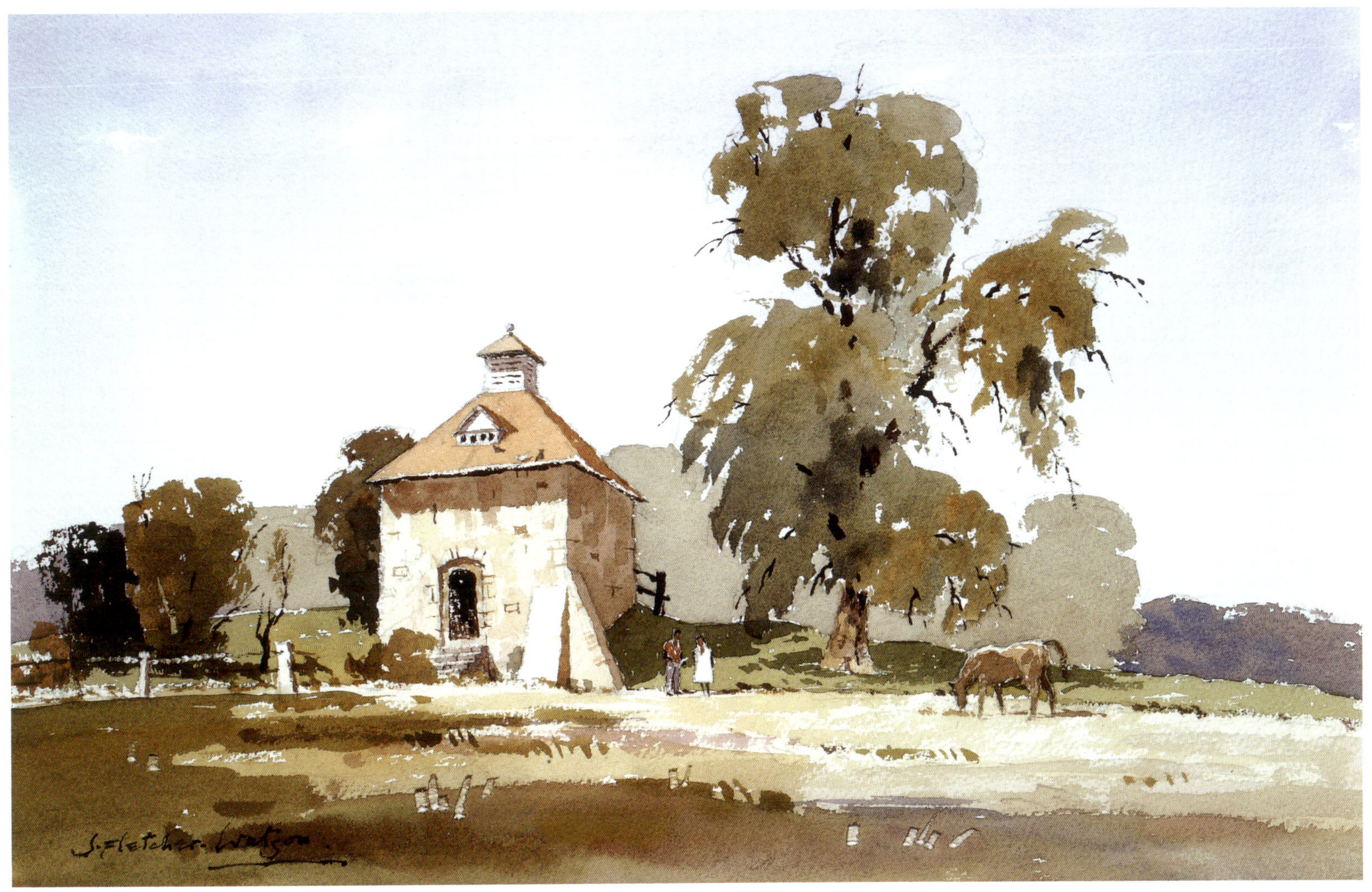

*Dovecote, Surrey   18.5 x 12.5 inches*
*James's concentration when painting was total.   Halfway through this*
*picture one of his group was rushed to hospital to give birth to her baby.   He*
*had no idea of the excitement until the picture was finished!*

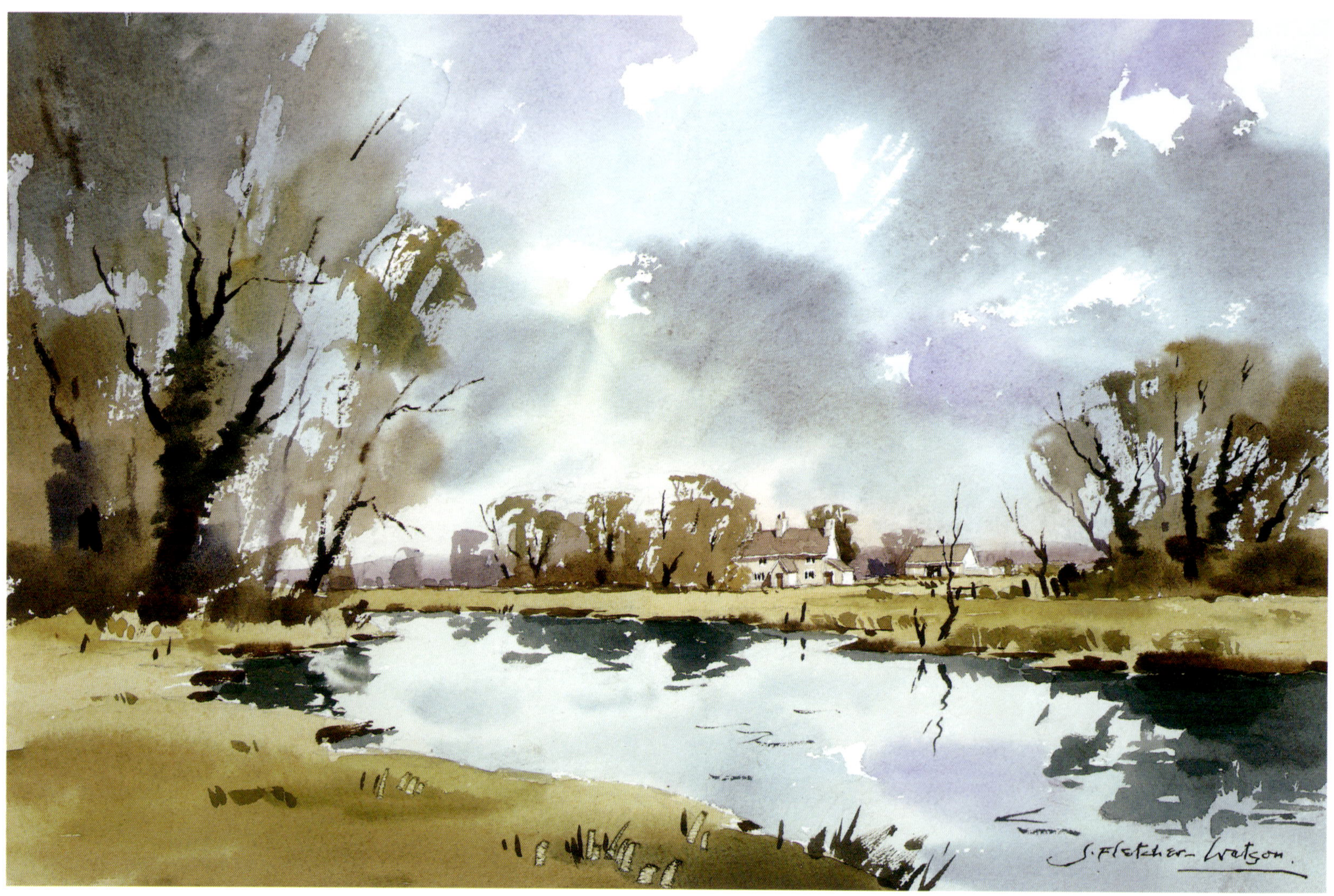

*River Windrush  18.5 x 12.5 inches*

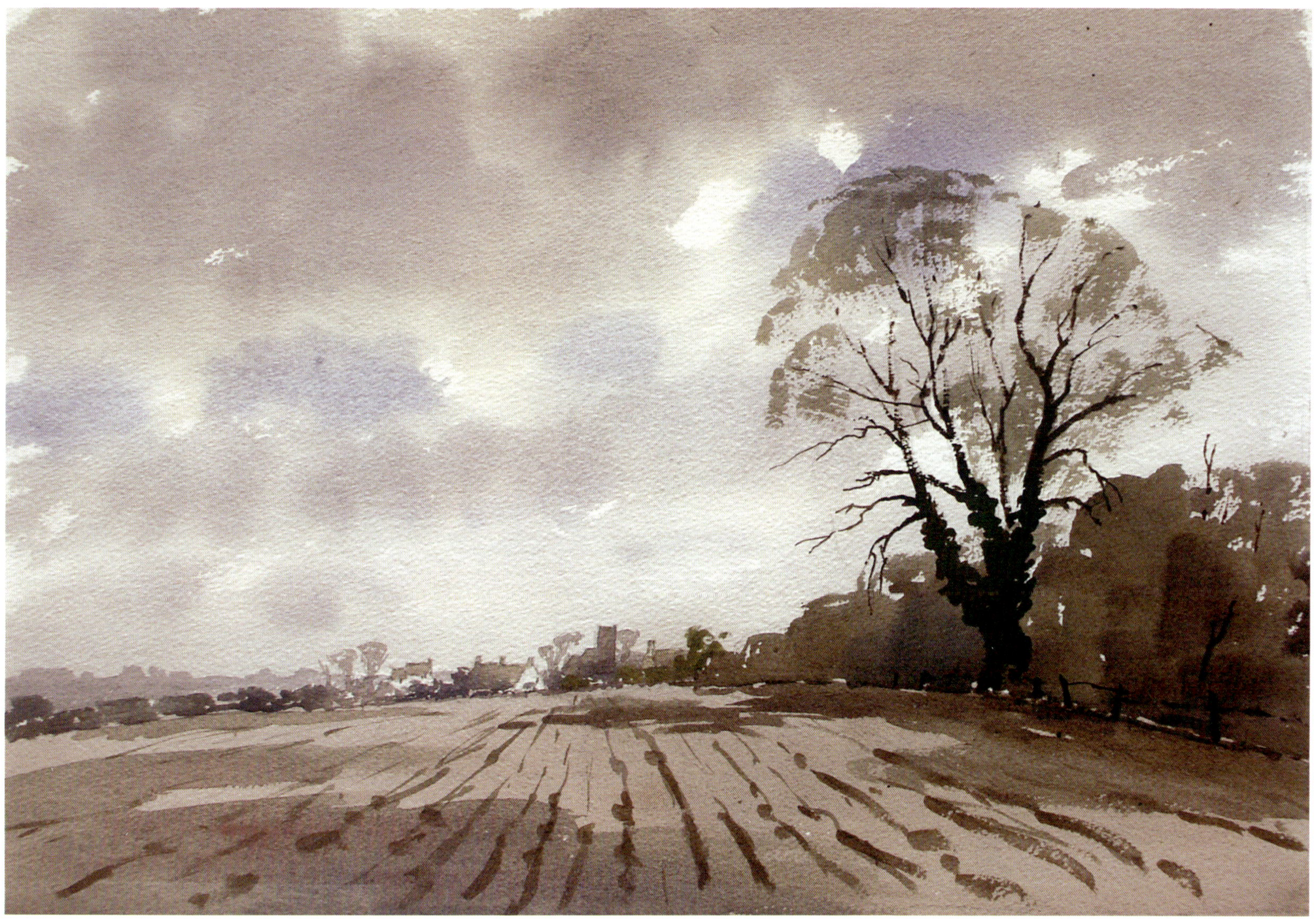

*Ploughed Field, Windrush  18.5 x 12.5 inches*

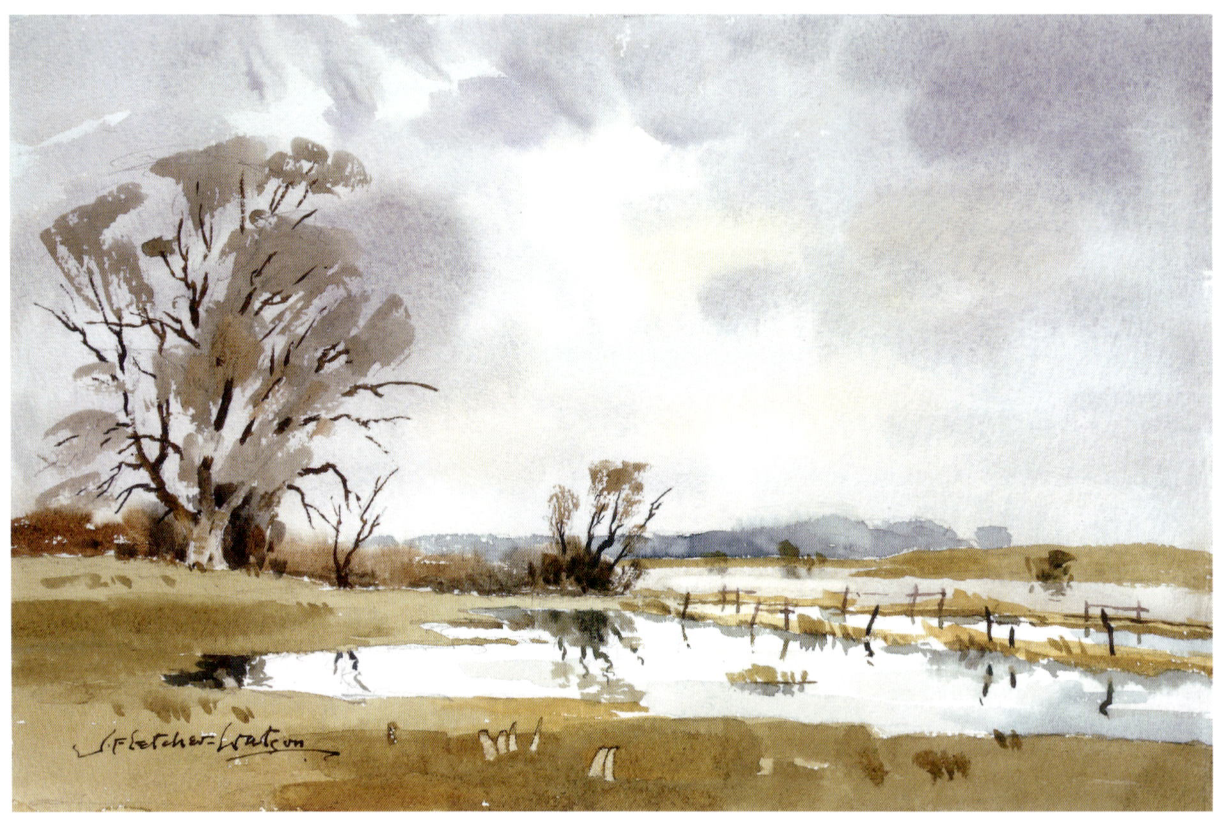

*Winter Floodwater  10 x 14 inches*

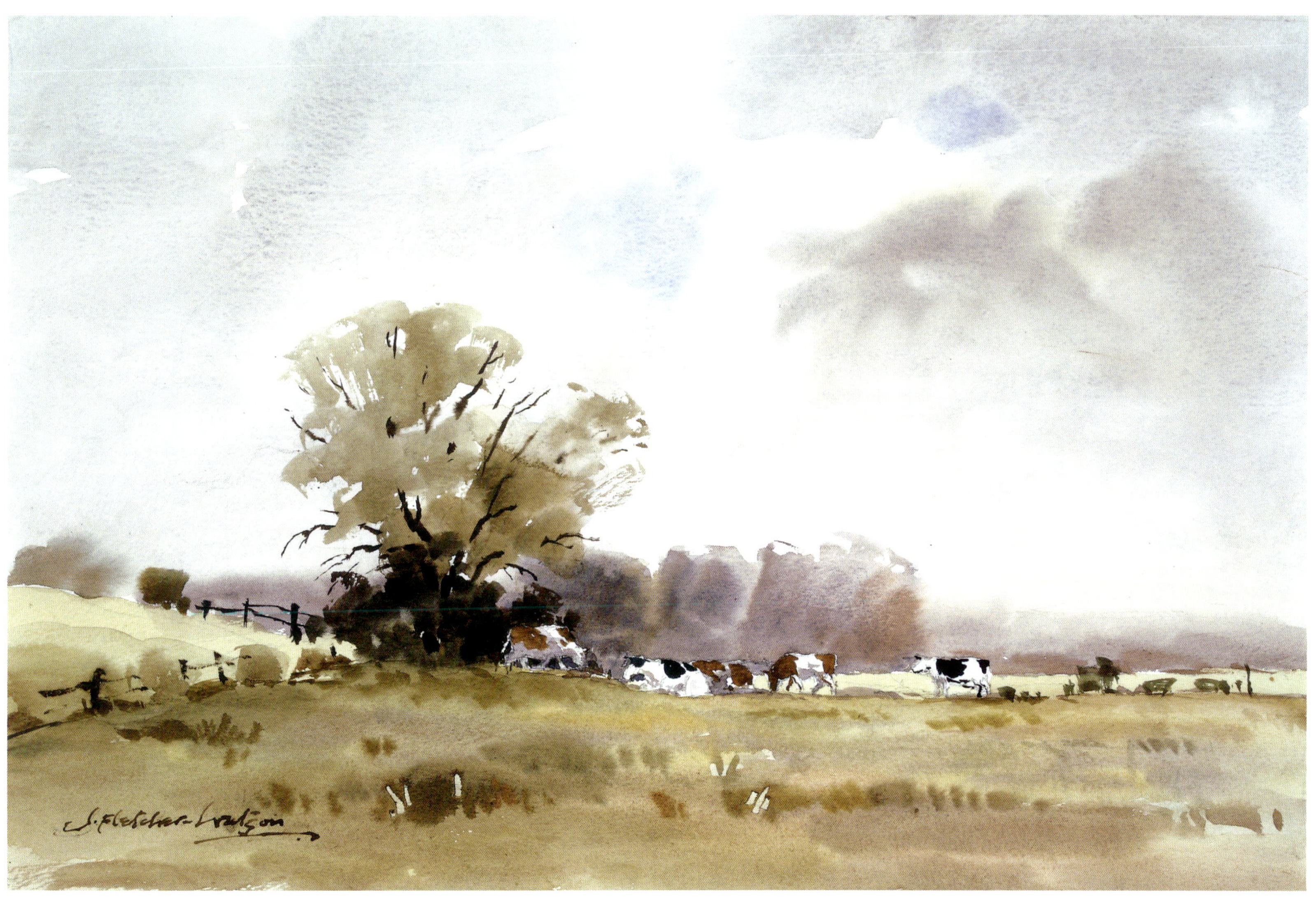

*Summer Landscape  18.5 x 12.5 inches*

'Enthusiasm is half the battle with watercolours; it is
a very exciting medium once you start.  My advice to
a beginner is never give up or be depressed if you do a
bad picture; you will have learnt something and
success is waiting for you just around the corner.'

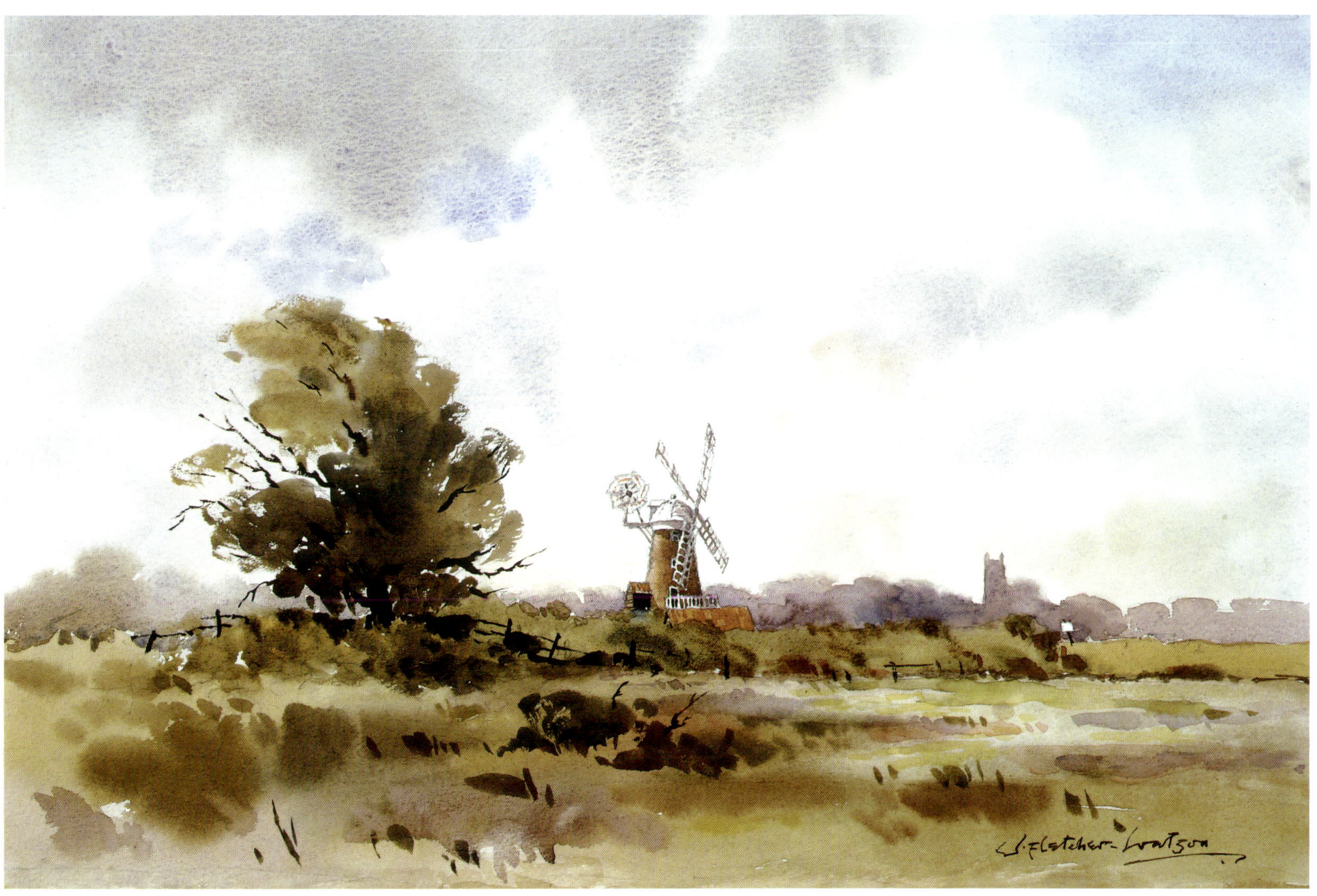

*Cley Mill, Norfolk  18.5 x 12.5 inches*

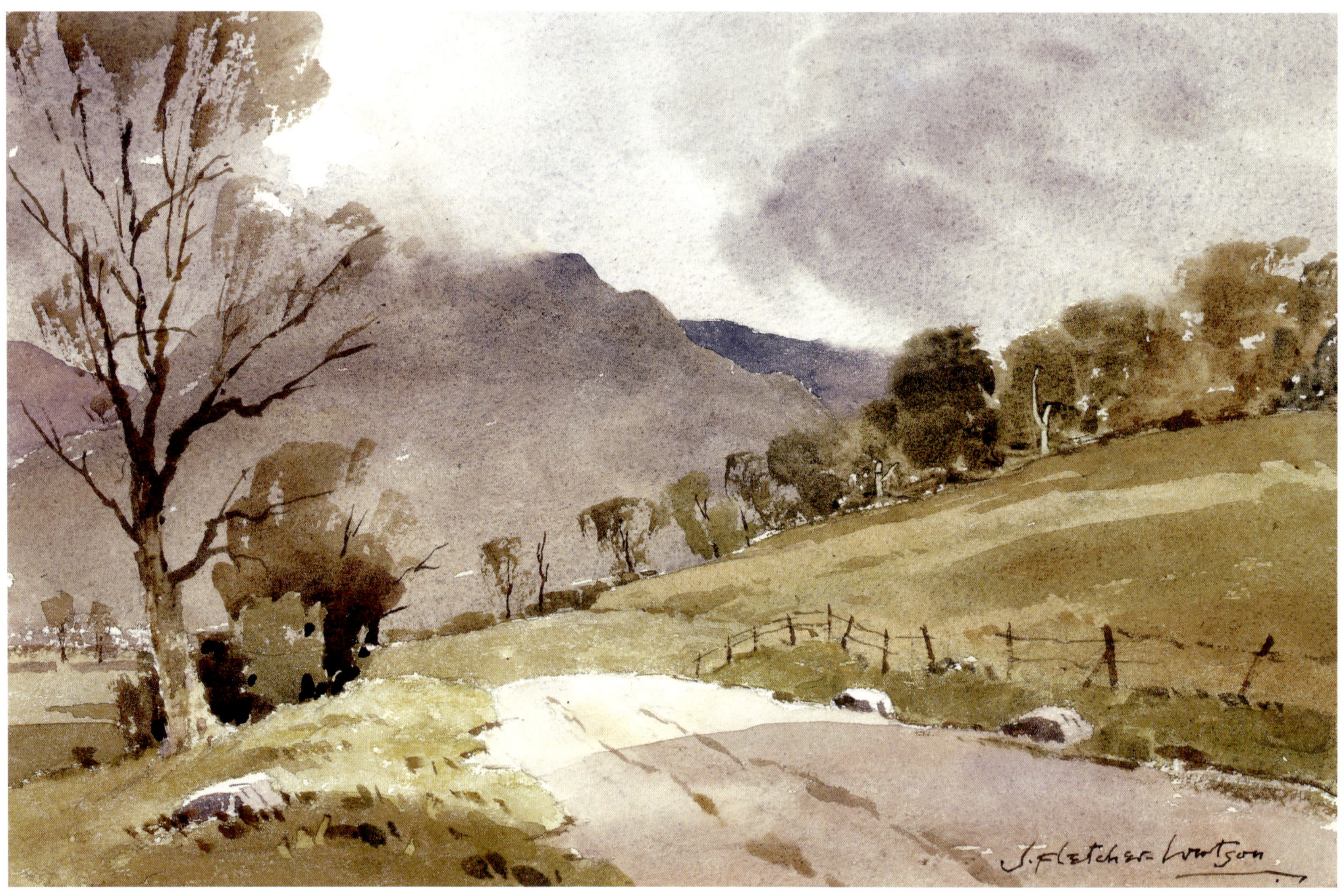

*Lake District Landscape  18.5 x 12.5 inches*

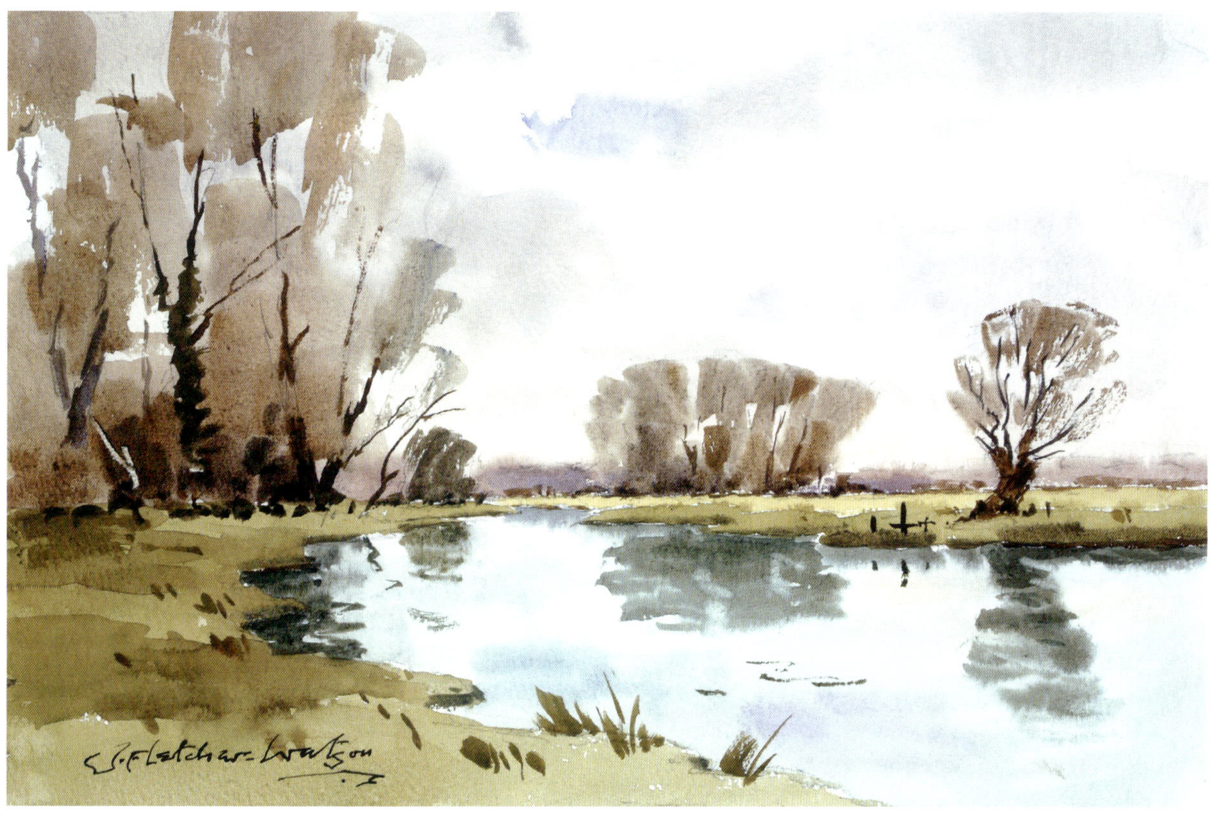

*Winter Reflections  12.5 x 9.5 inches*

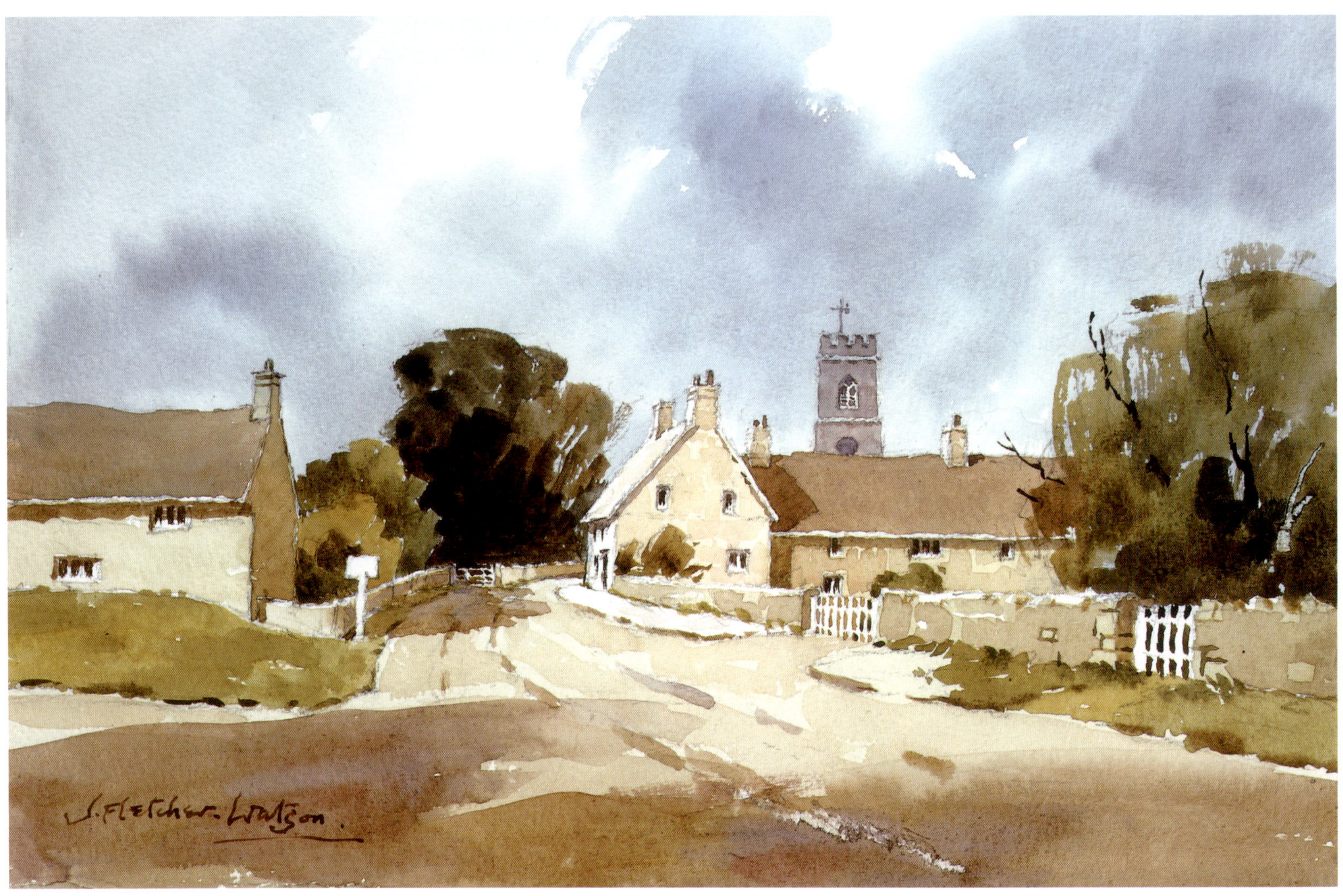

*Cotswold Village  18.5 x 12.5 inches*

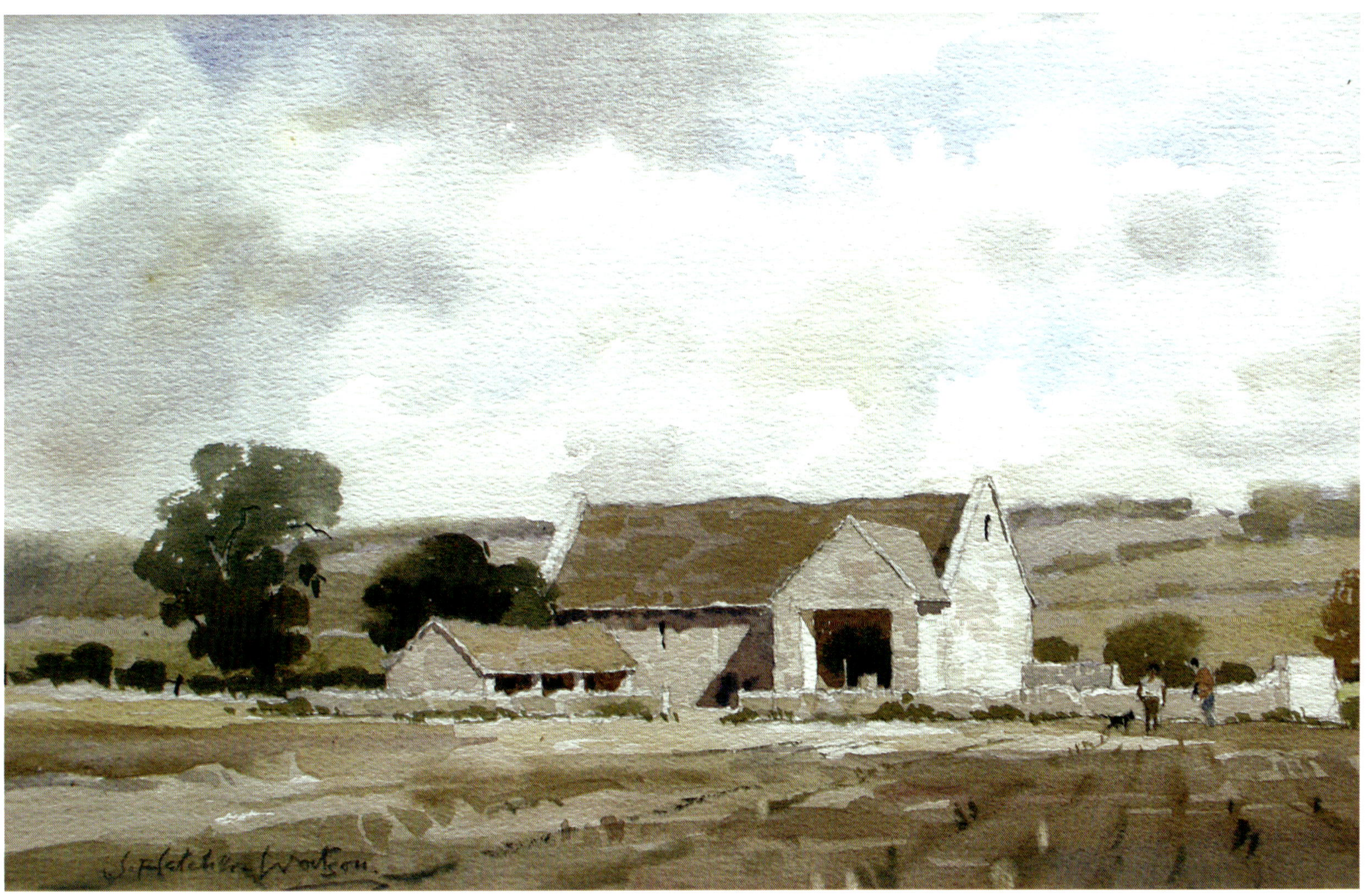

*Cotswold Barn  18.5 x 12.5 inches*

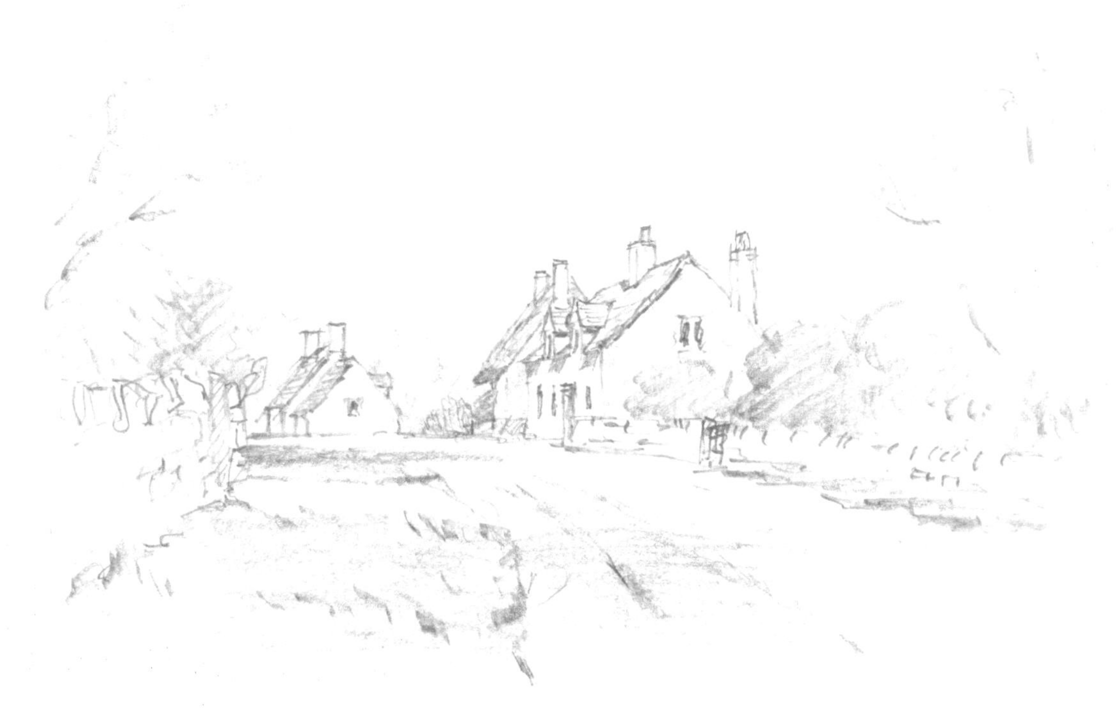

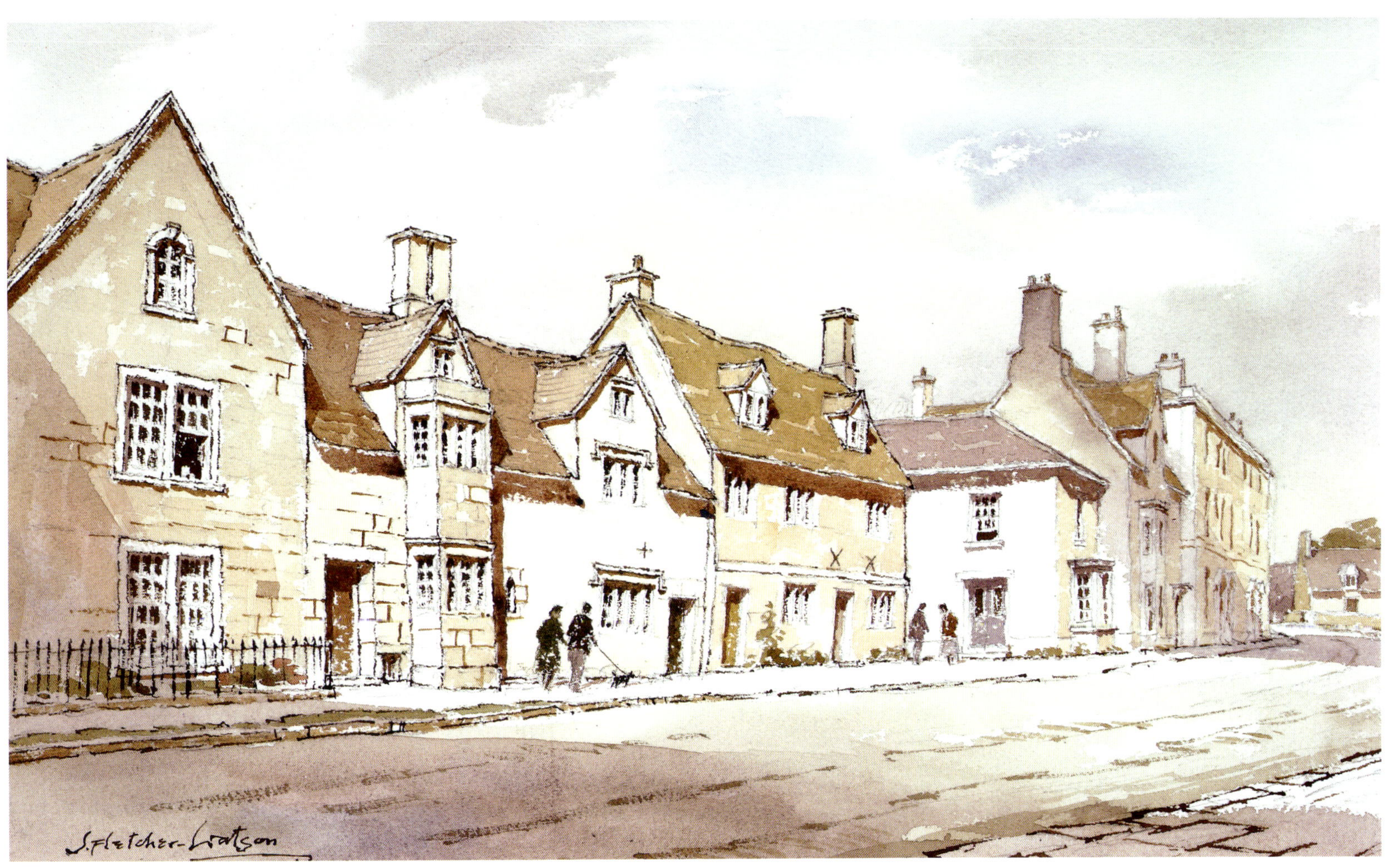

*Cirencester  18 x 10 inches*

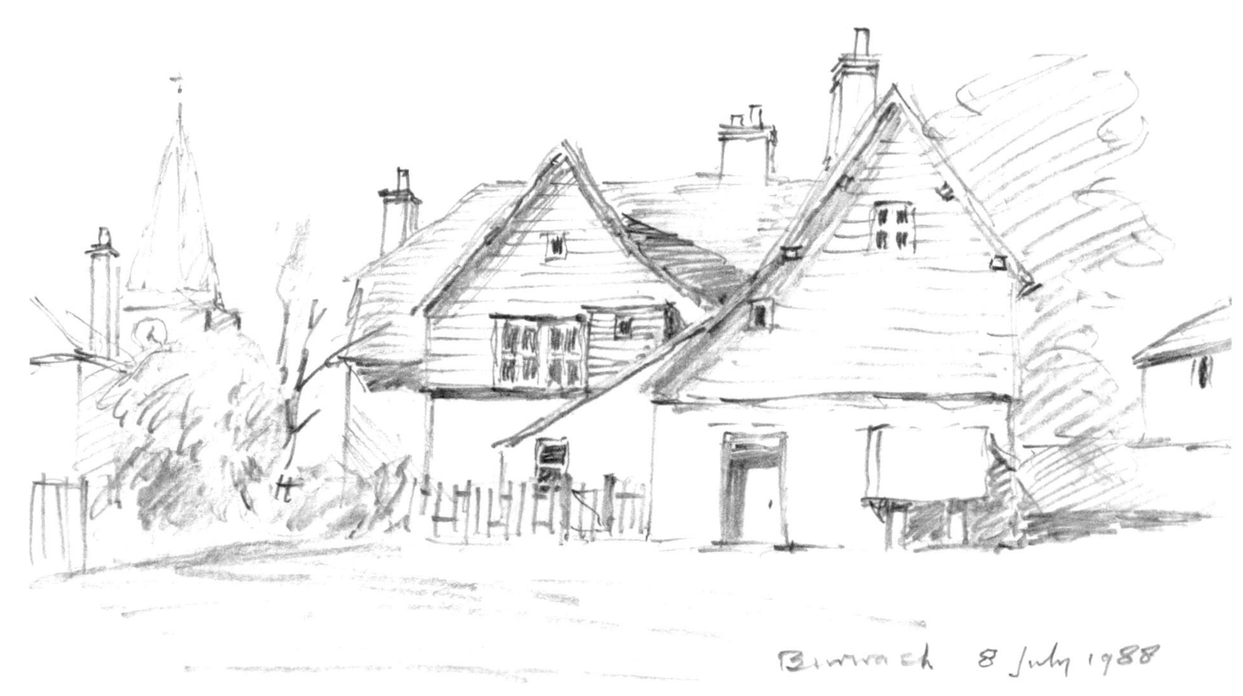



*James always had a sketch book in his pocket and
he often took a shooting stick which had a convenient
device so that the seat could be lowered to just the right
sitting position.  He found it easier to draw with
a sketch book when sitting.*

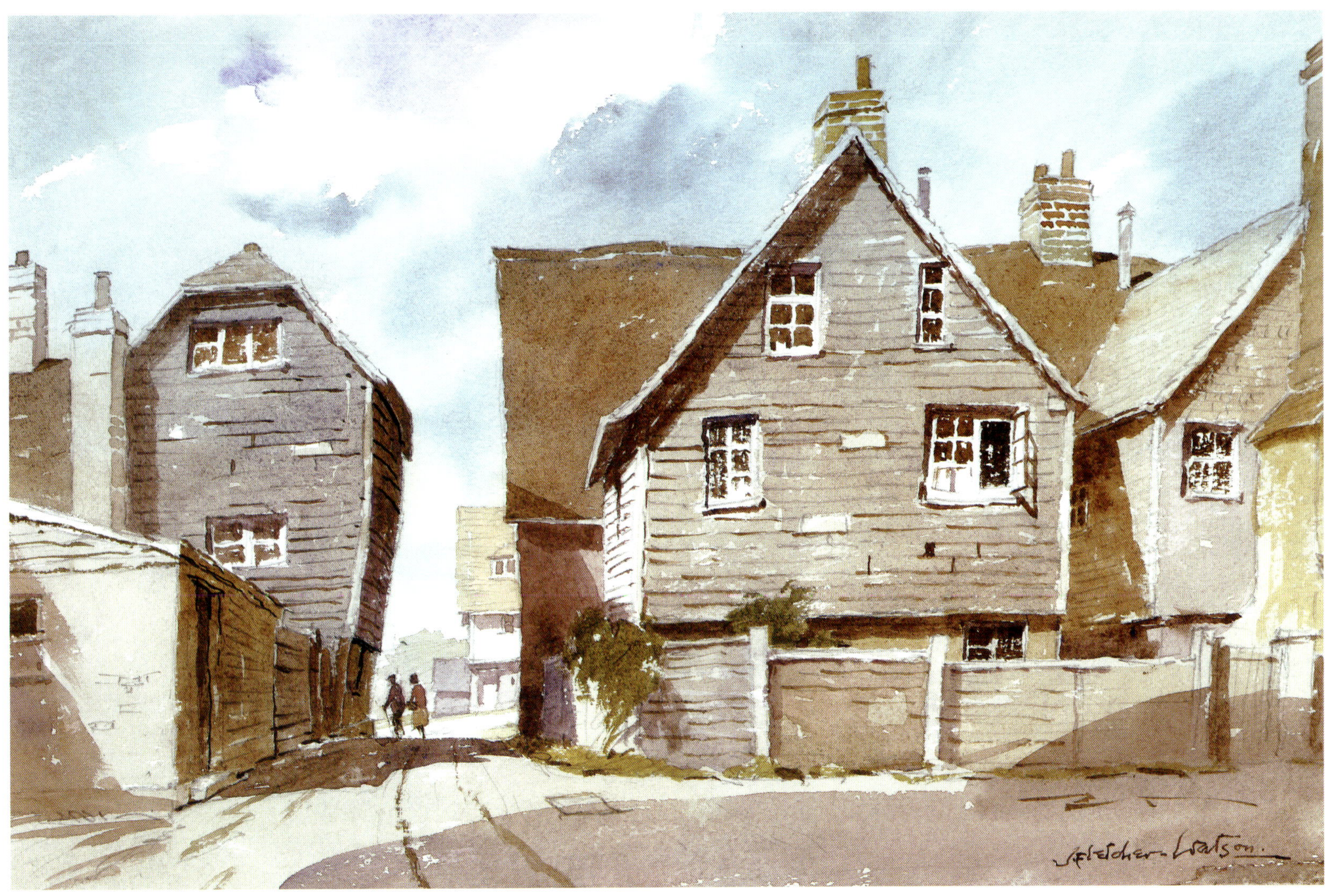

*Burwash, Sussex  18.5 x 12.5 inches*

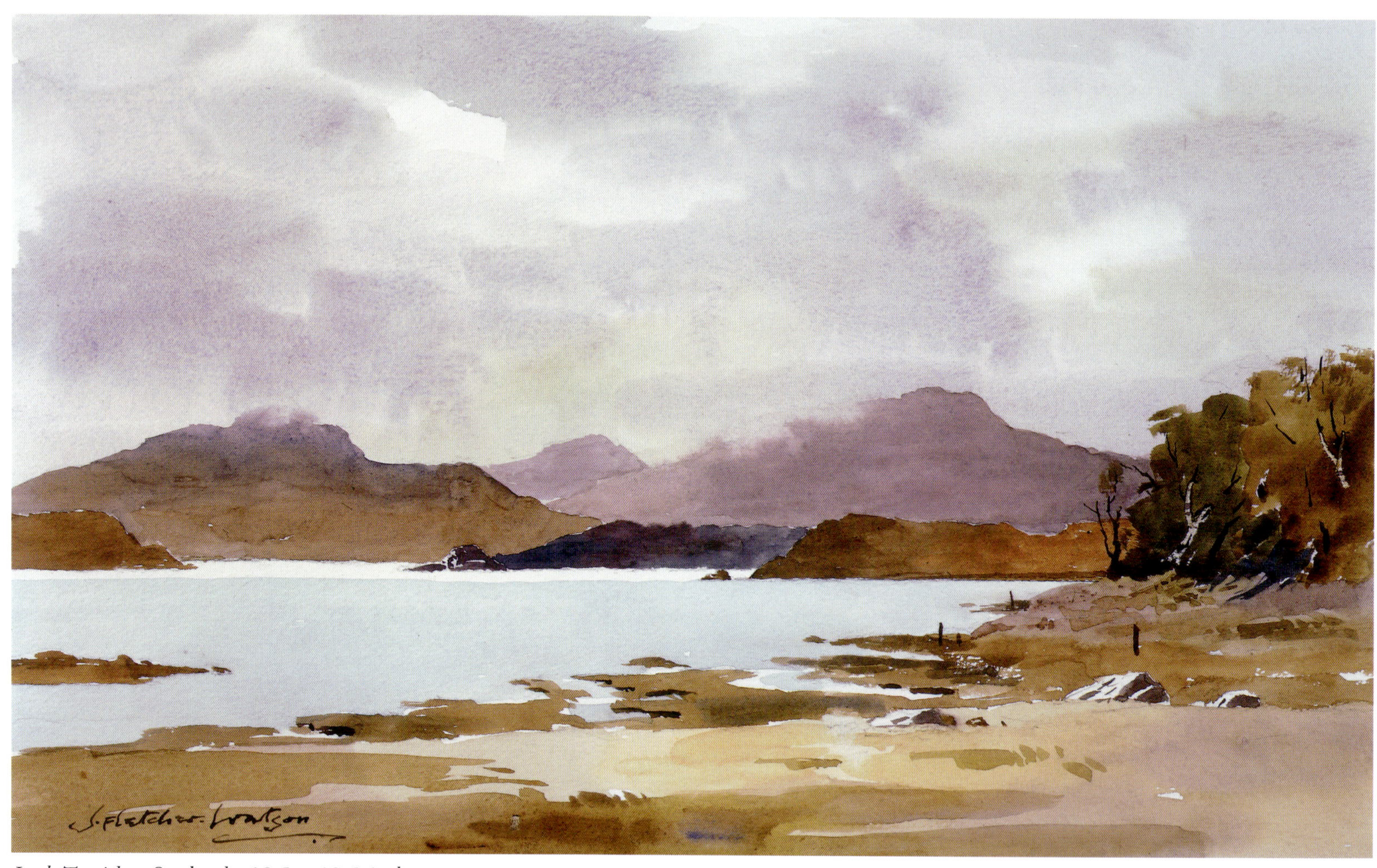

*Loch Torridon, Scotland   18.5 x 12.5 inches*

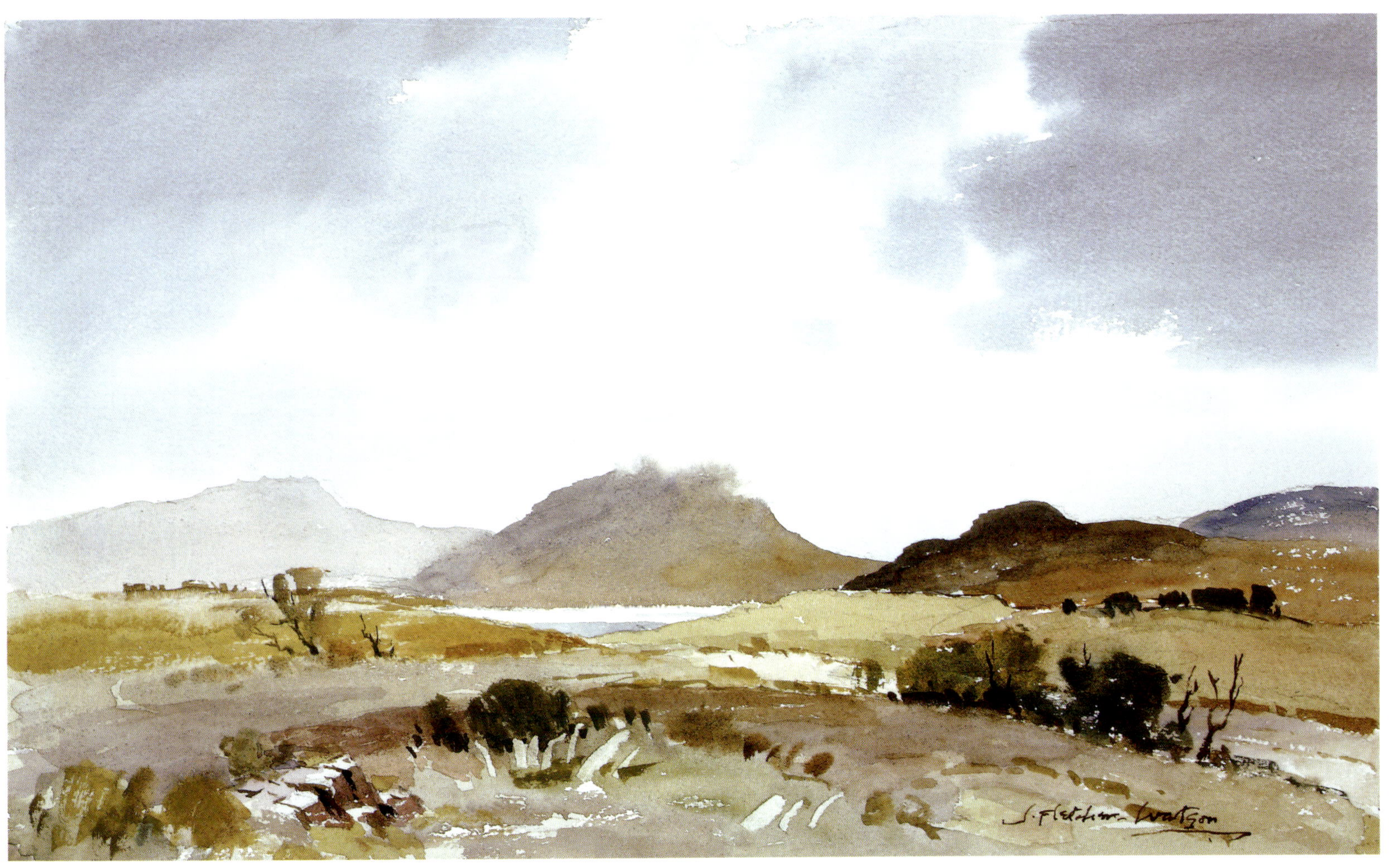

*West Highlands, Scotland  18.5 x 12.5 inches*

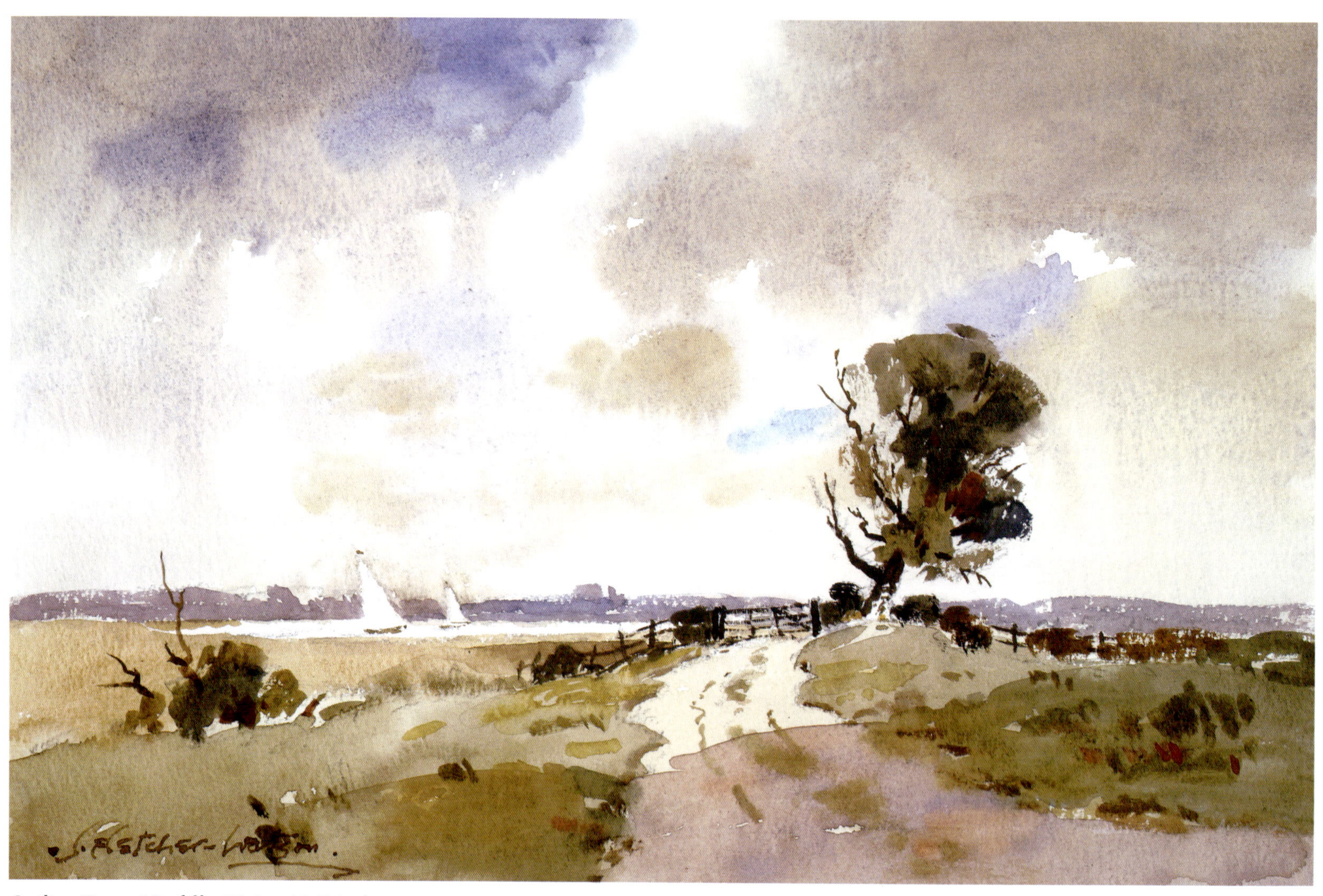

*Sailing Boats, Norfolk  18.5 x 12.5 inches*

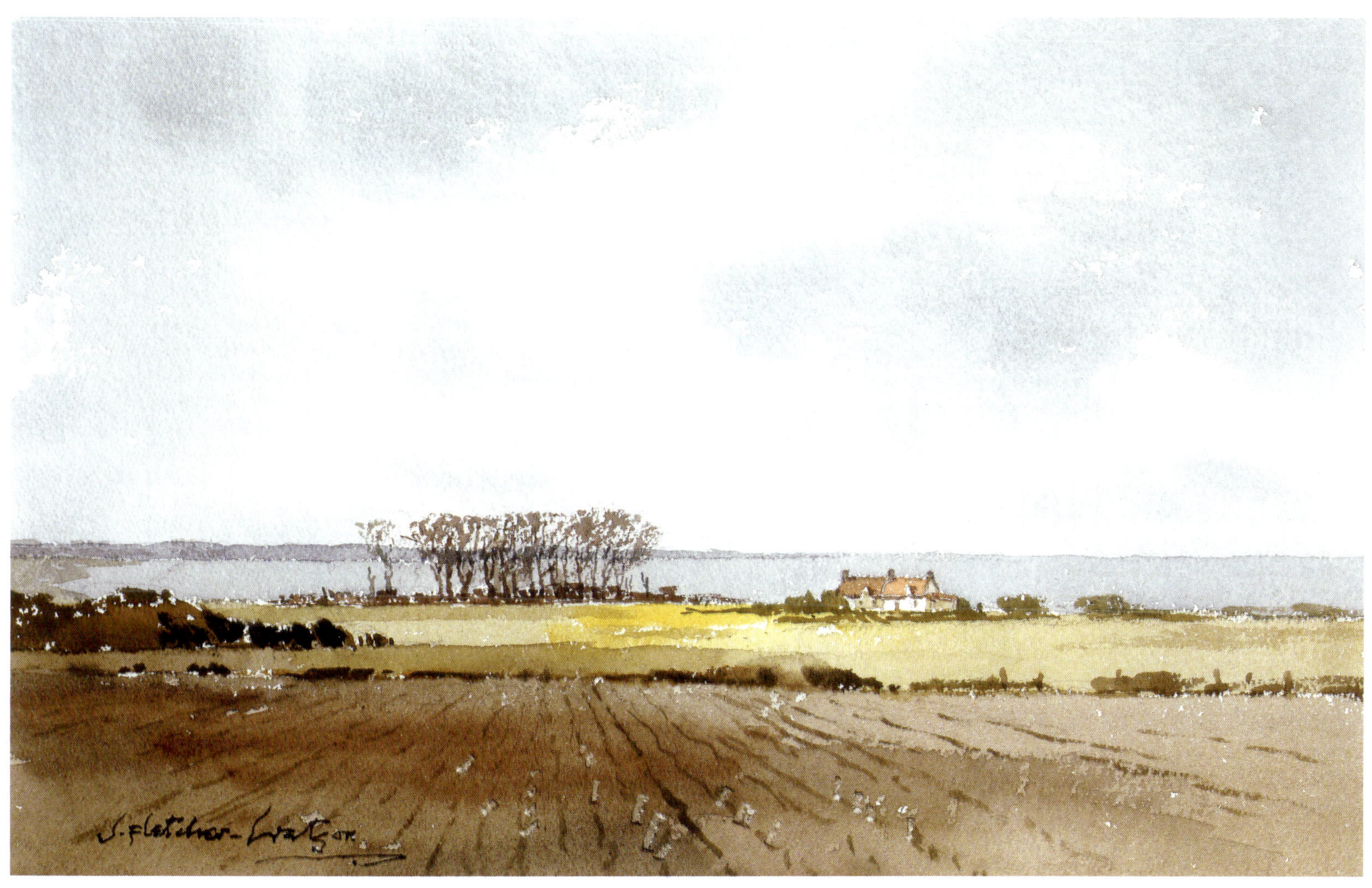

*North Norfolk Coast  18.5 x 12.5 inches*

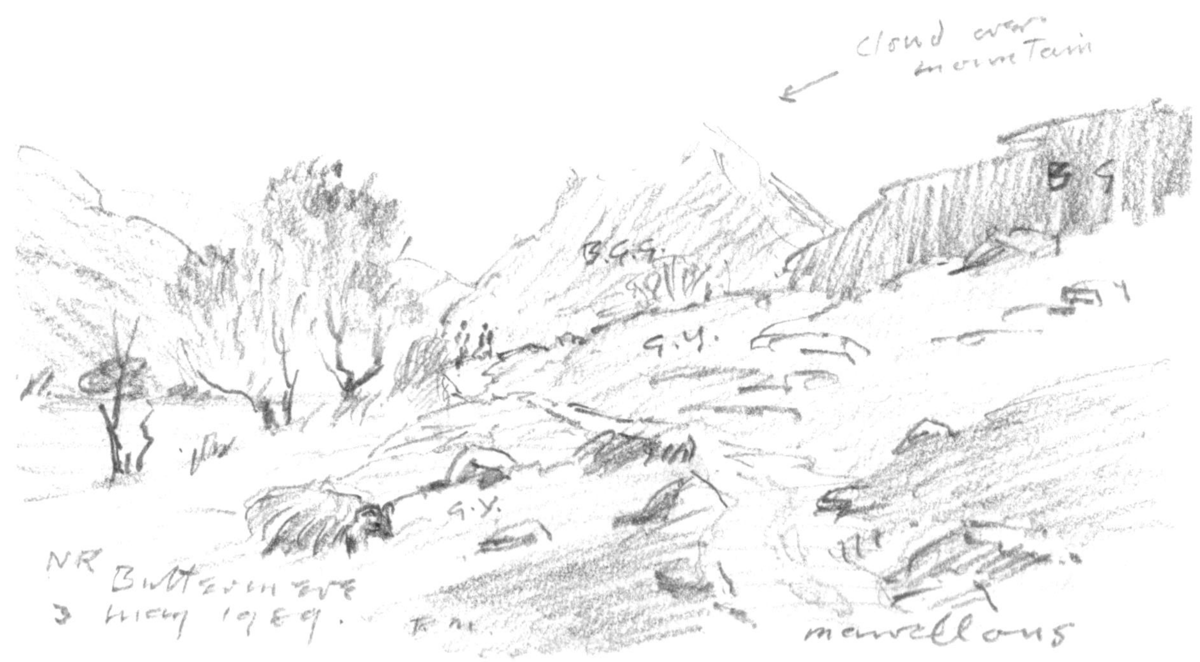
B.G.G = Blue green grey
G.Y = green-yellow
B.G = Brown grey
cloud over mountain
B.G
B.G.G
G.Y
G.Y
NR Buttermere
3 May 1989.
marvellous

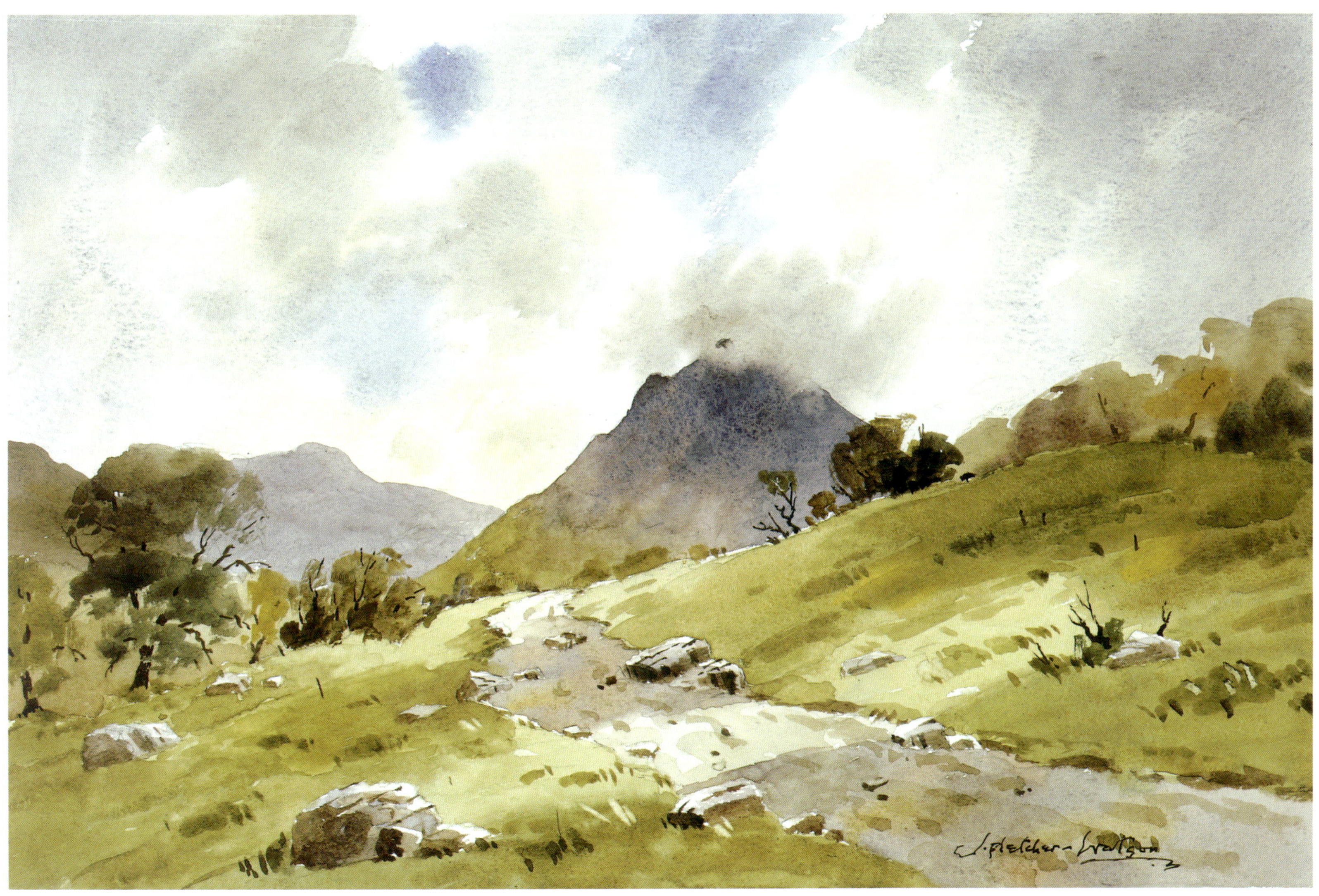

*Track between Buttermere and Crummock Water, Cumbria  18.5 x 12.5 inches*

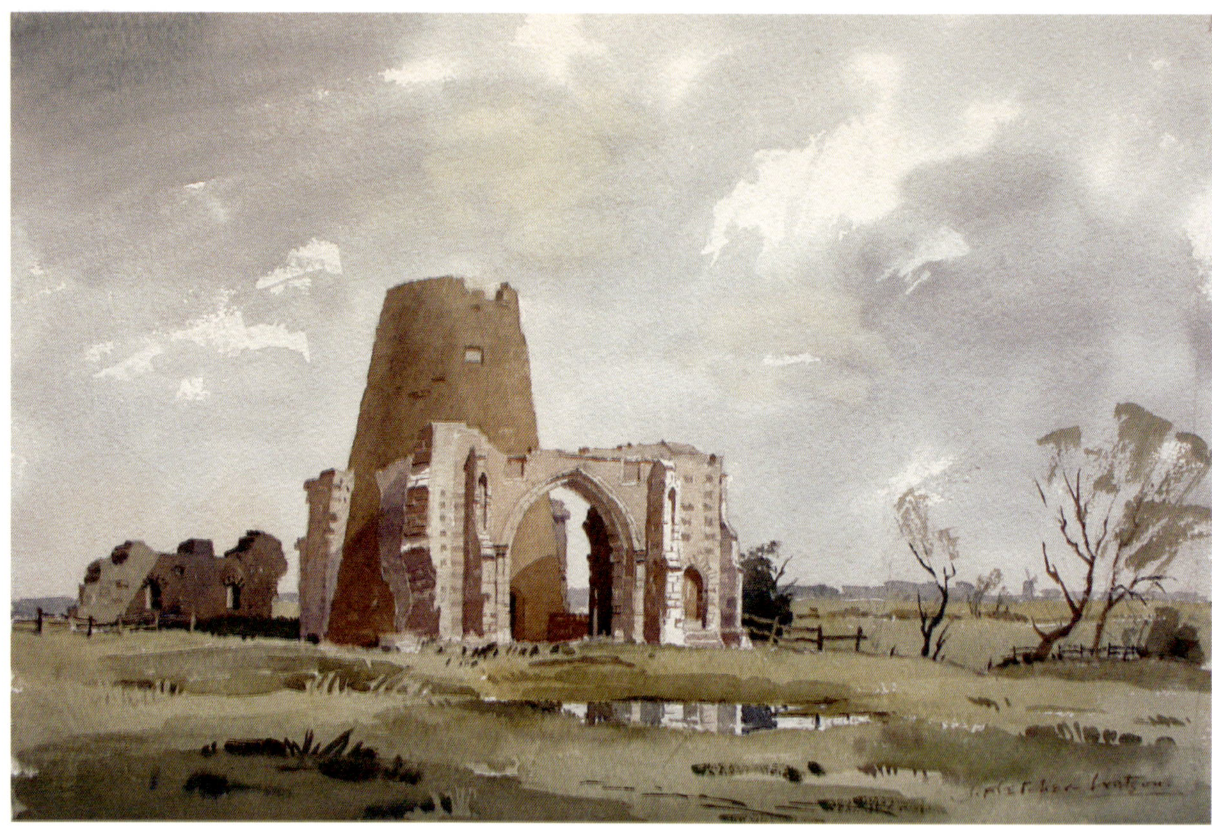

*St Benet's Abbey, Norfolk  14 x 10 inches*

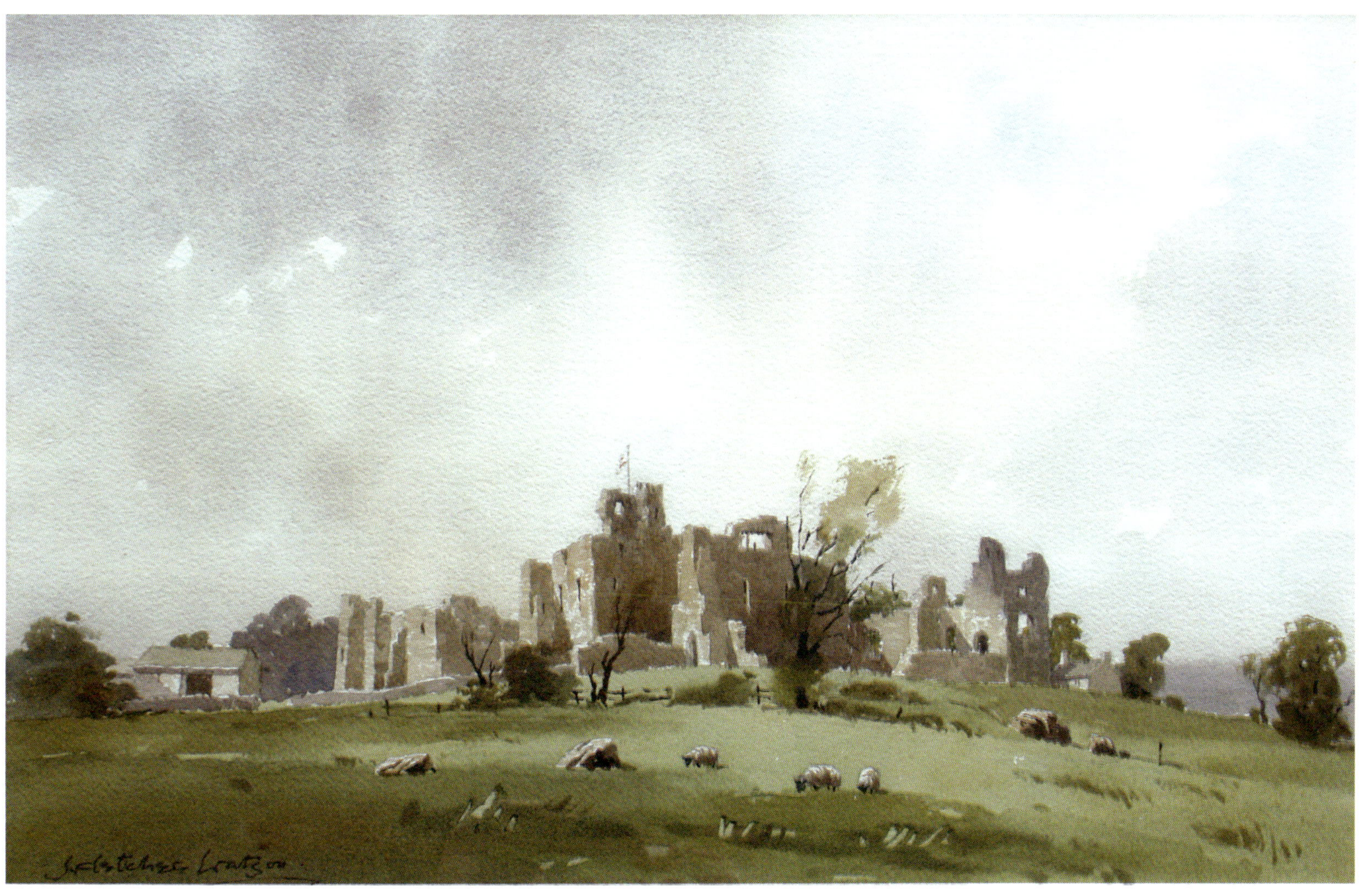

*Middleham Castle, Yorkshire  18.5 x 12.5 inches*

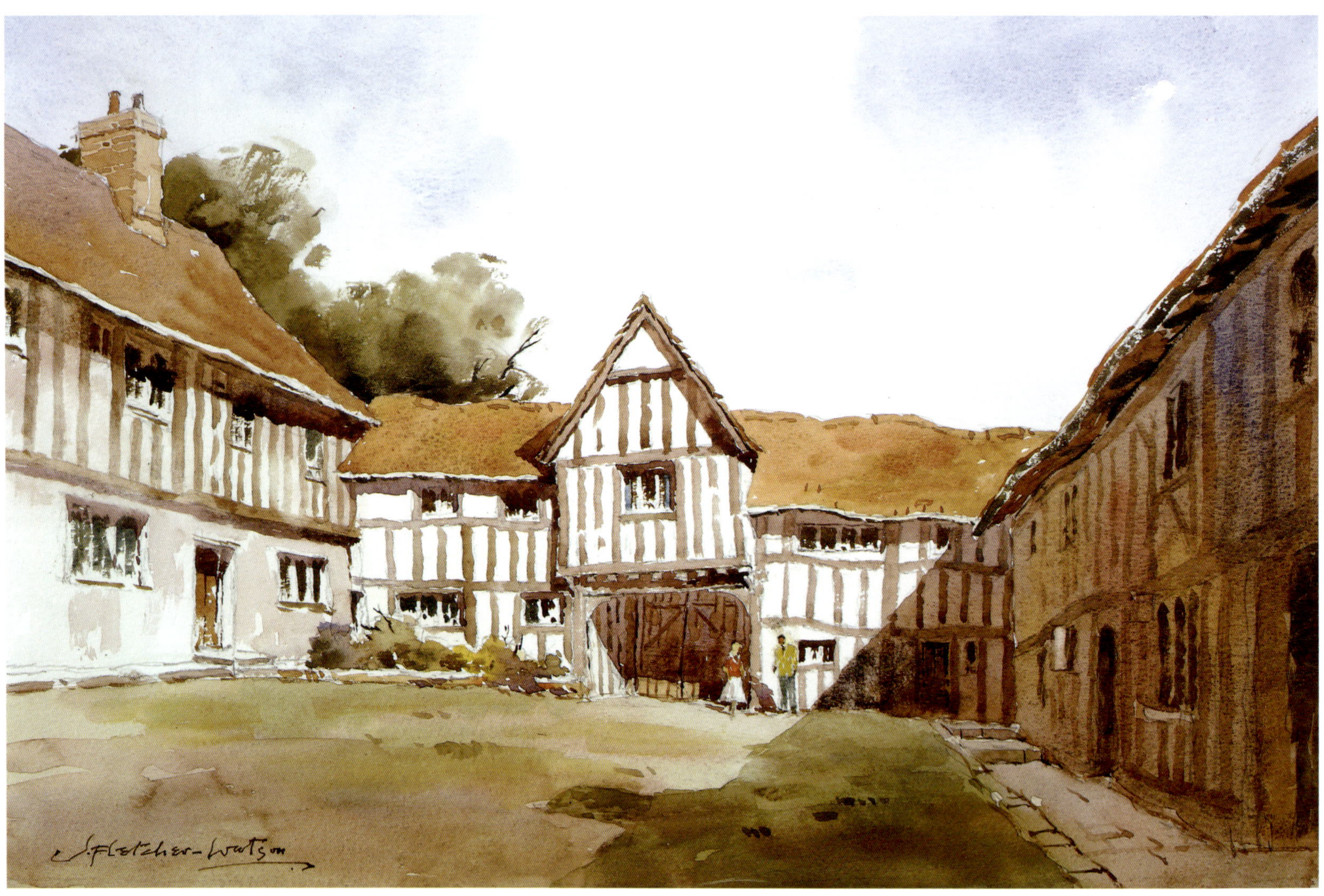

*Flemish Cottages, Dedham  18.5 x 12.5 inches*

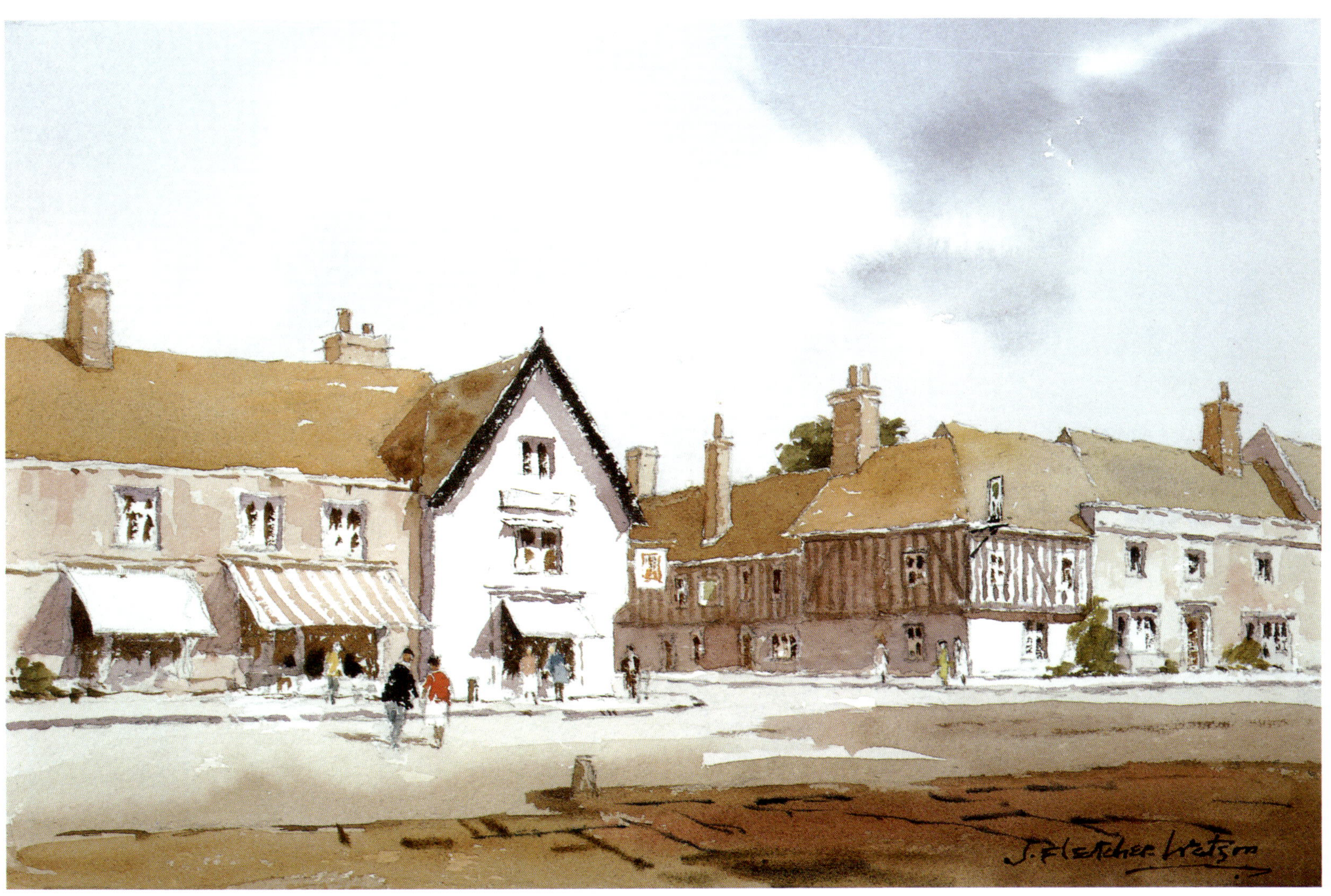

*Dedham Village  18.5 x 12.5 inches*

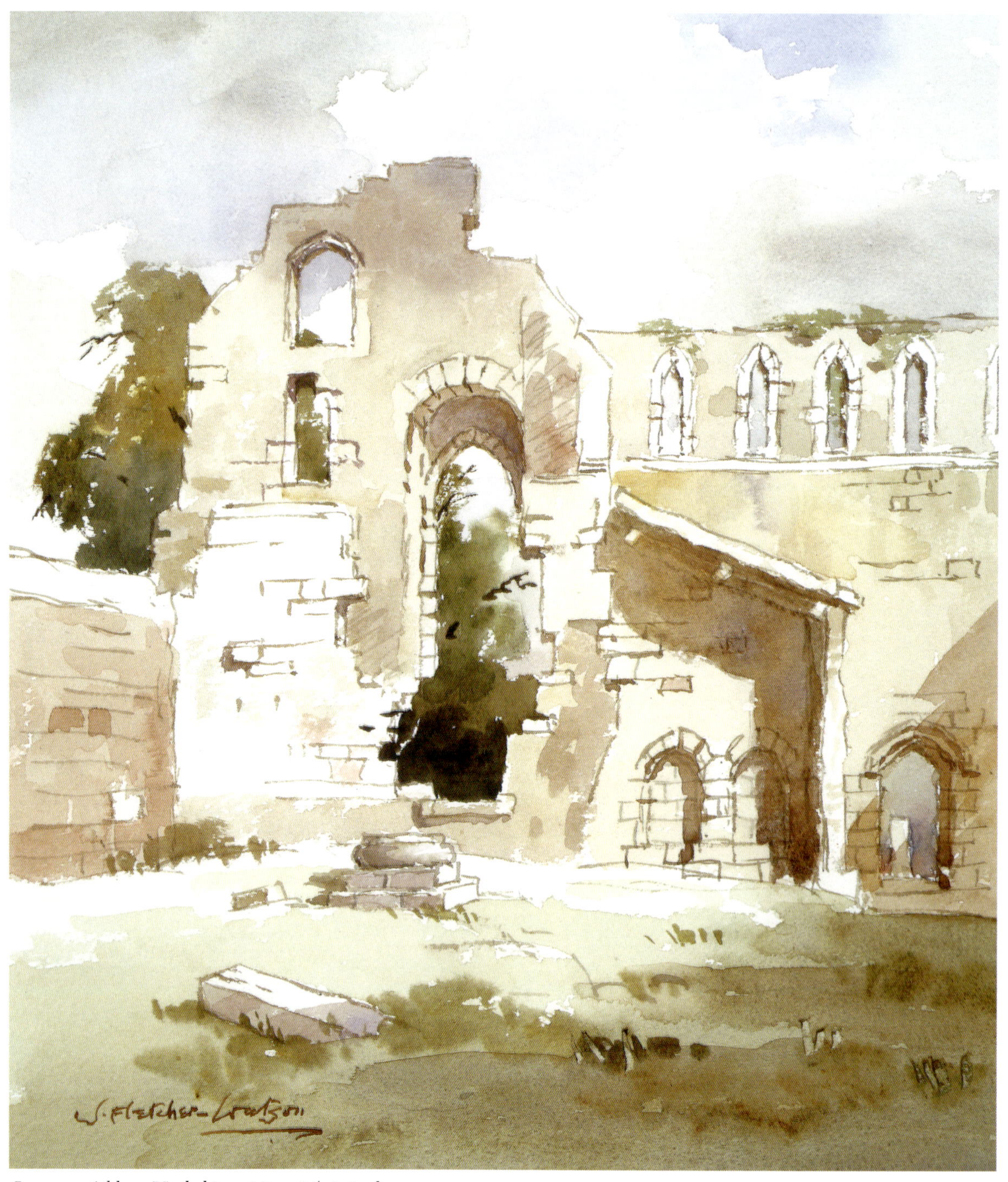

*Jervaux Abbey, Yorkshire  12 x 14.5 inches*

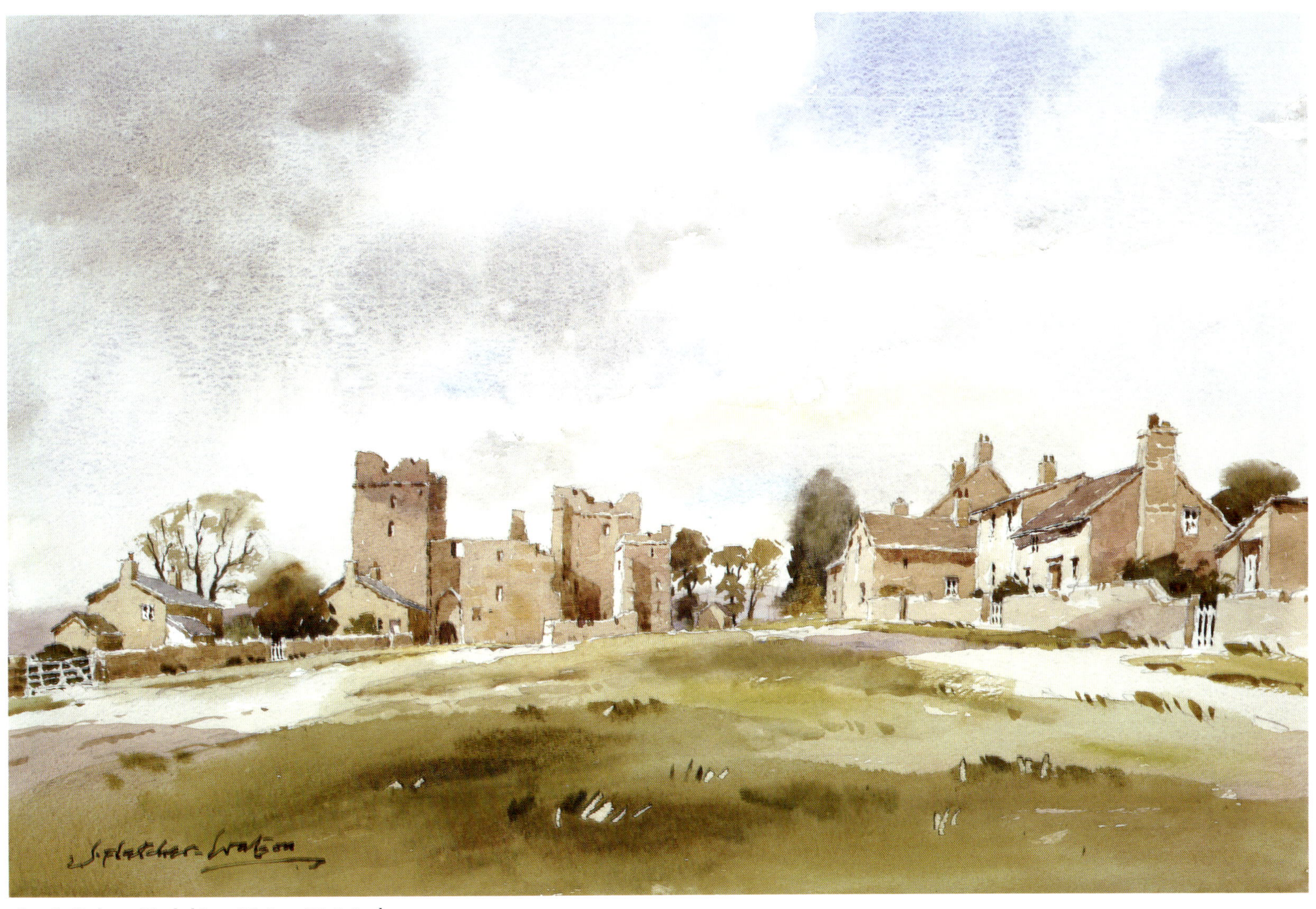

*Castle Bolton, Yorkshire  18.5 x 12.5 inches*

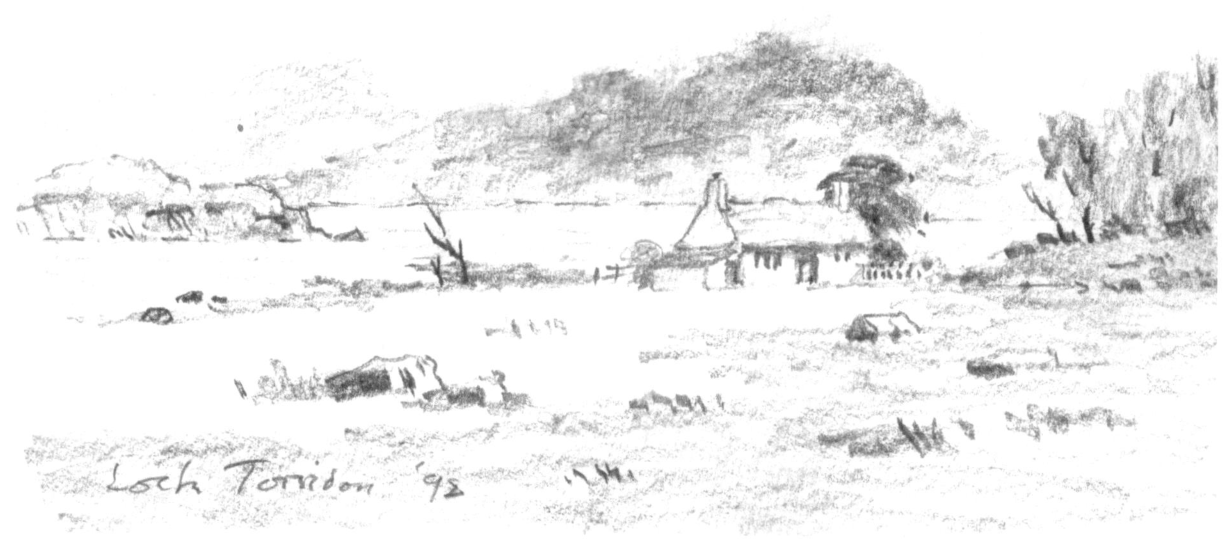
Loch Torridon '92

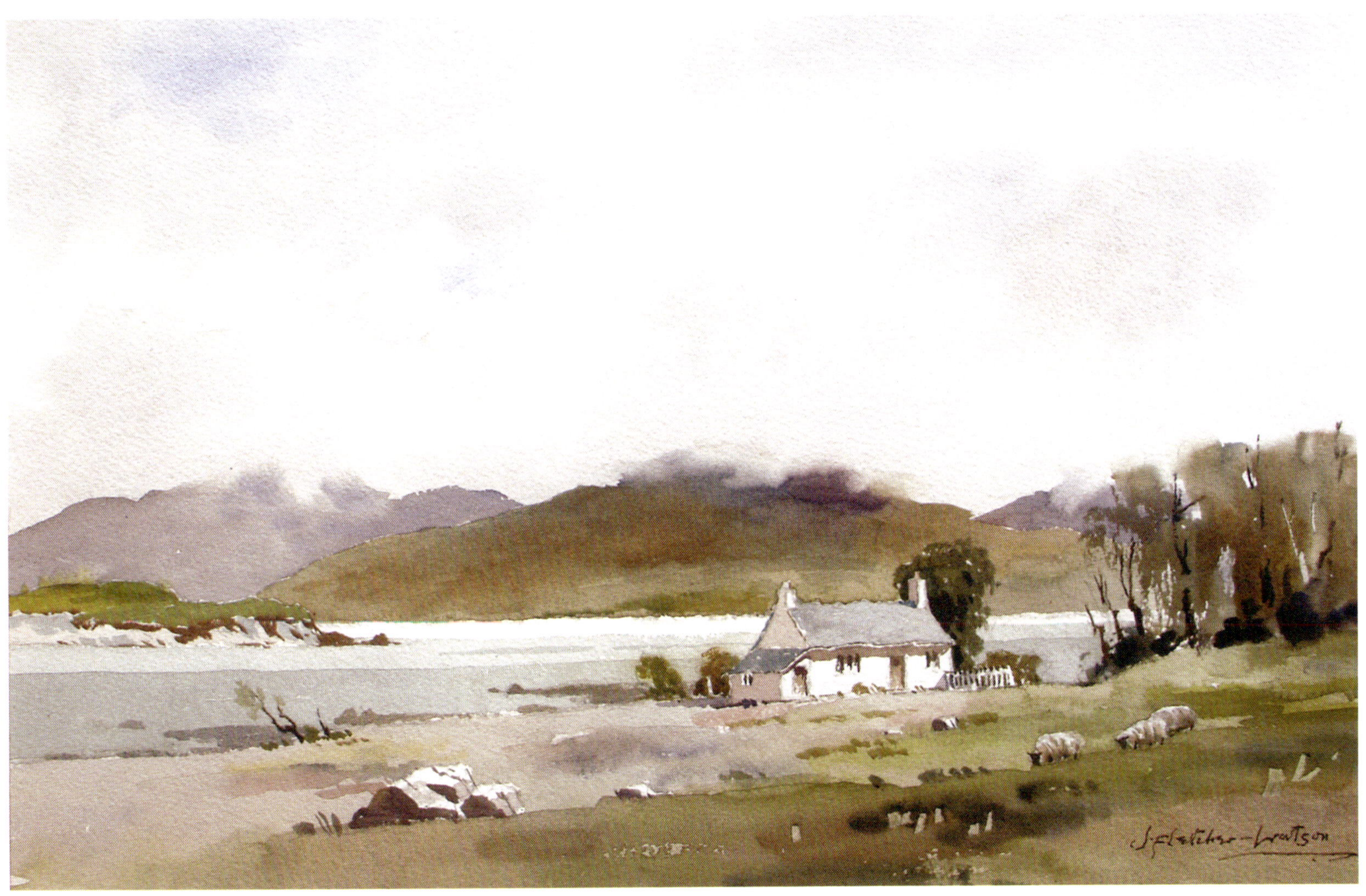

*Loch Torridon, Scotland   18.5 x 12.5 inches*

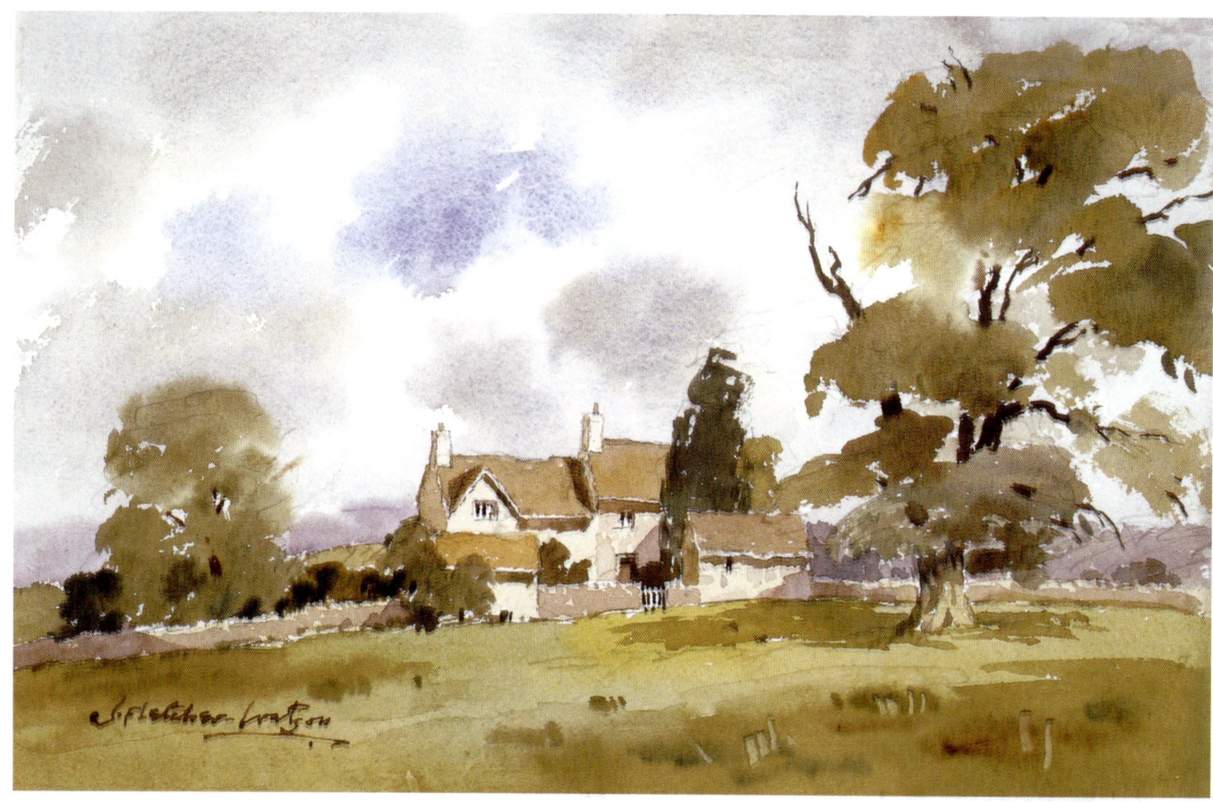

*Cotswold Farmhouse  14 x 10 inches*

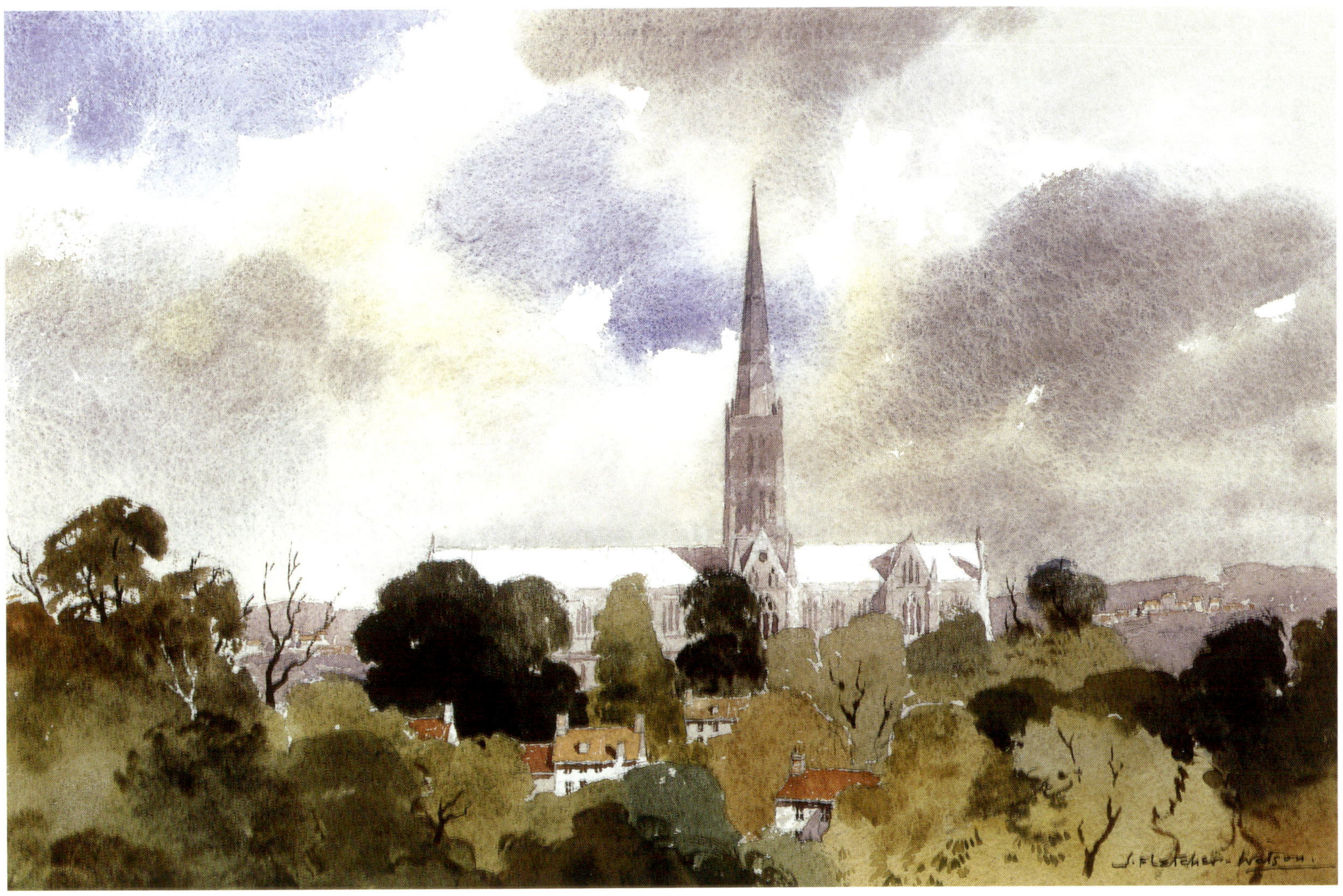

*Salisbury Cathedral from the south, painted for the Salisbury Cathedral Trust Fund   18.5 x 12.5 inches*

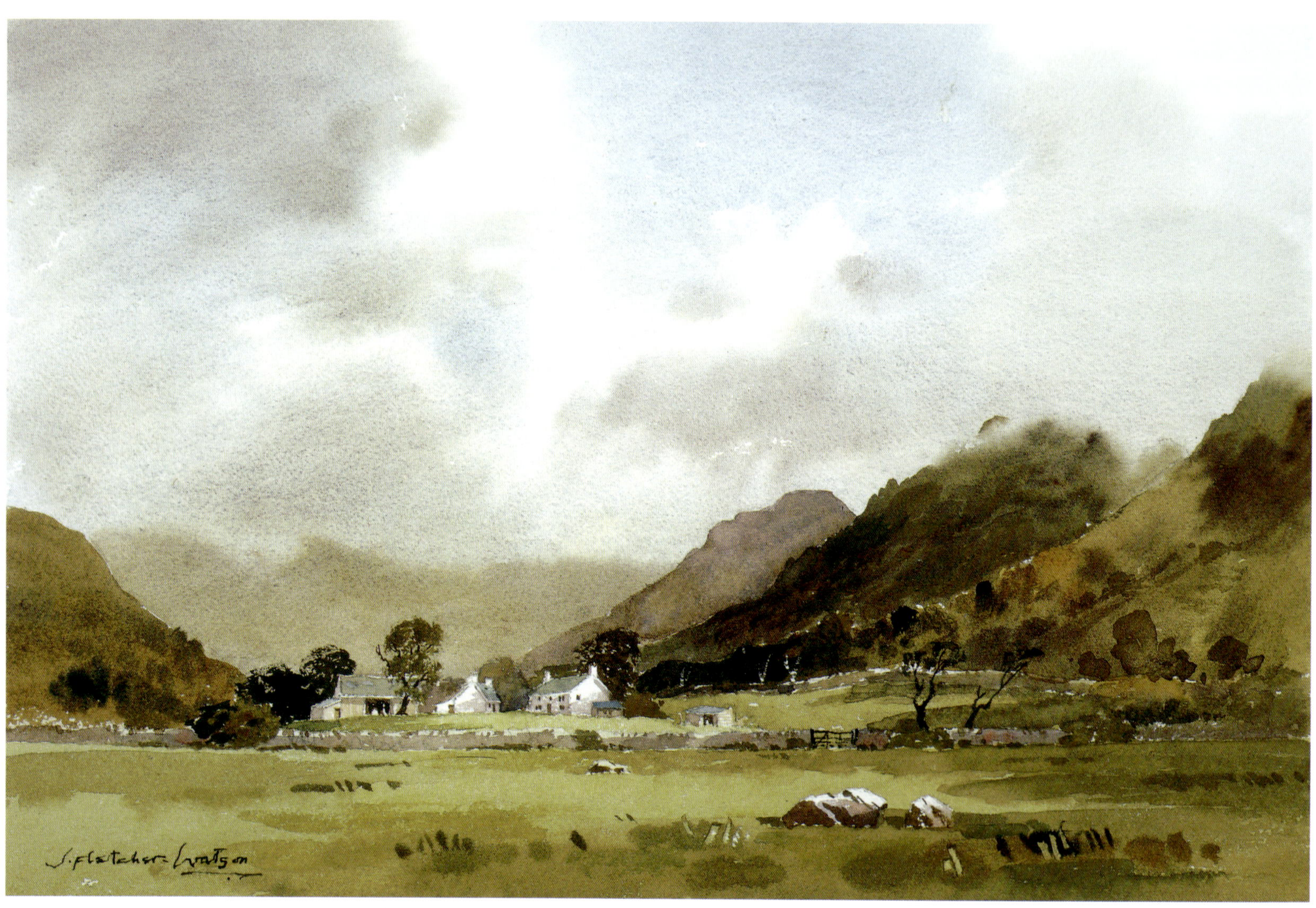

*Stonethwaite Valley, Cumbria  18.5 x 12.5 inches*

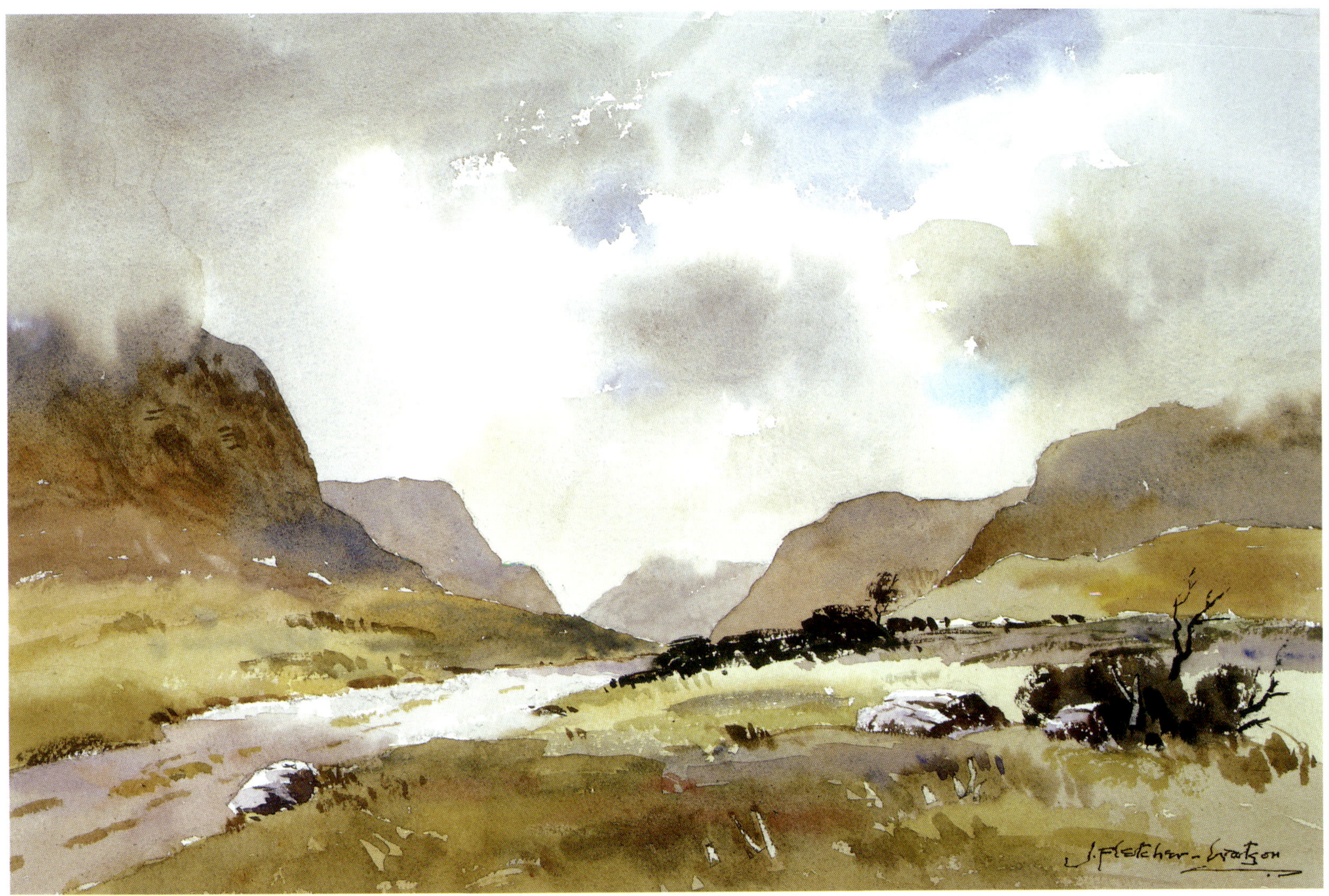

*Old Road, Glen Coe   18.5 x 12.5 inches*

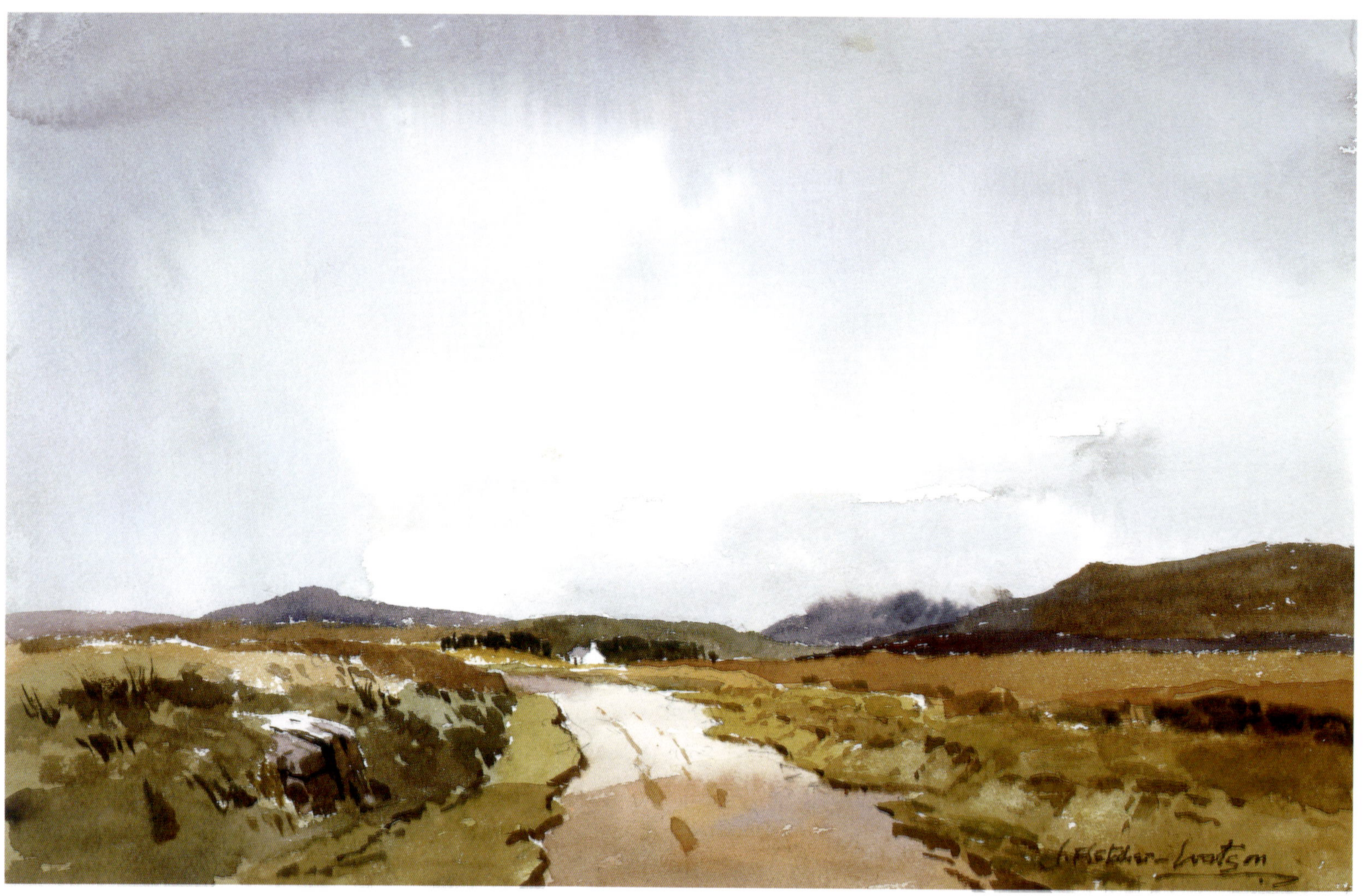

*North Skye  18.5 x 12.5 inches*

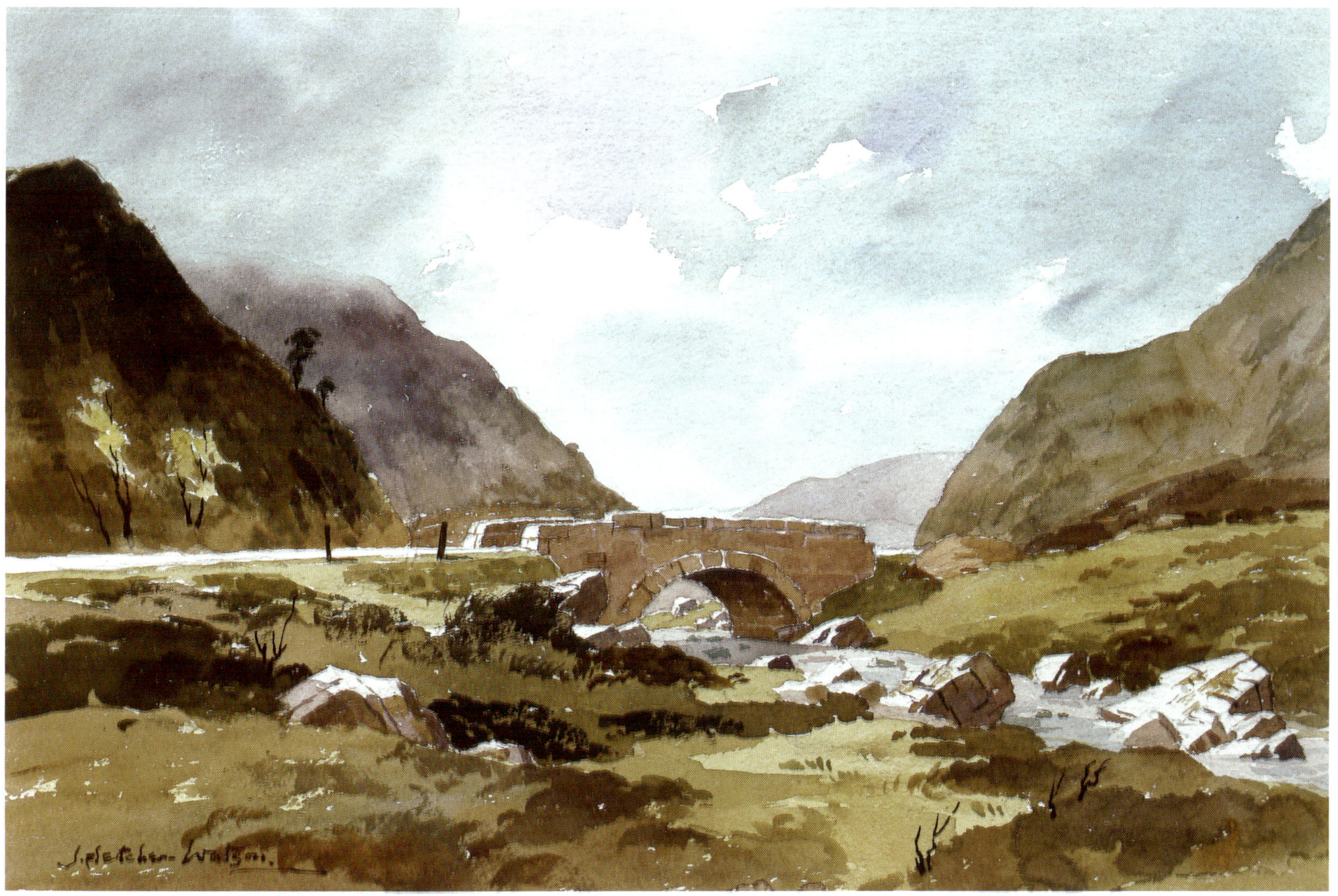

*Bridge, West Highlands  18.5 x 12.5 inches*

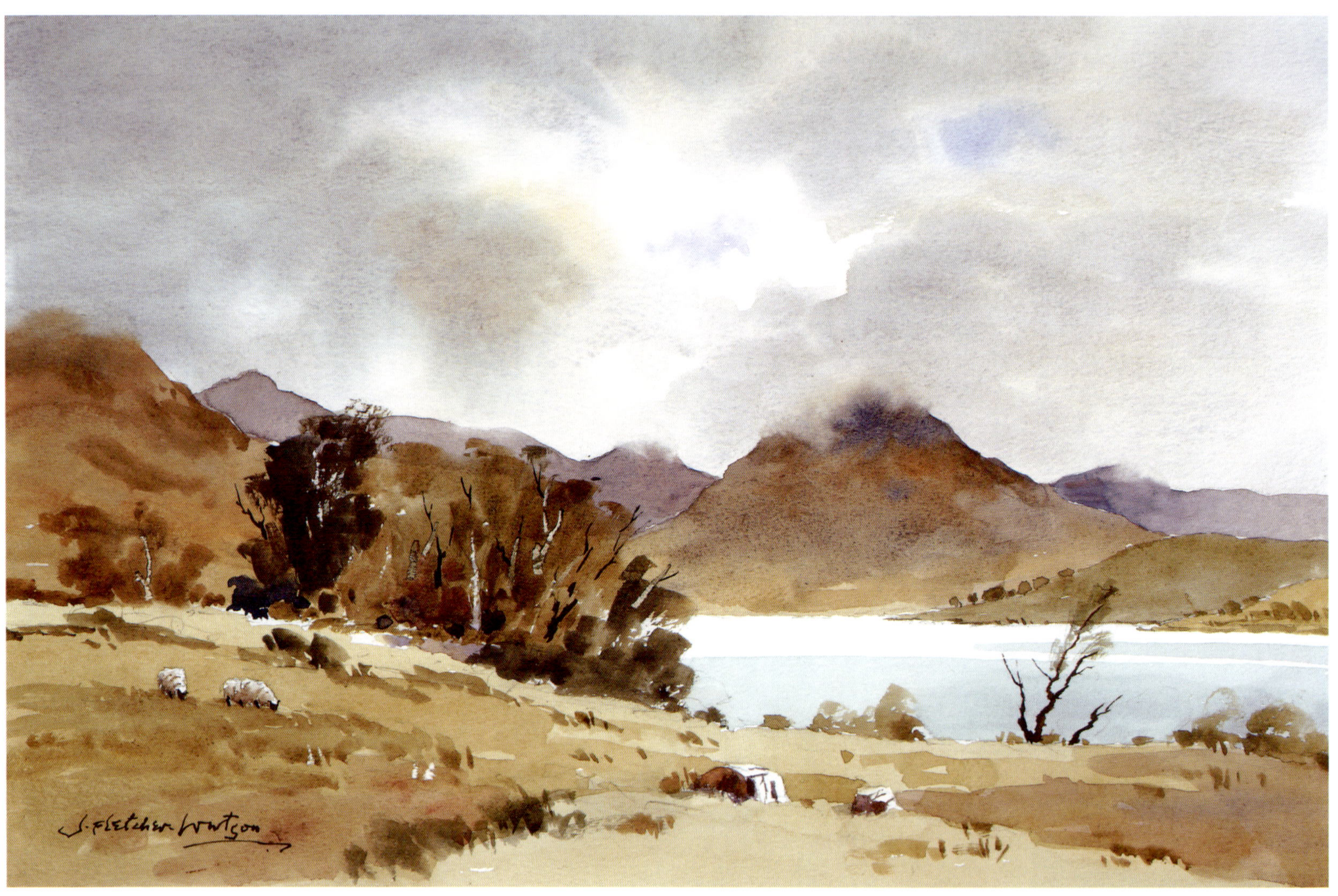

*Loweswater, Cumbria  18.5 x 12.5 inches*

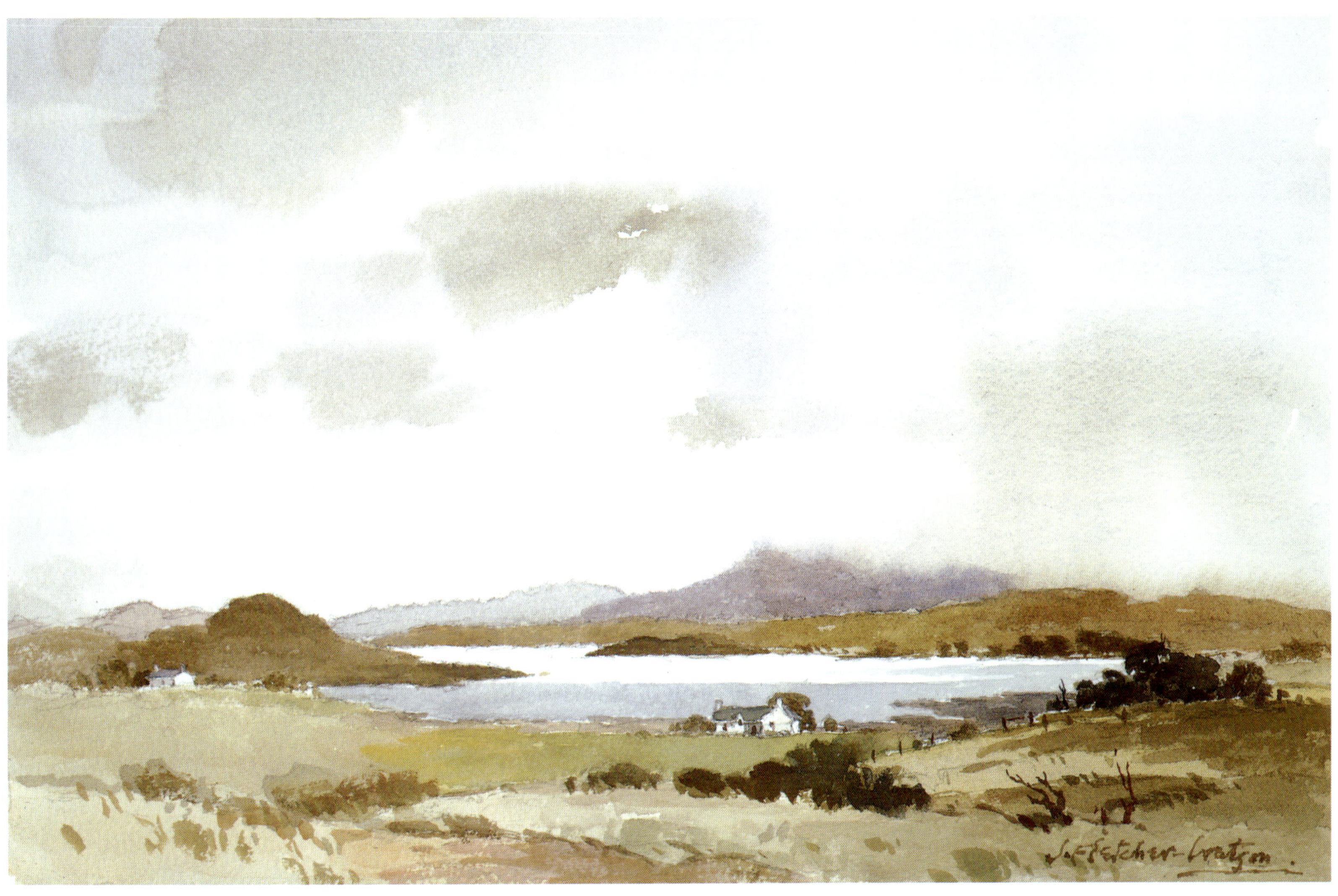

*Rain in Skye  18.5 x 12.5 inches*

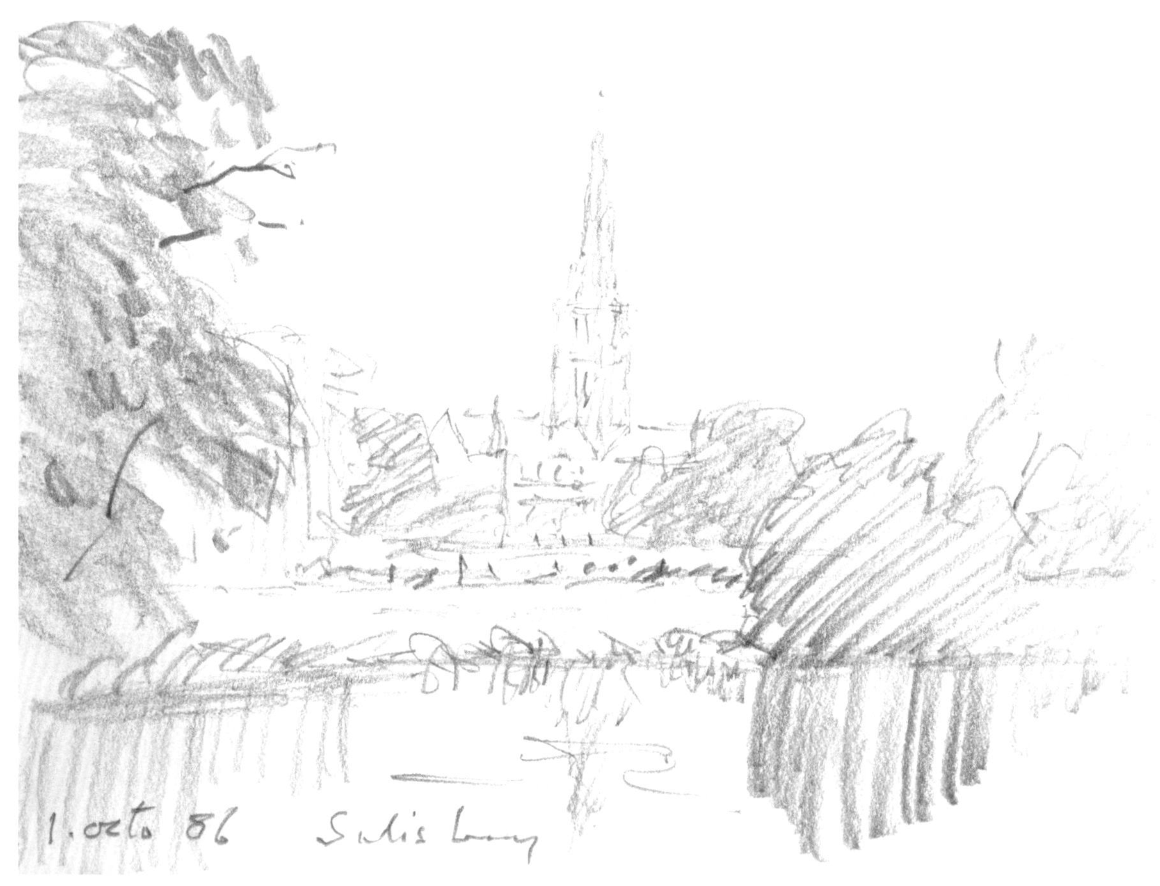


1. octo 86    Salisbury

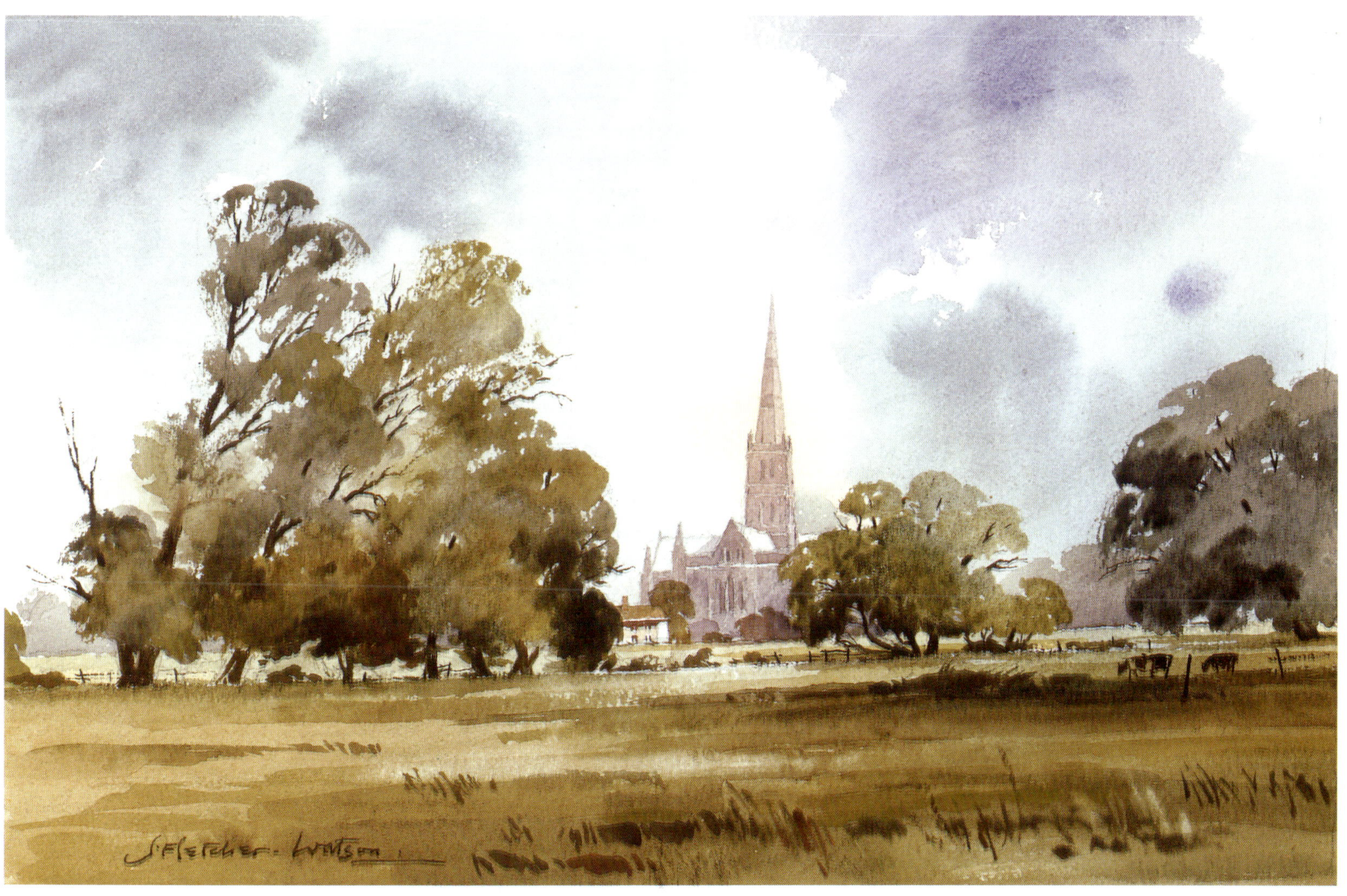

*Salisbury from the Watermeadows*  18.5 x 12.5 inches

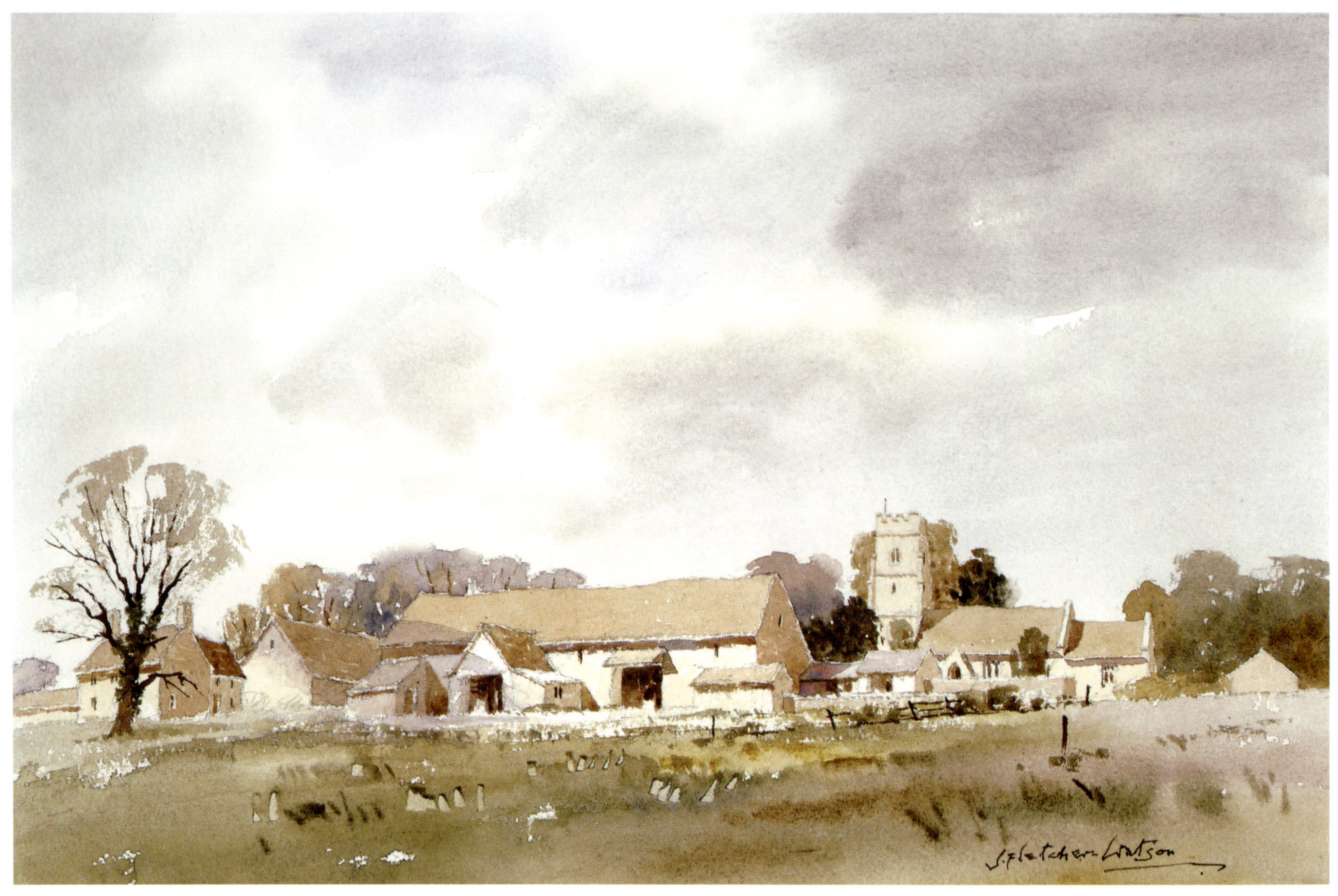

*Cotswold Barns.  Painted for the Countryside Commission's Christmas Card, 1984   18.5 x 12.5 inches*

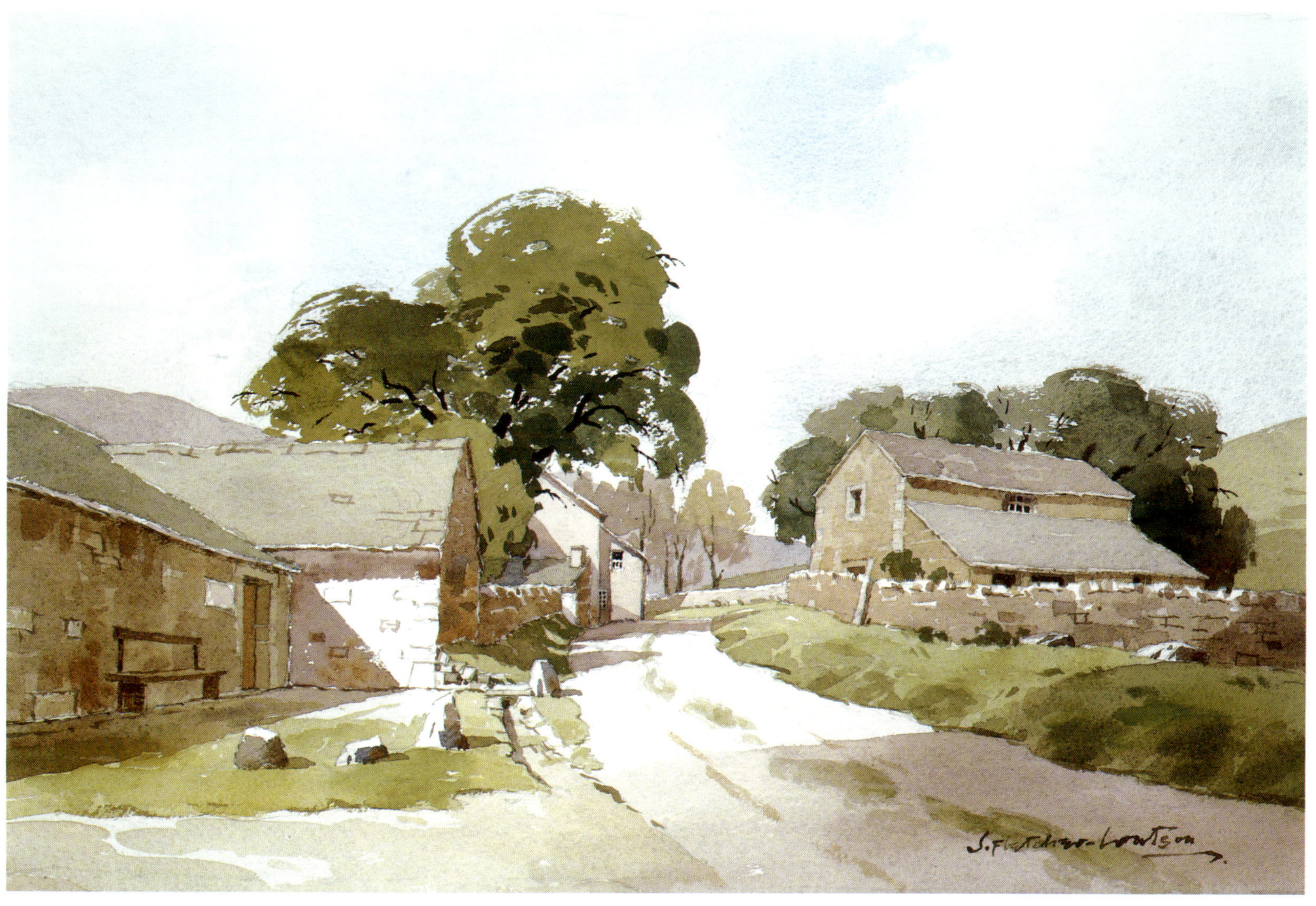

*Mosedale, Cumbria  18.5 x 12.5 inches*
*The building on the right was a delightful Quaker Meeting House, dispensing hospitality to passing travellers.*

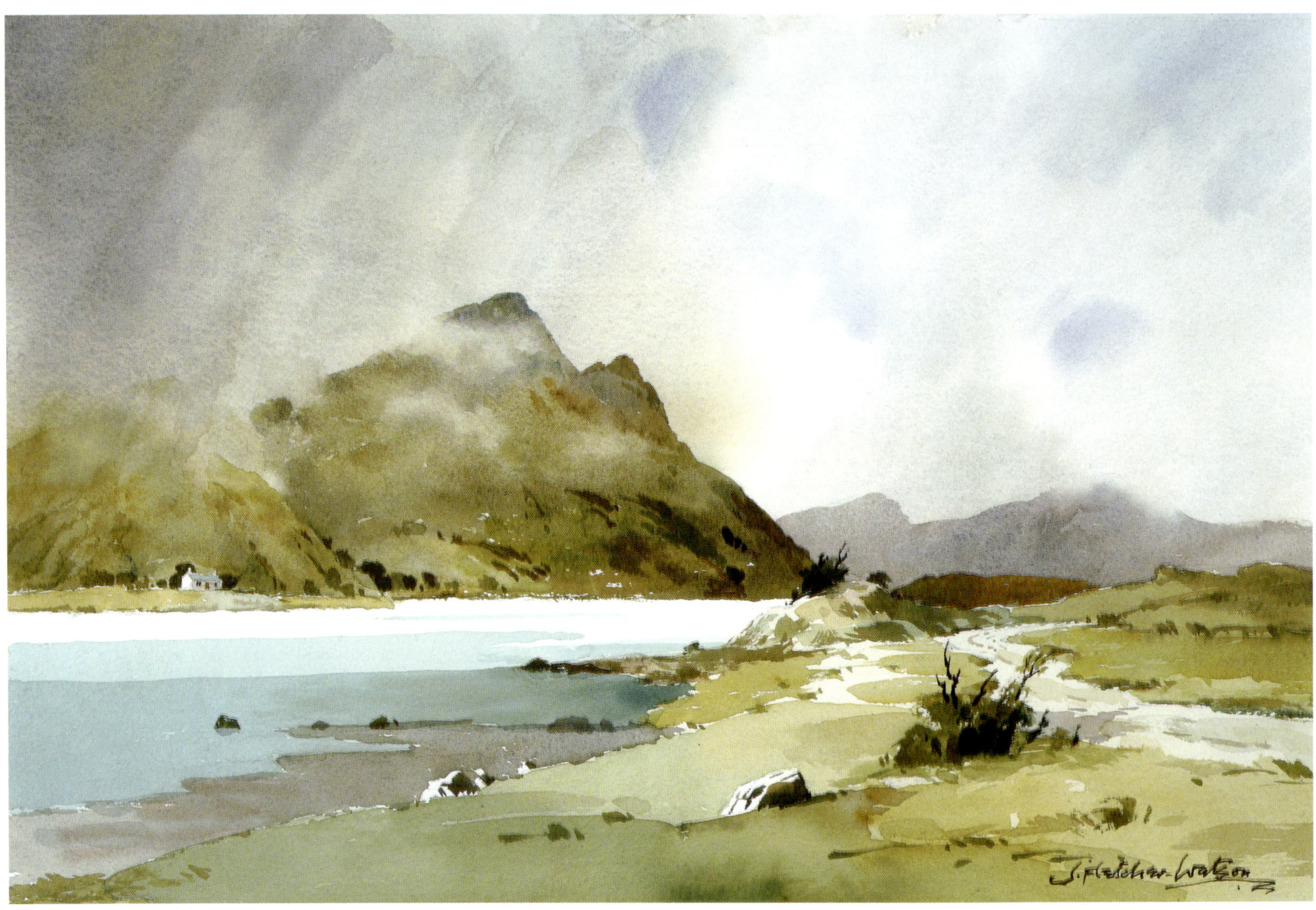

*Upper Loch Torridon, Scotland   18.5  x 12.5 inches*

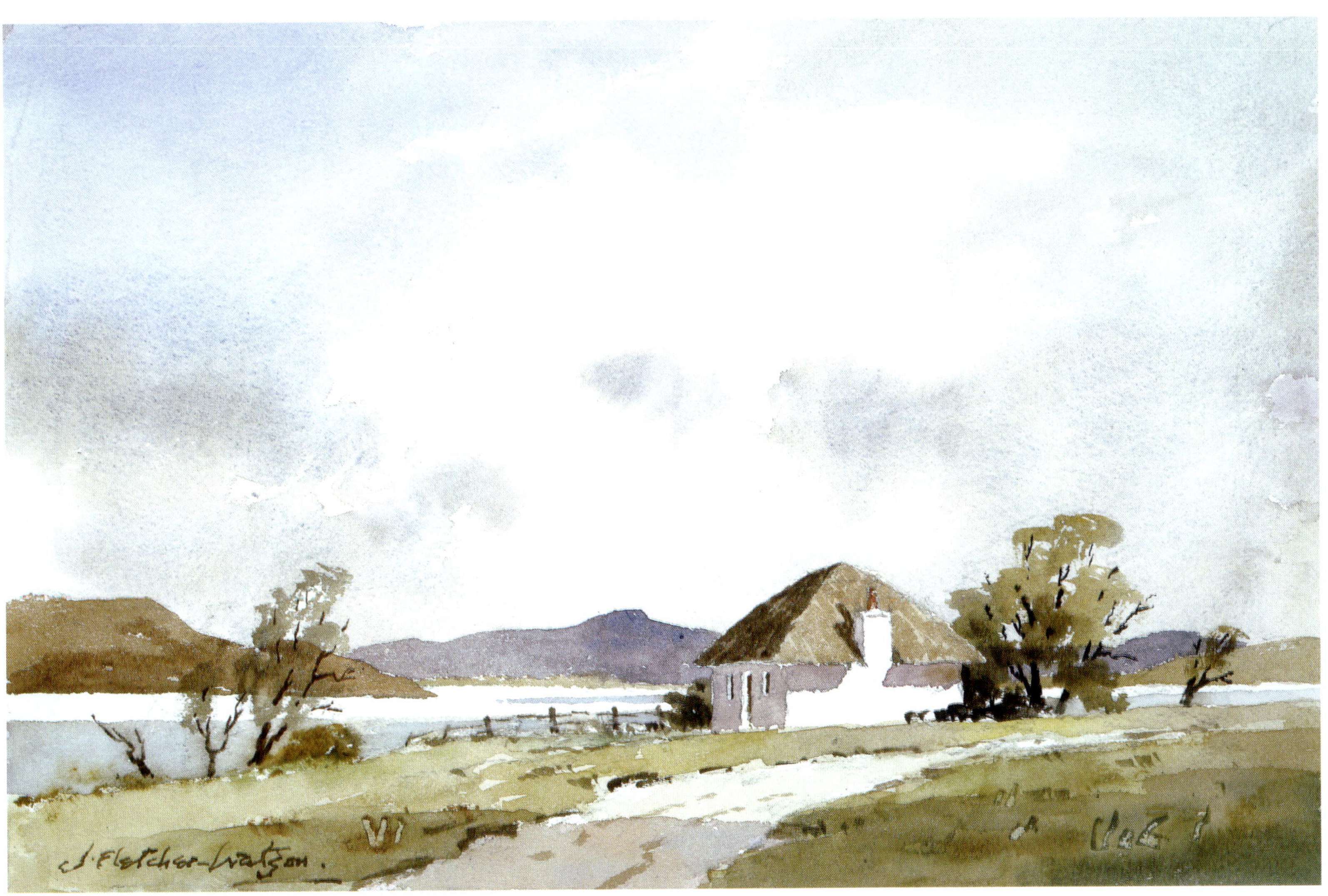

*Loch Ainort, Skye  18.5  x 12.5 inches*

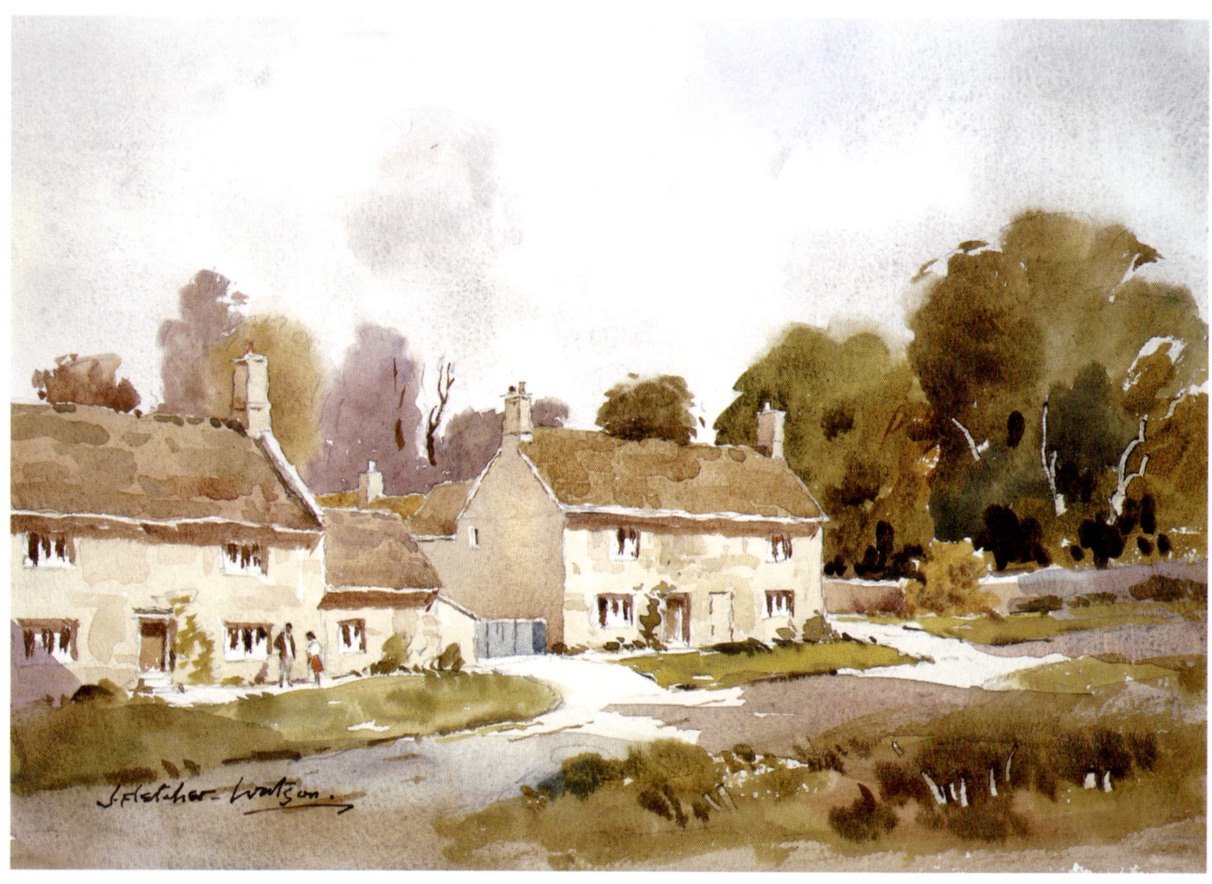

*Little Barrington, Gloucestershire  14 x 10 inches*

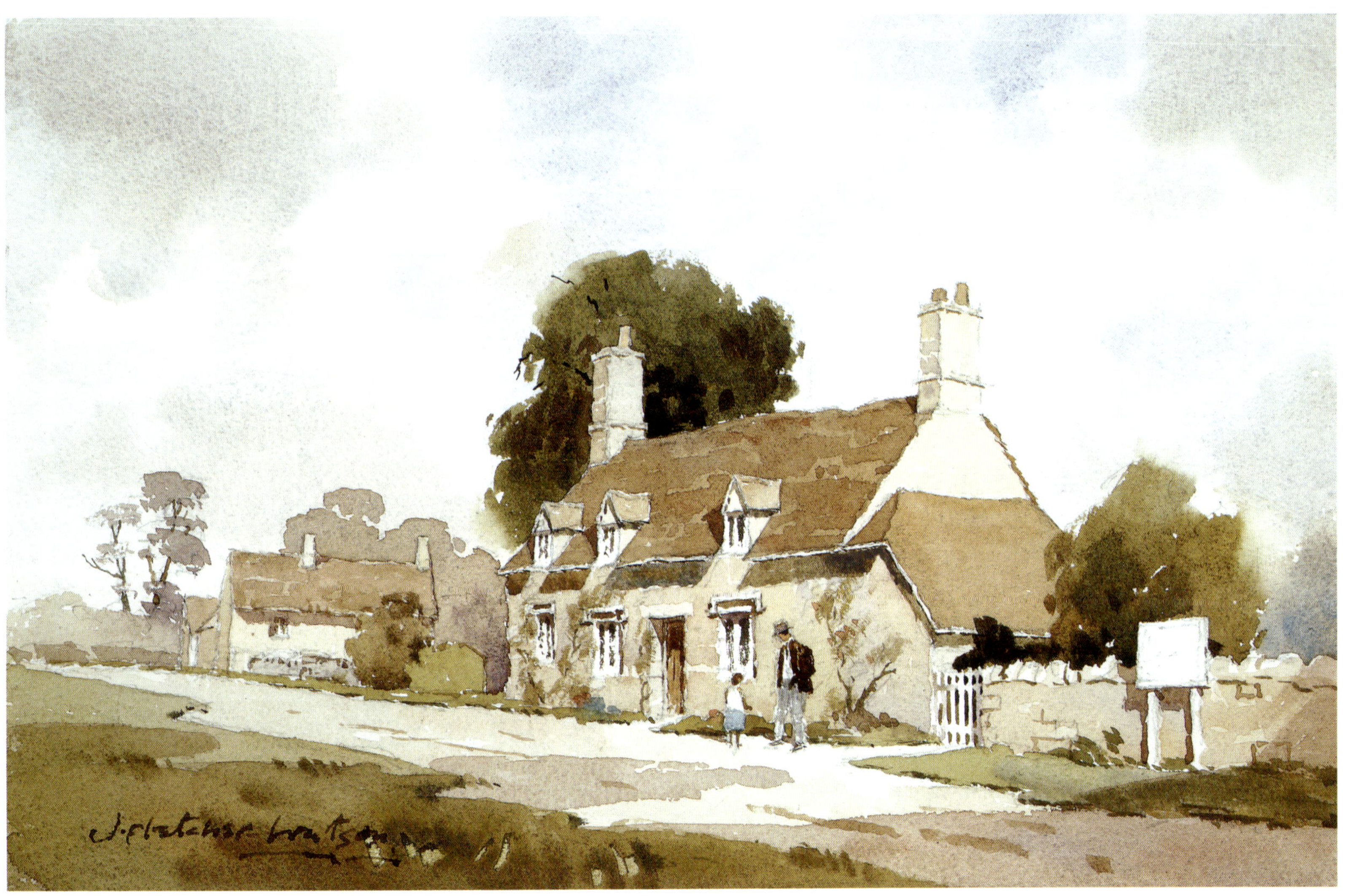

*Taynton, Oxfordshire 16 x 12 inches*

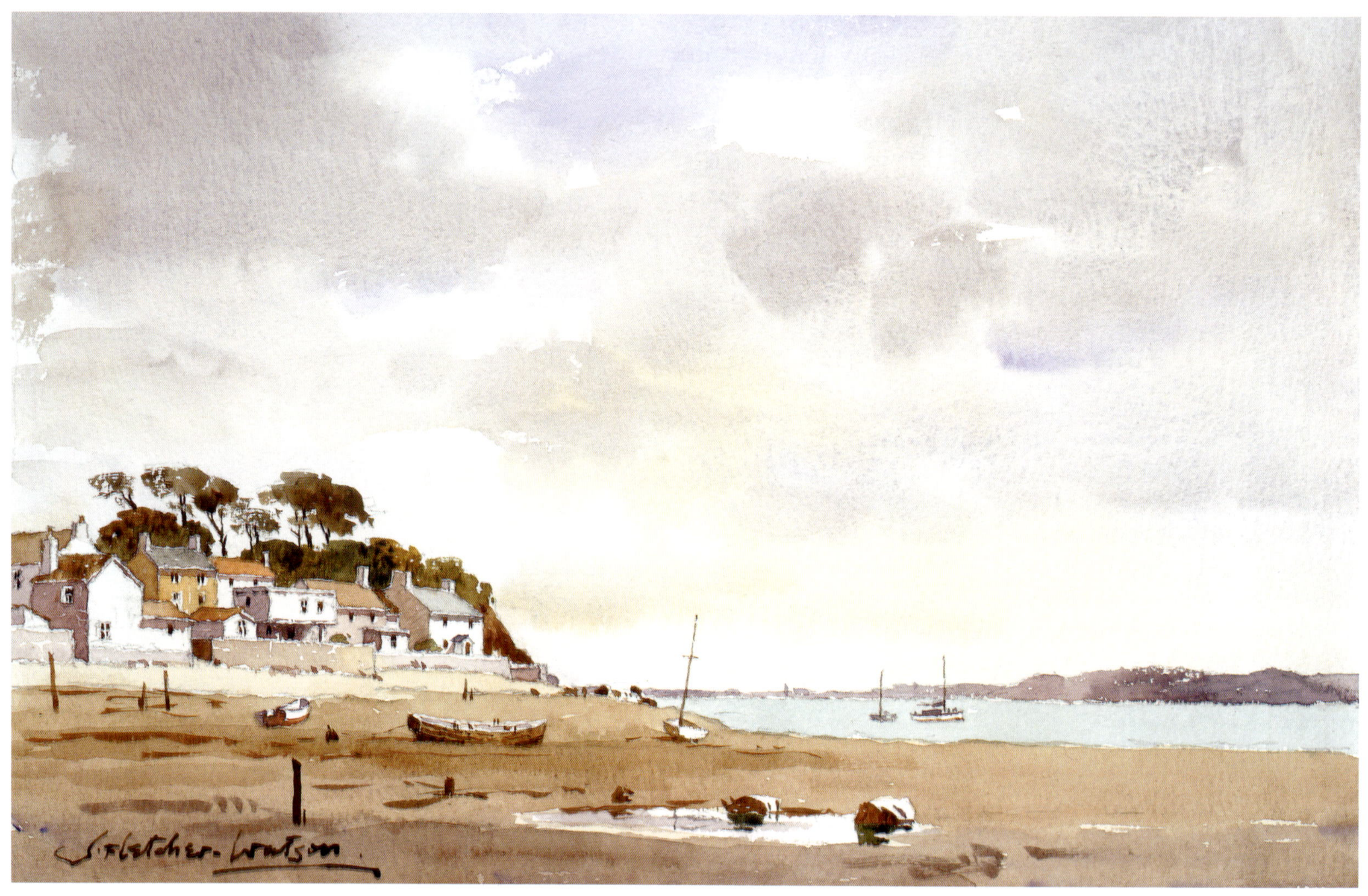

*Lympstone, Devon (Exe Estuary)   14 x 9 inches*

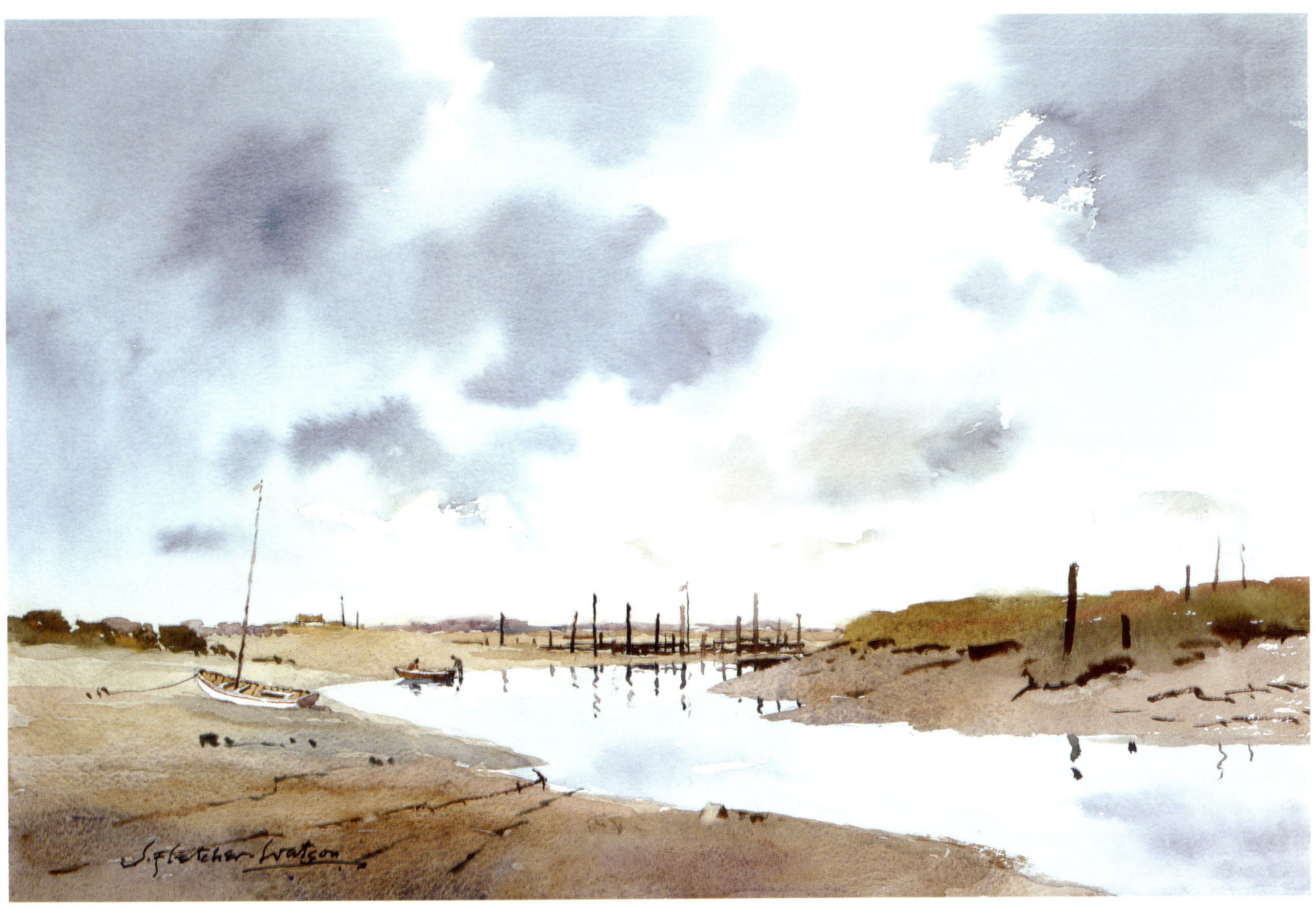

*Blakeney Estuary, Norfolk  18.5 x 12.5 inches*

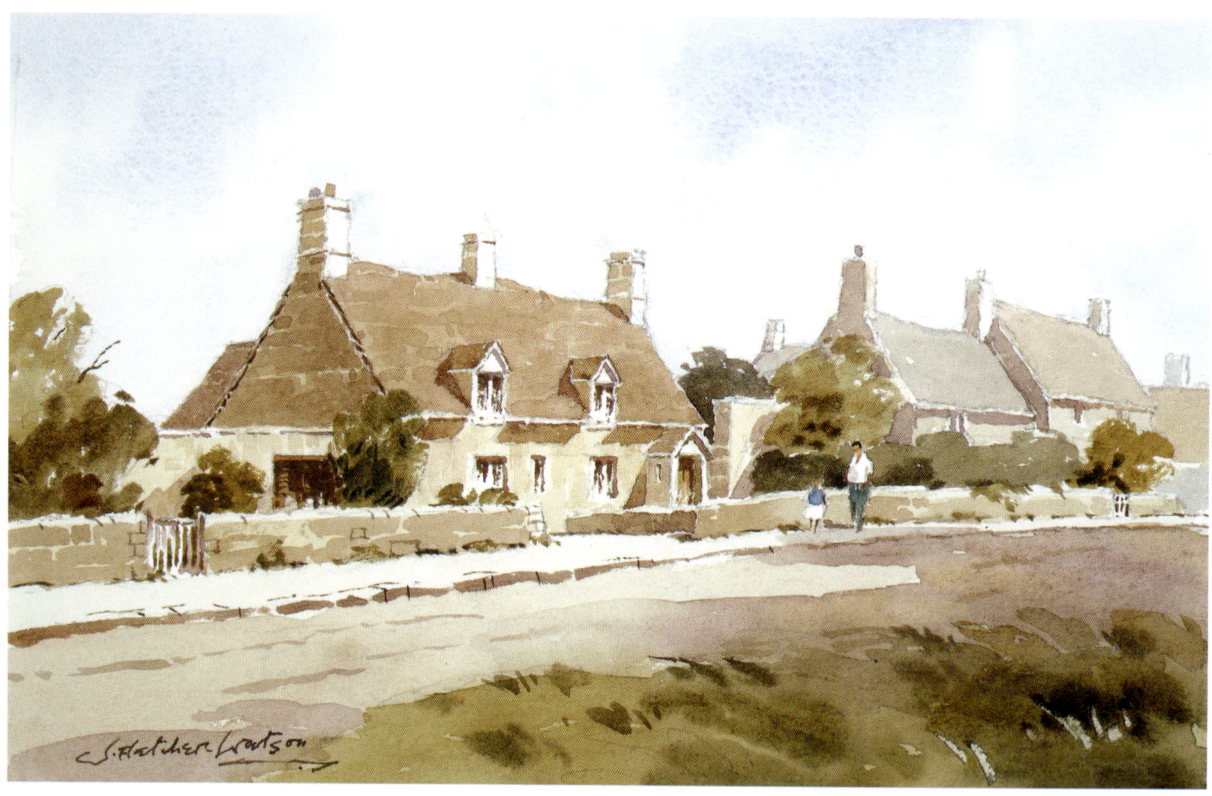

*Cottages in Windrush  14 x 10 inches*

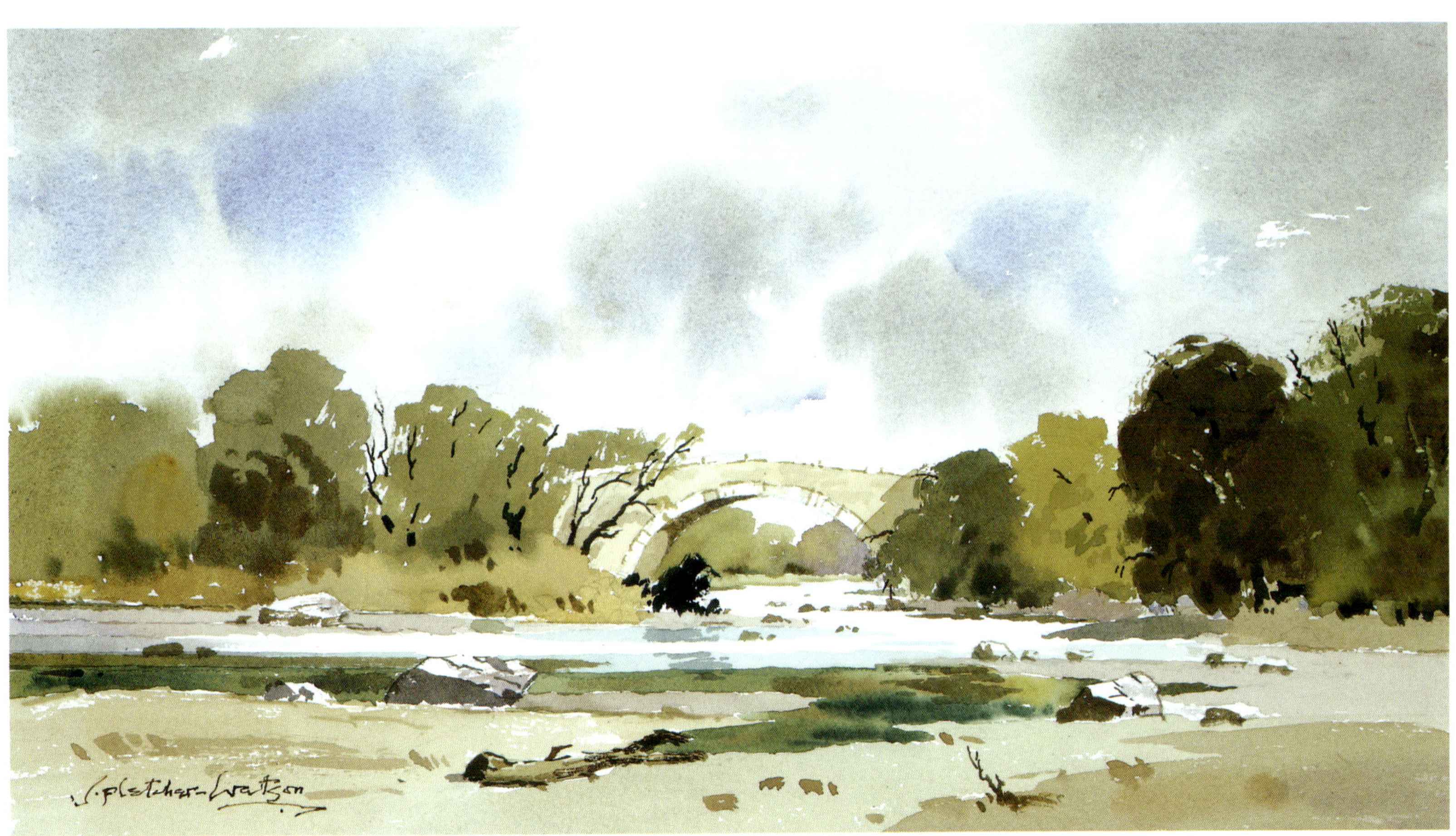

*On the Tees  16 x 10 inches*

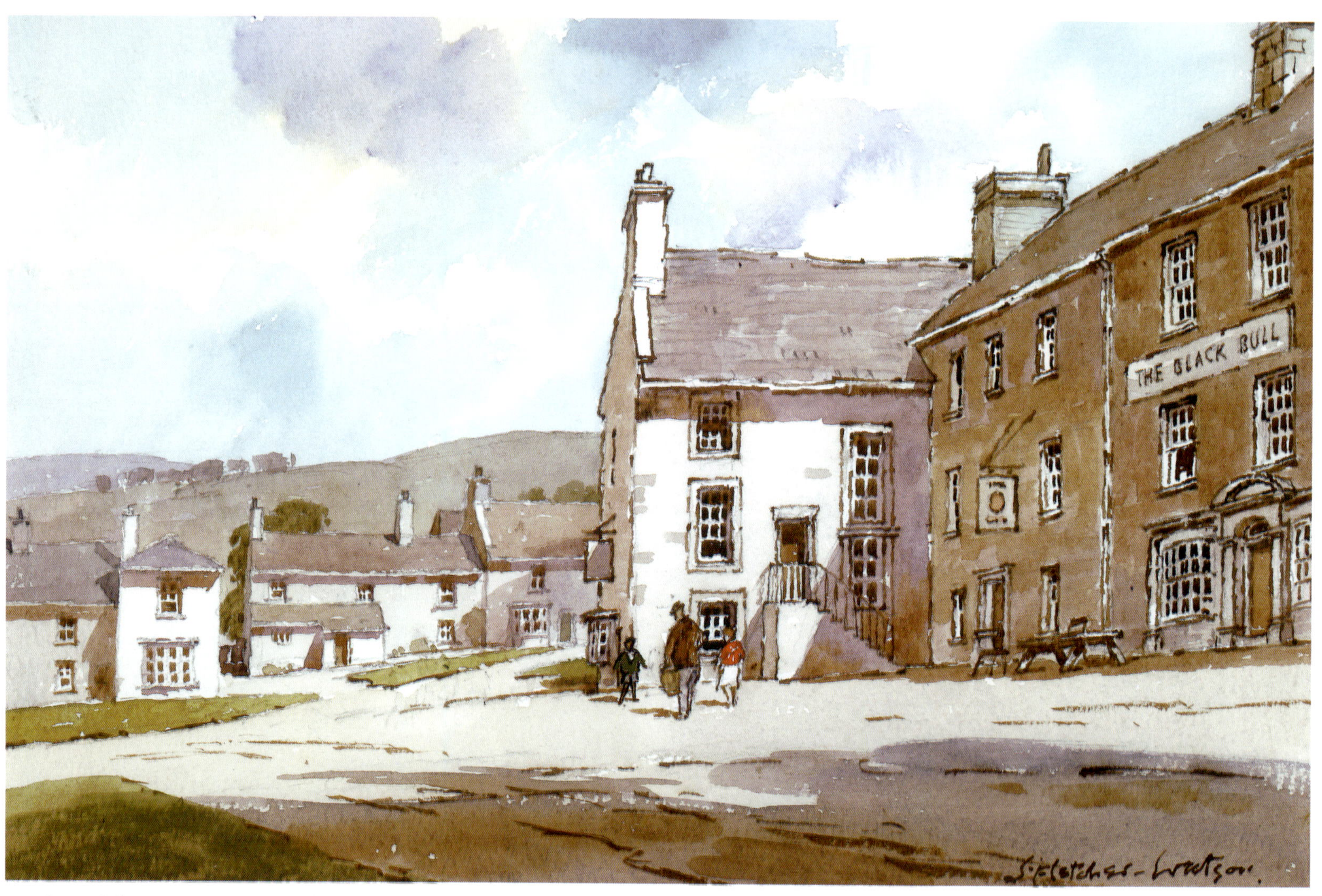


*Reeth, Yorkshire   18.5 x 12.5 inches*

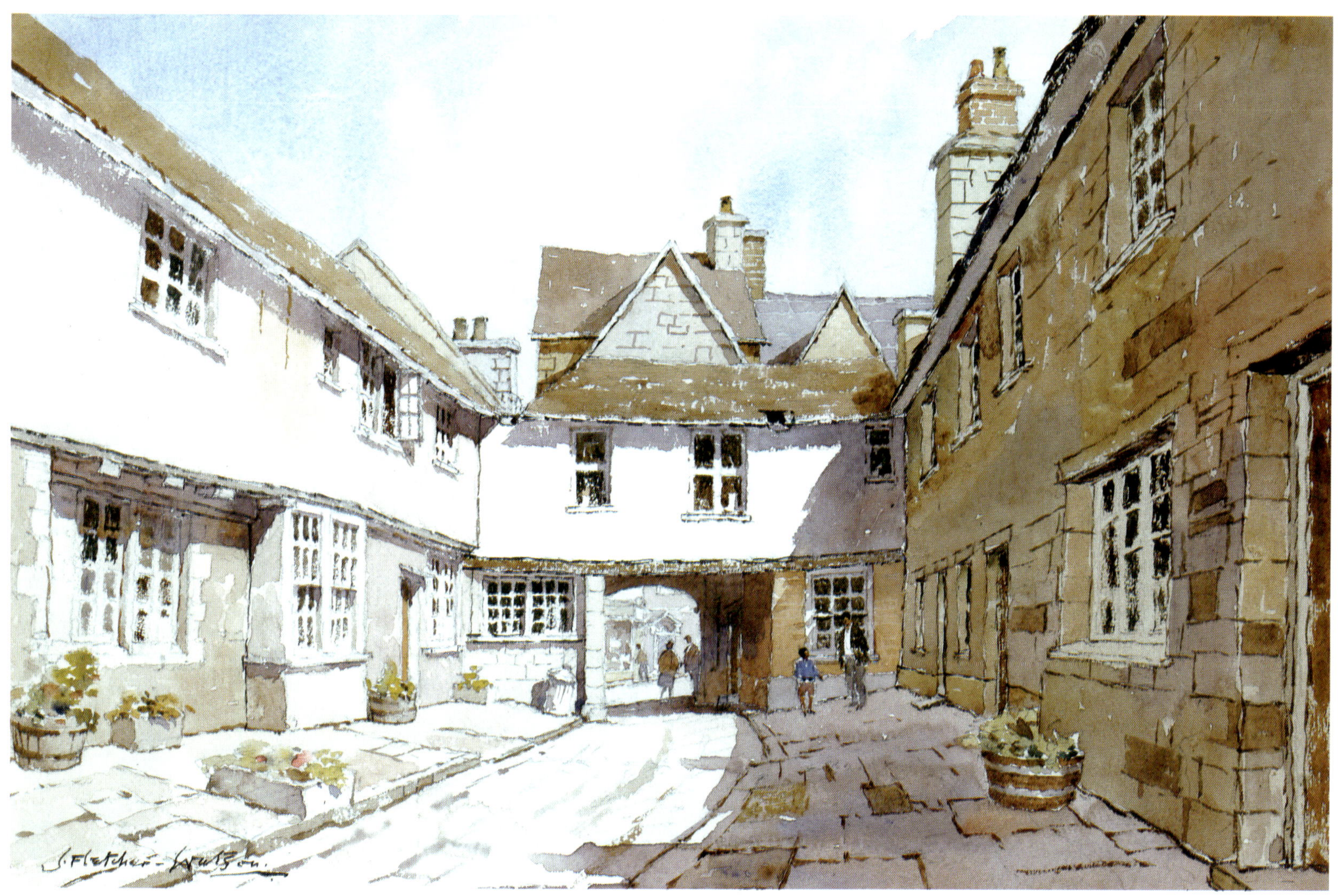

*The George Yard, Burford   18.5 x 12.5 inches*

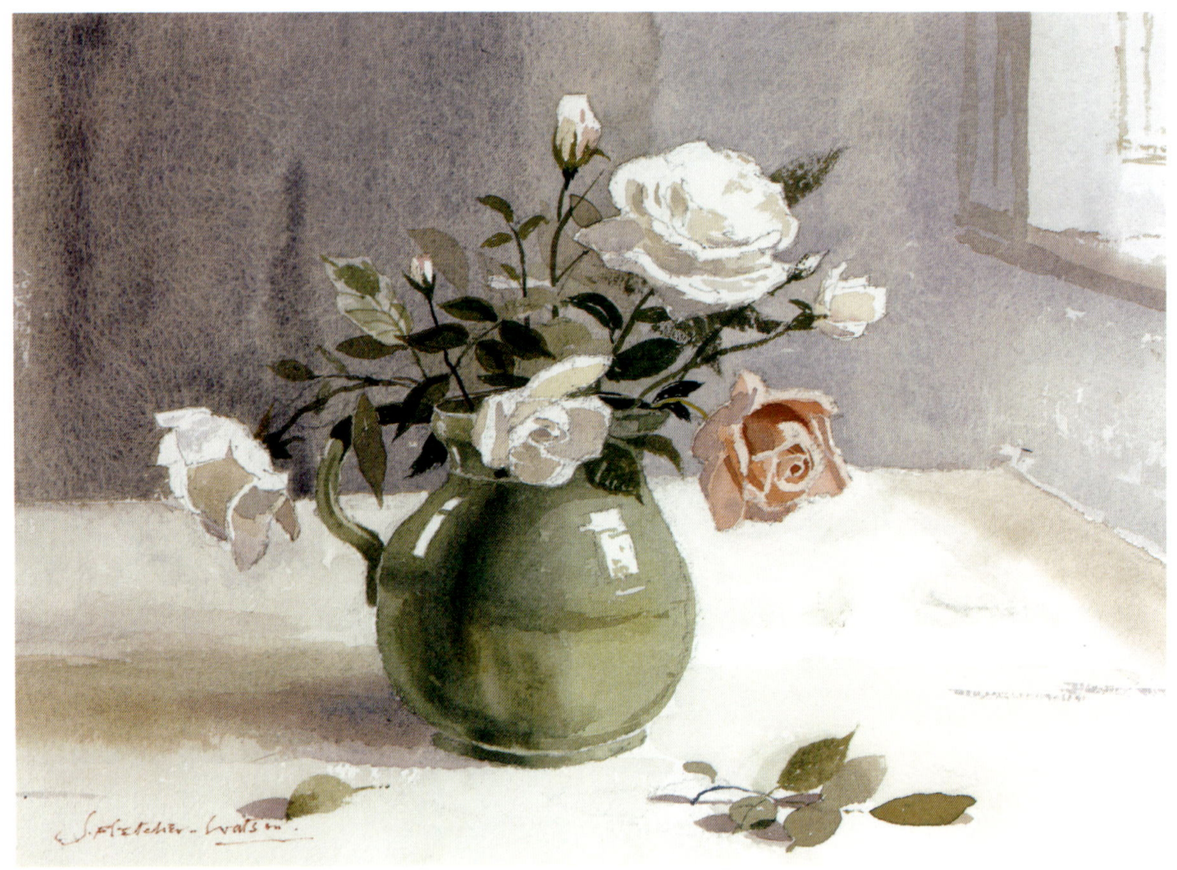

*Roses   15 x 11 inches*

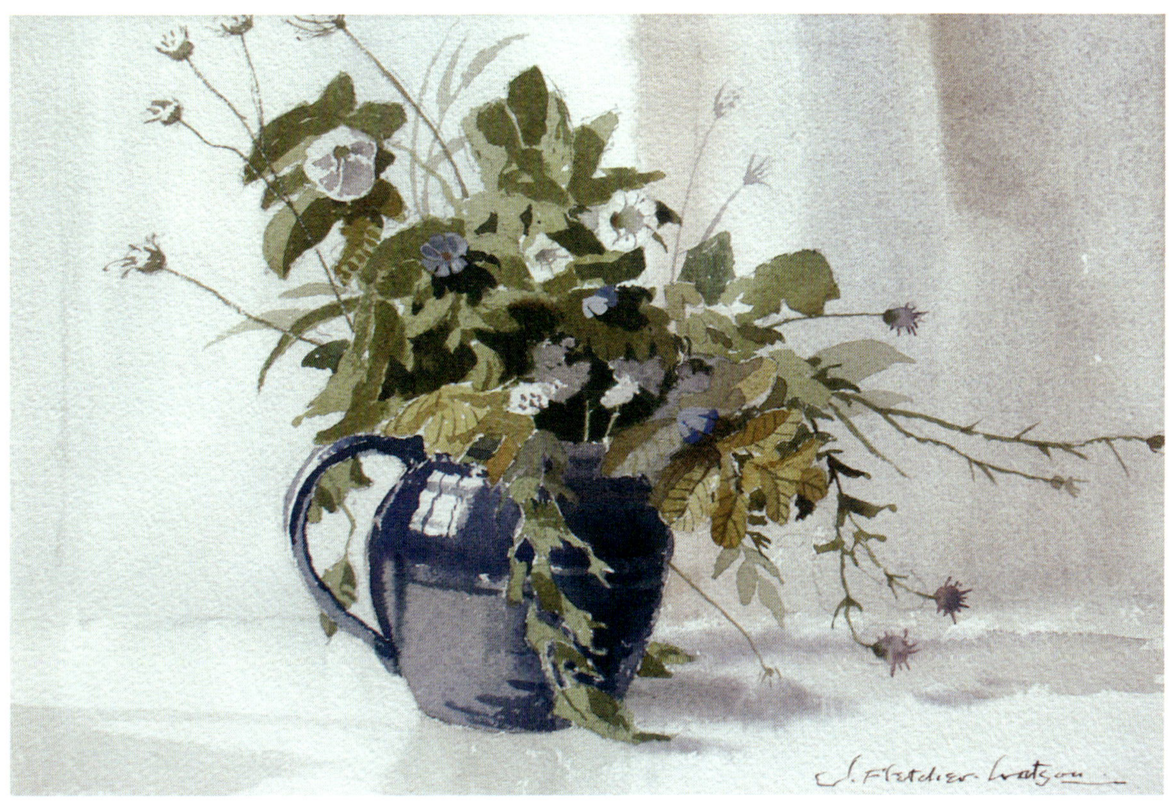

*Wild Flowers  15 x 11 inches*

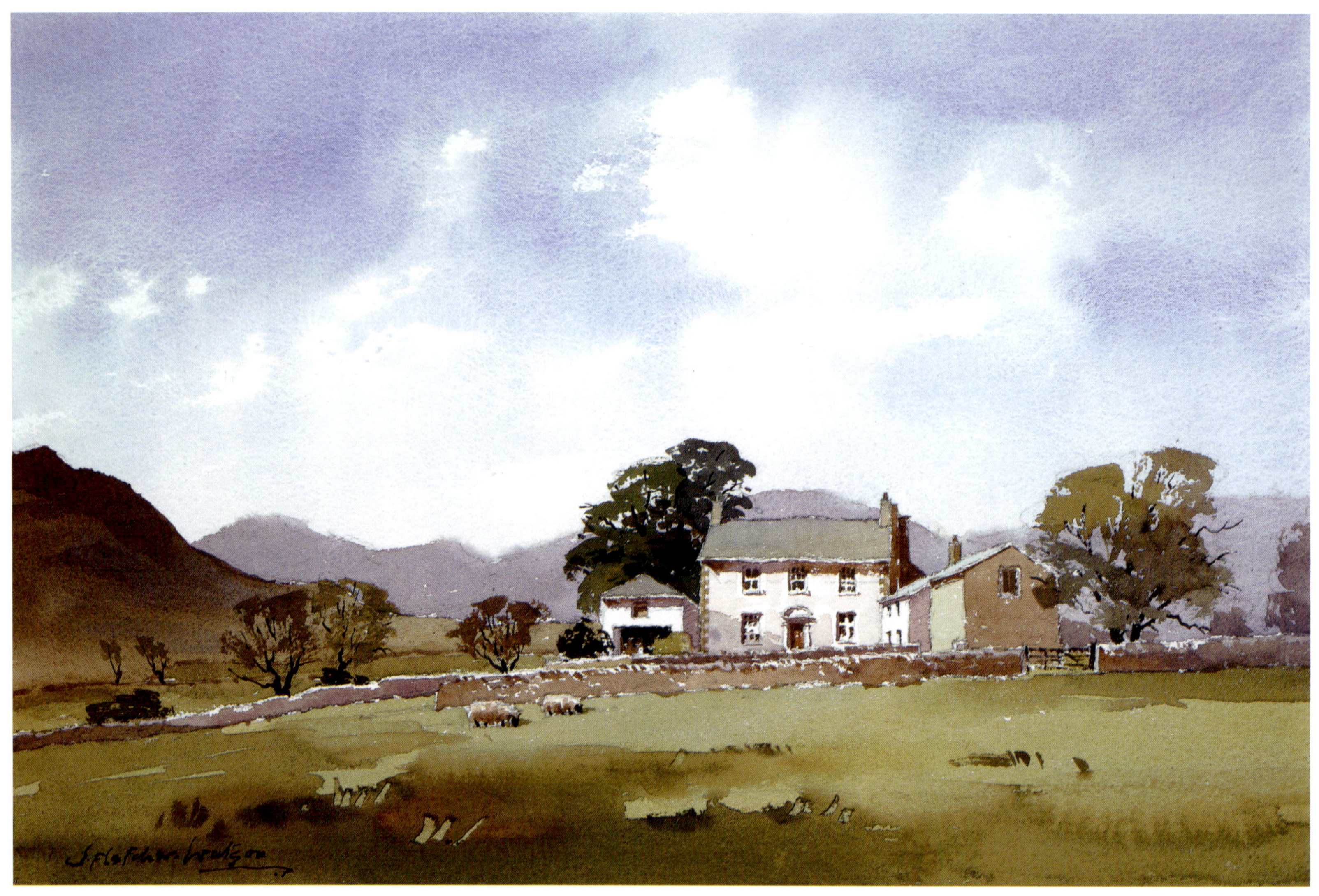

*Farmhouse near Loweswater, Cumbria   18.5 x 12.5 inches*

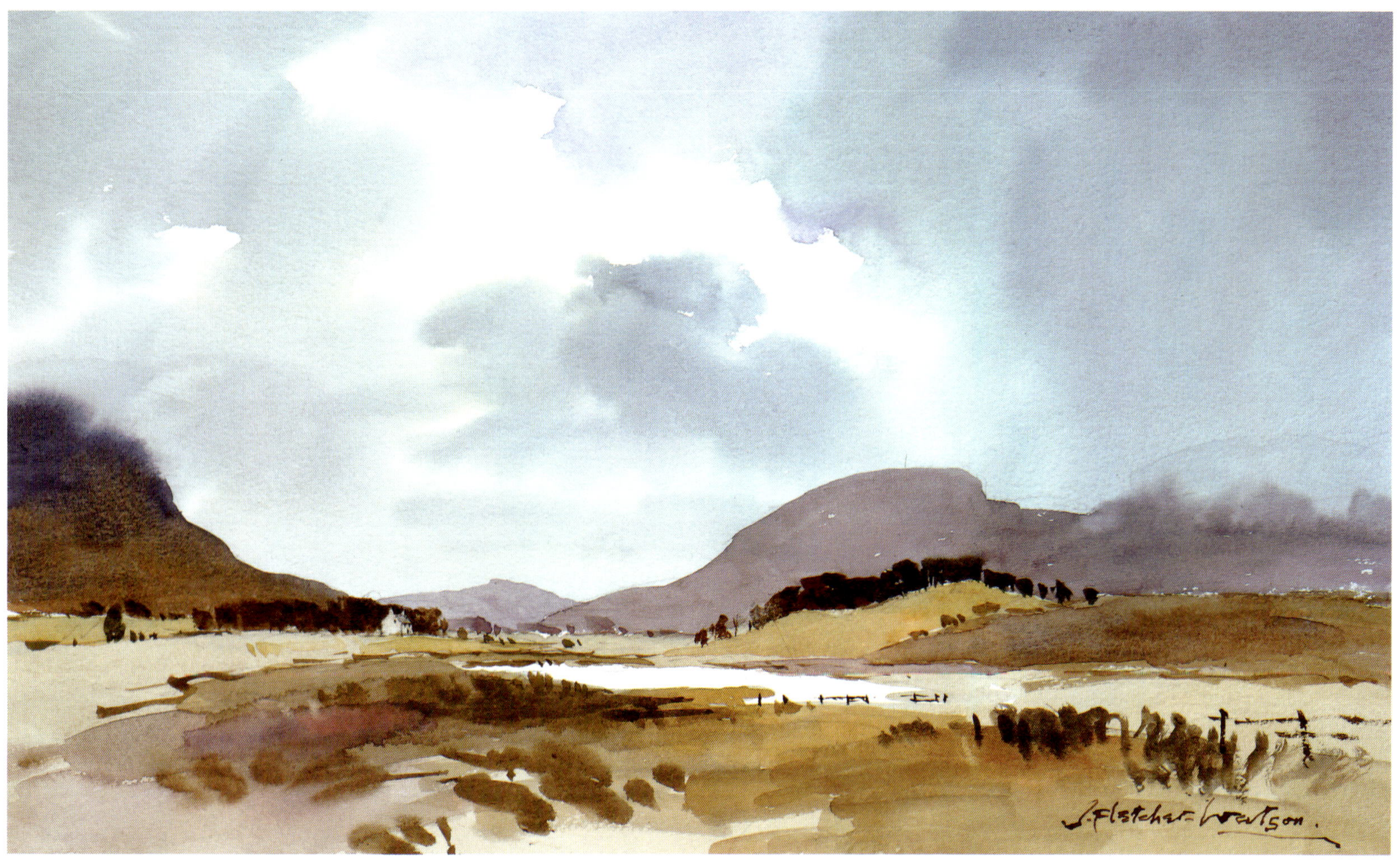

*Connemara, Southern Ireland   16 x 10 inches*

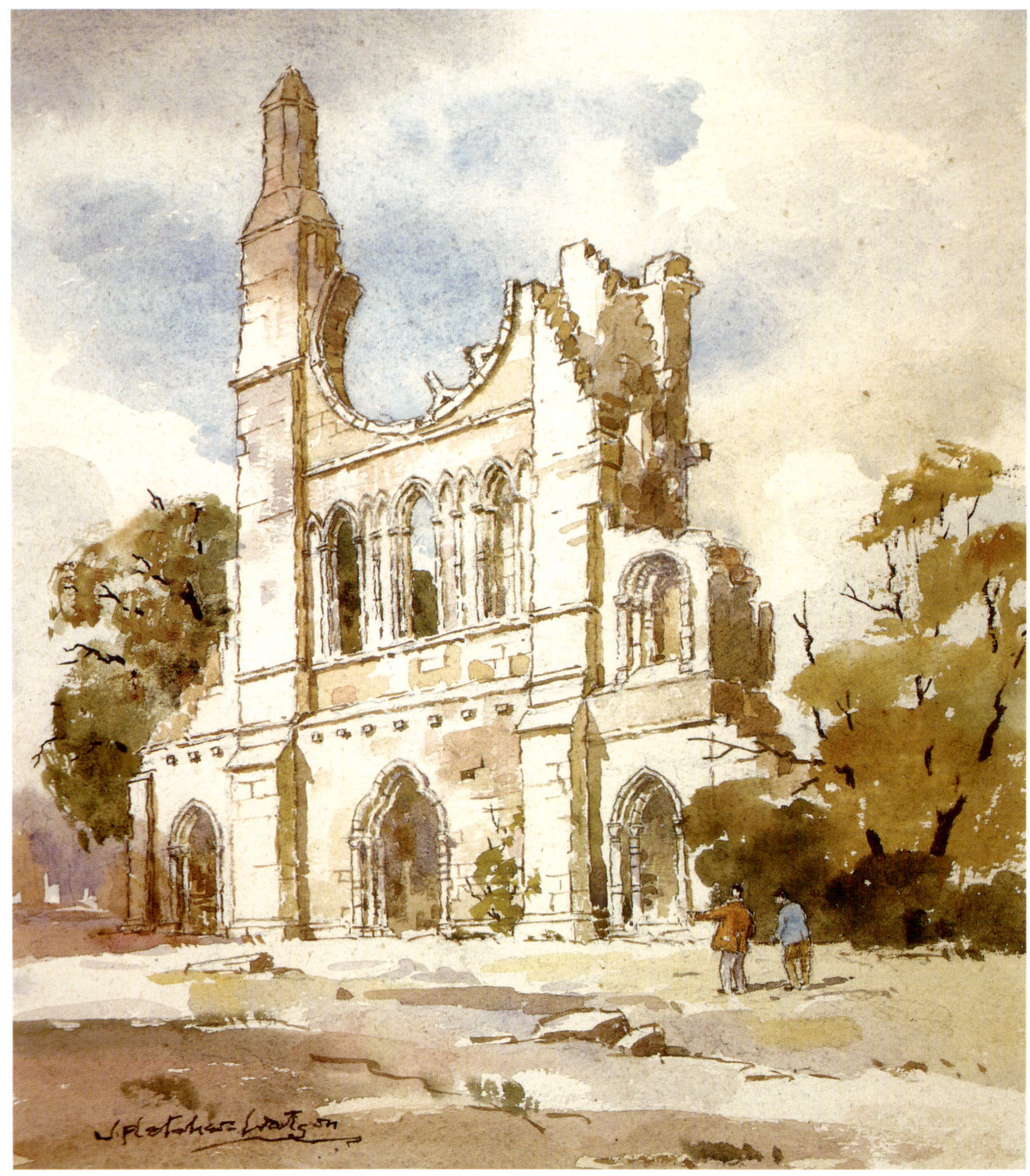

*Byland Abbey*

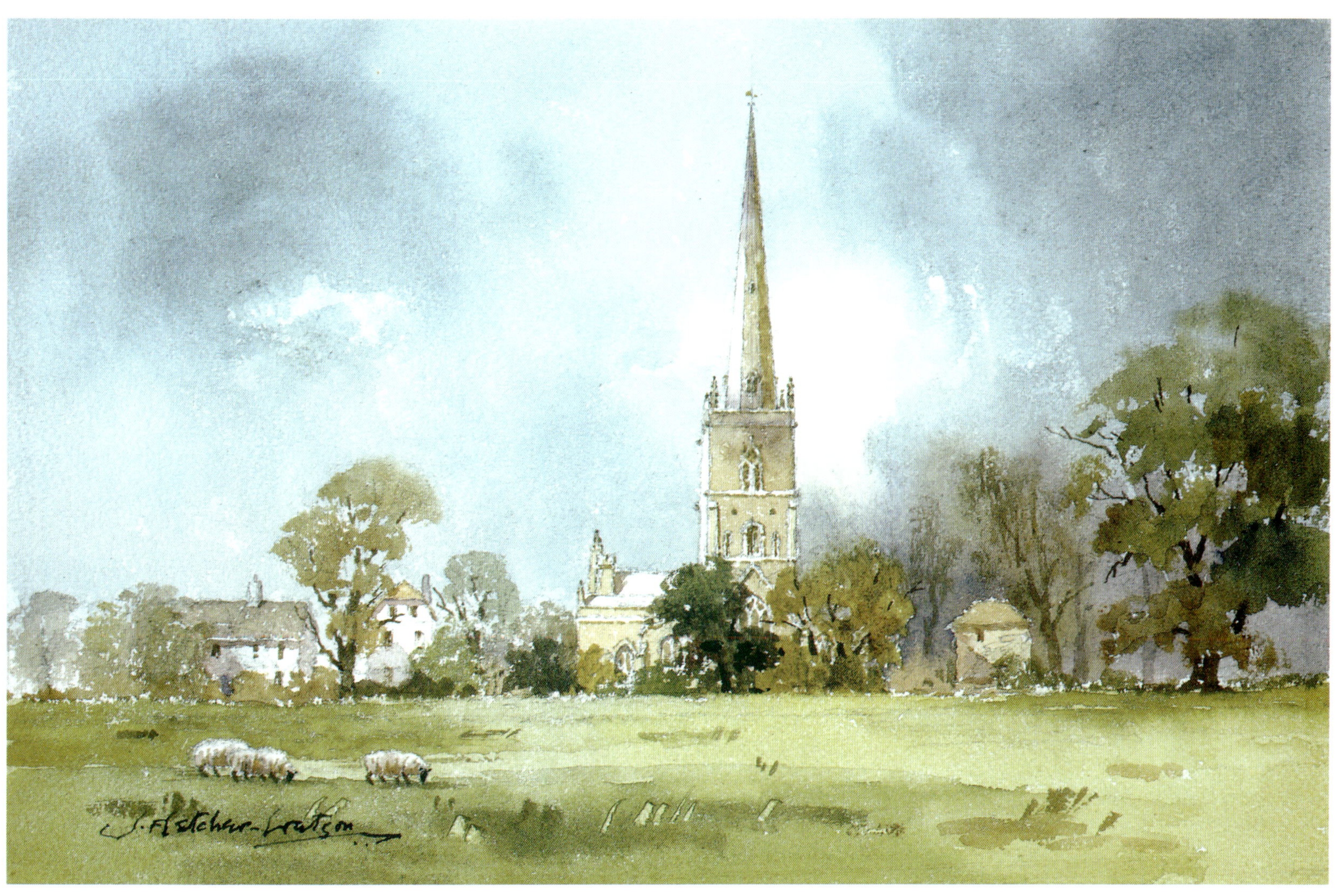

*Salisbury Cathedral   18.5 x 12.5 inches*

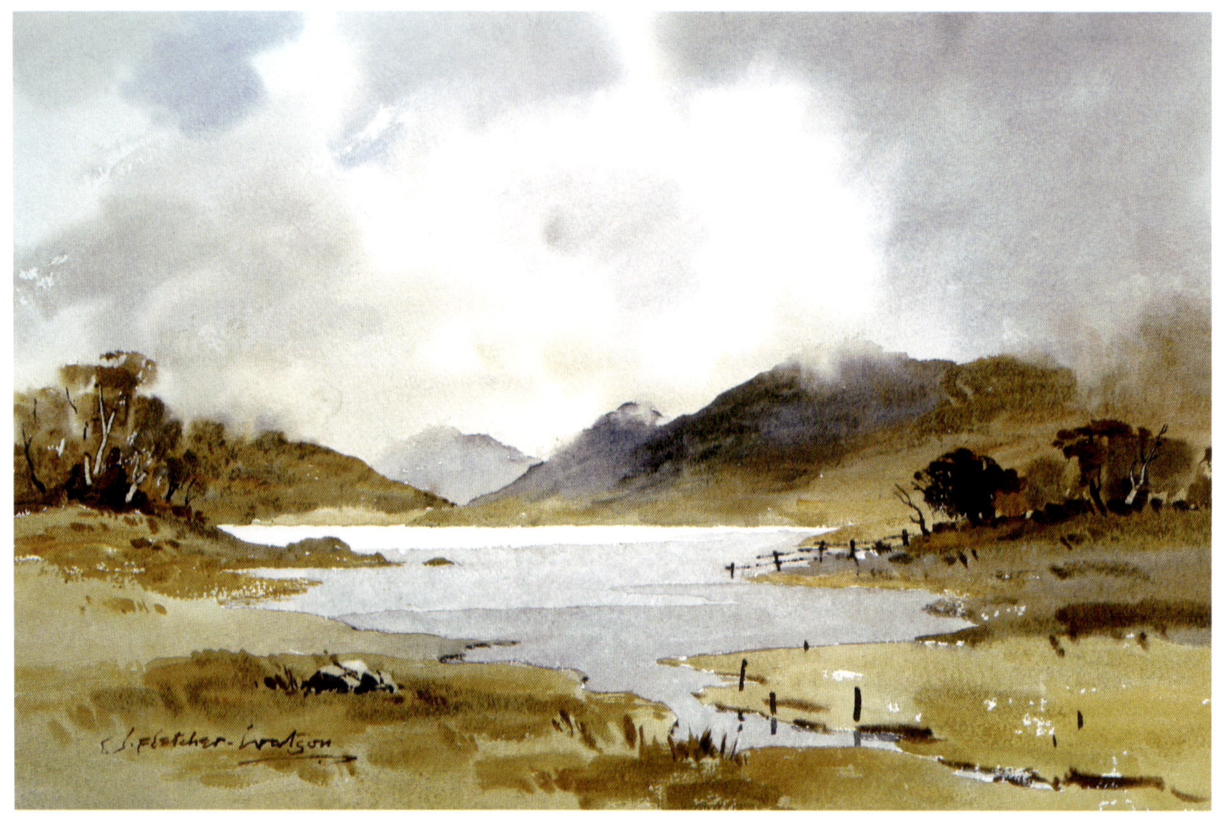

*Loch Long, North West Highlands   16 x 10.5 inches*

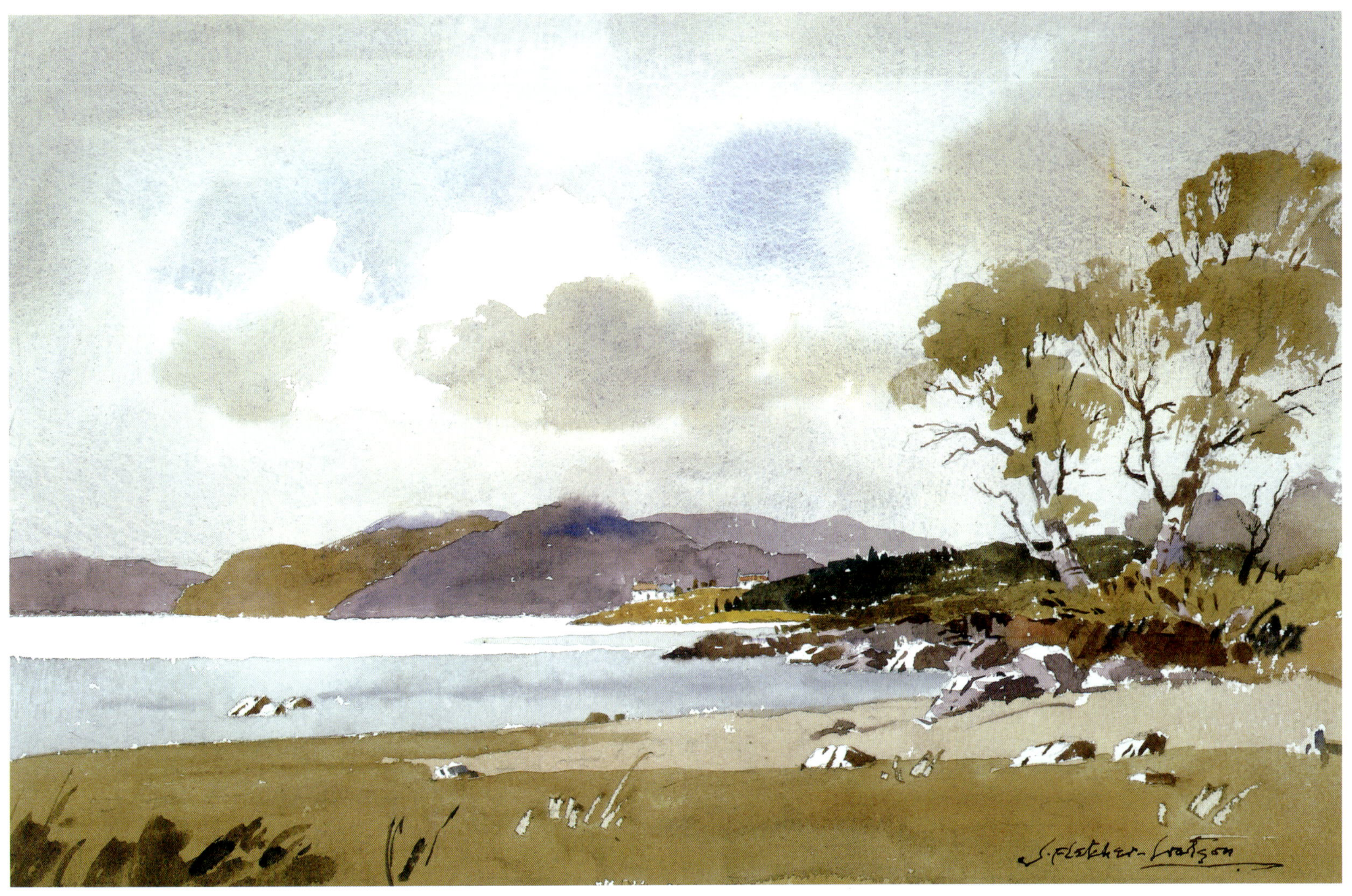

*Loch Linnhe, Scotland   18.5 x 12.5 inches*

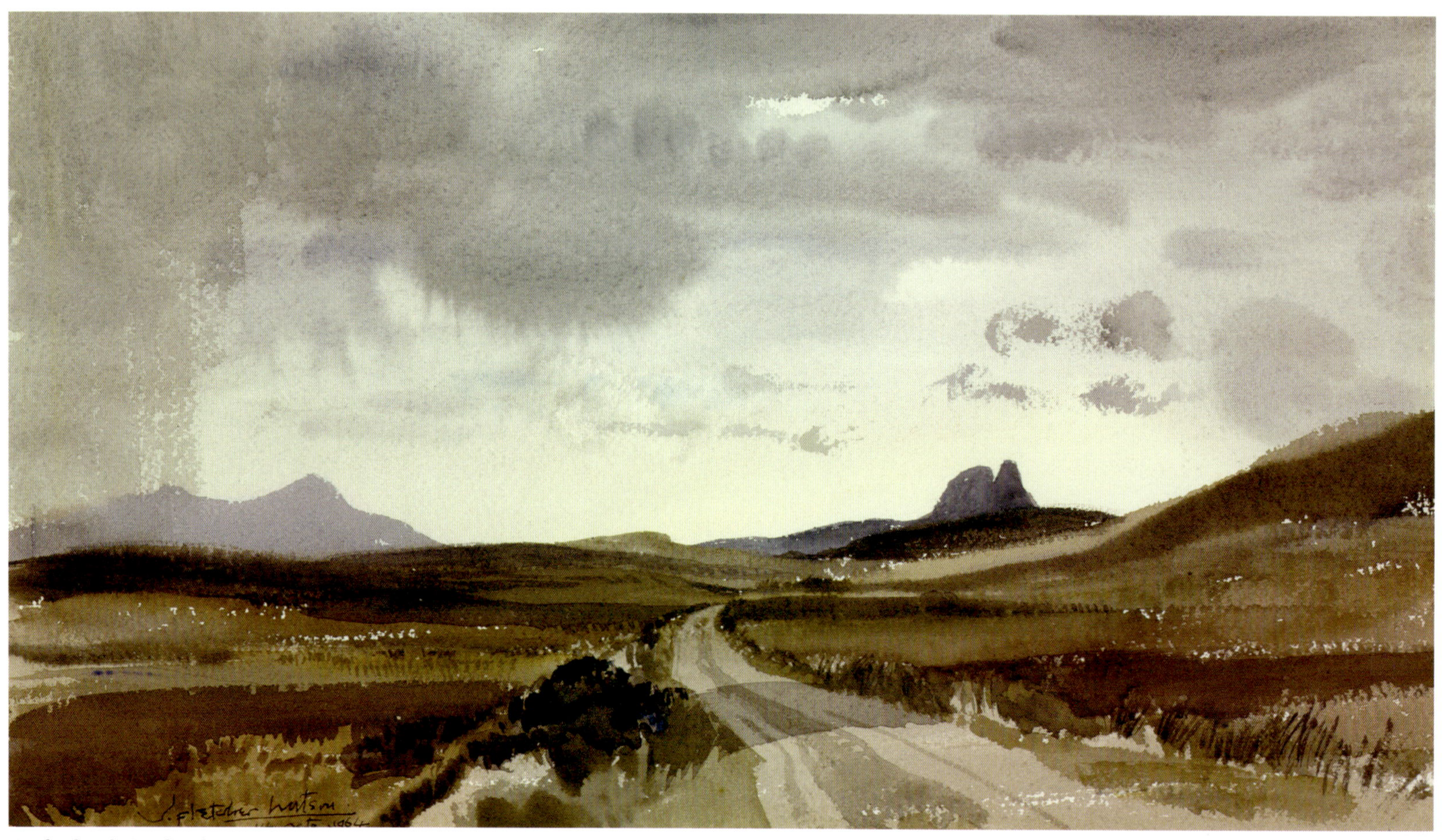

*Sutherland, Scotland*

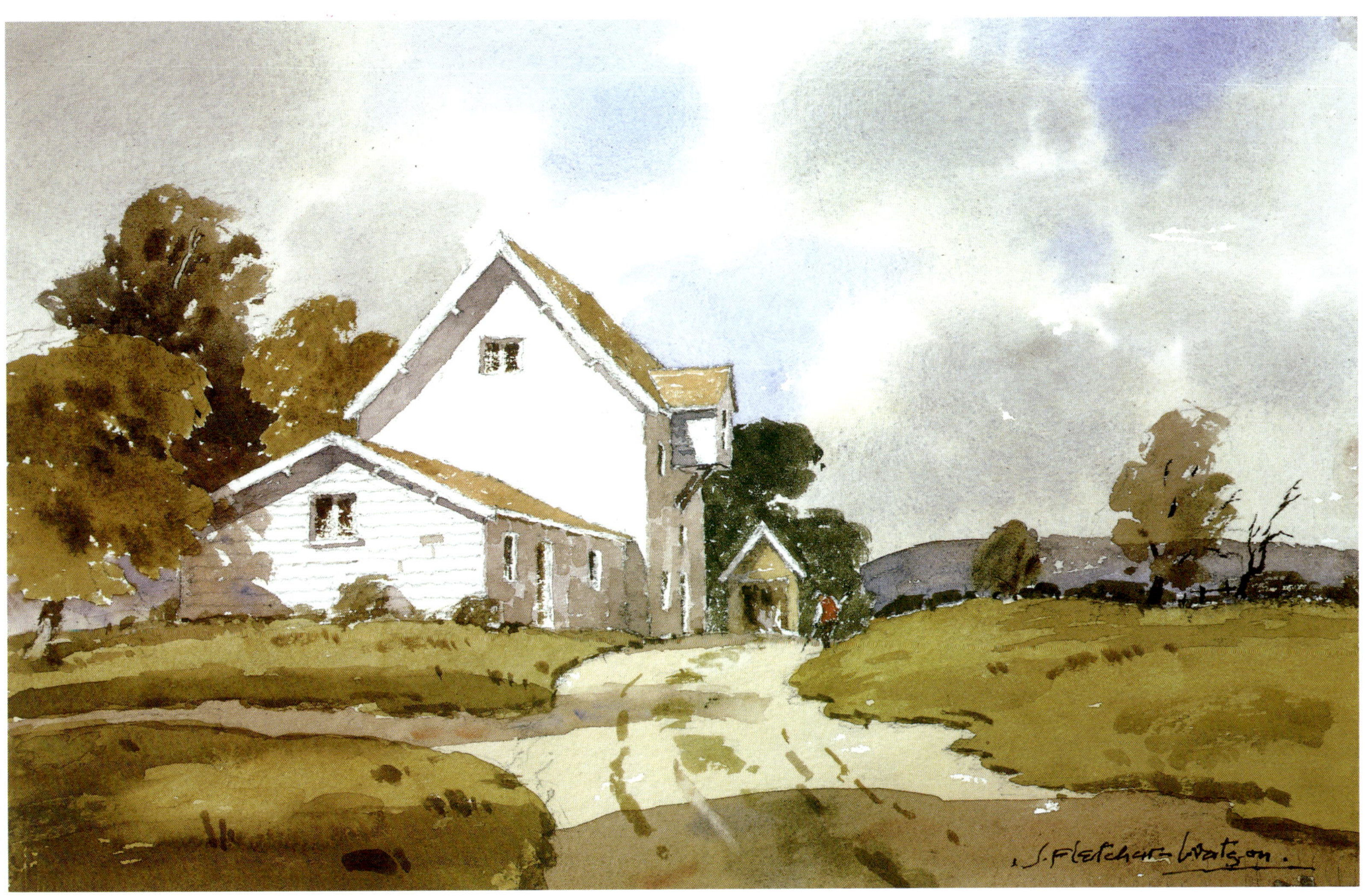

*Stoke Farthing Mill, Wiltshire    18.5 x 12.5 inches*

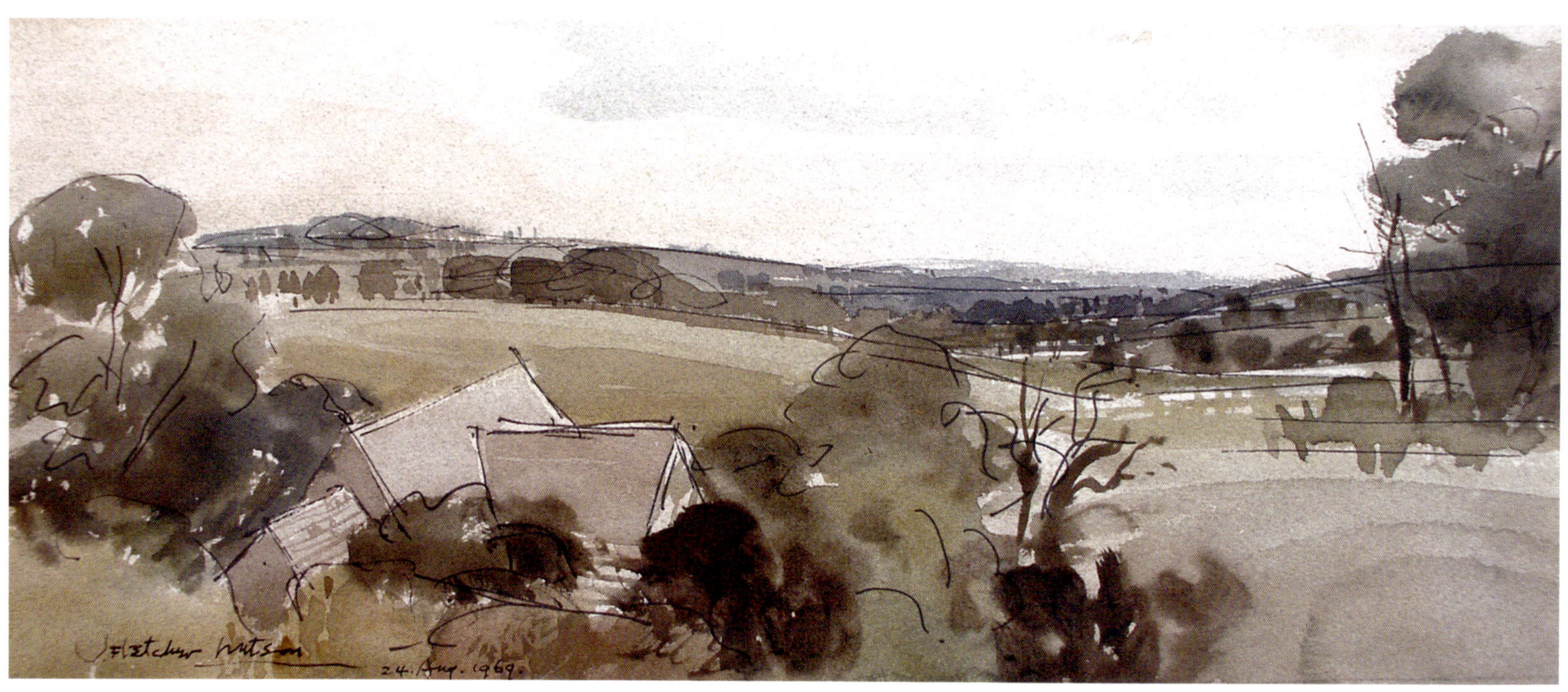

*Windrush   12 x 8 inches*

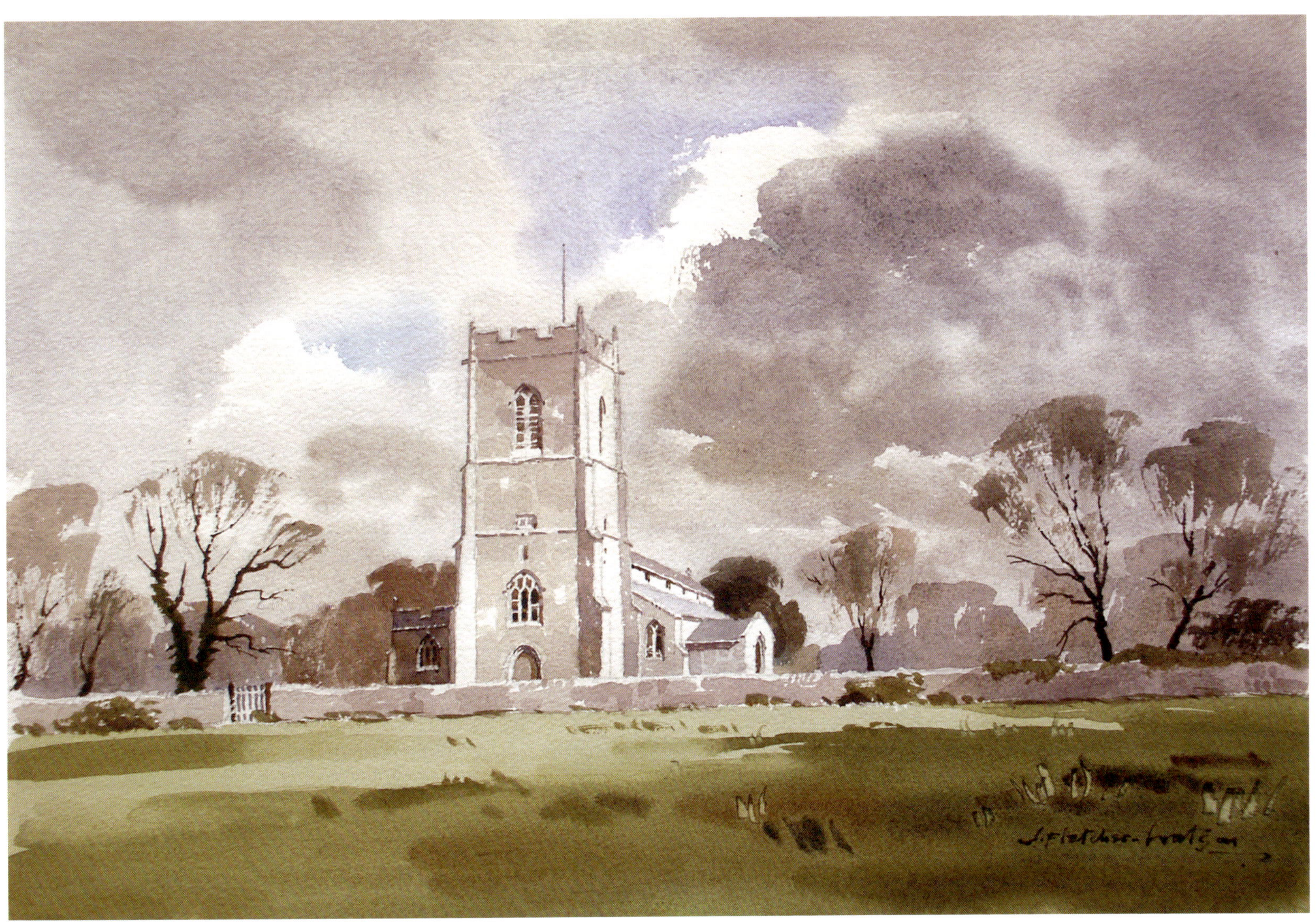

*Norfolk Church   18.5 x 12.5 inches*

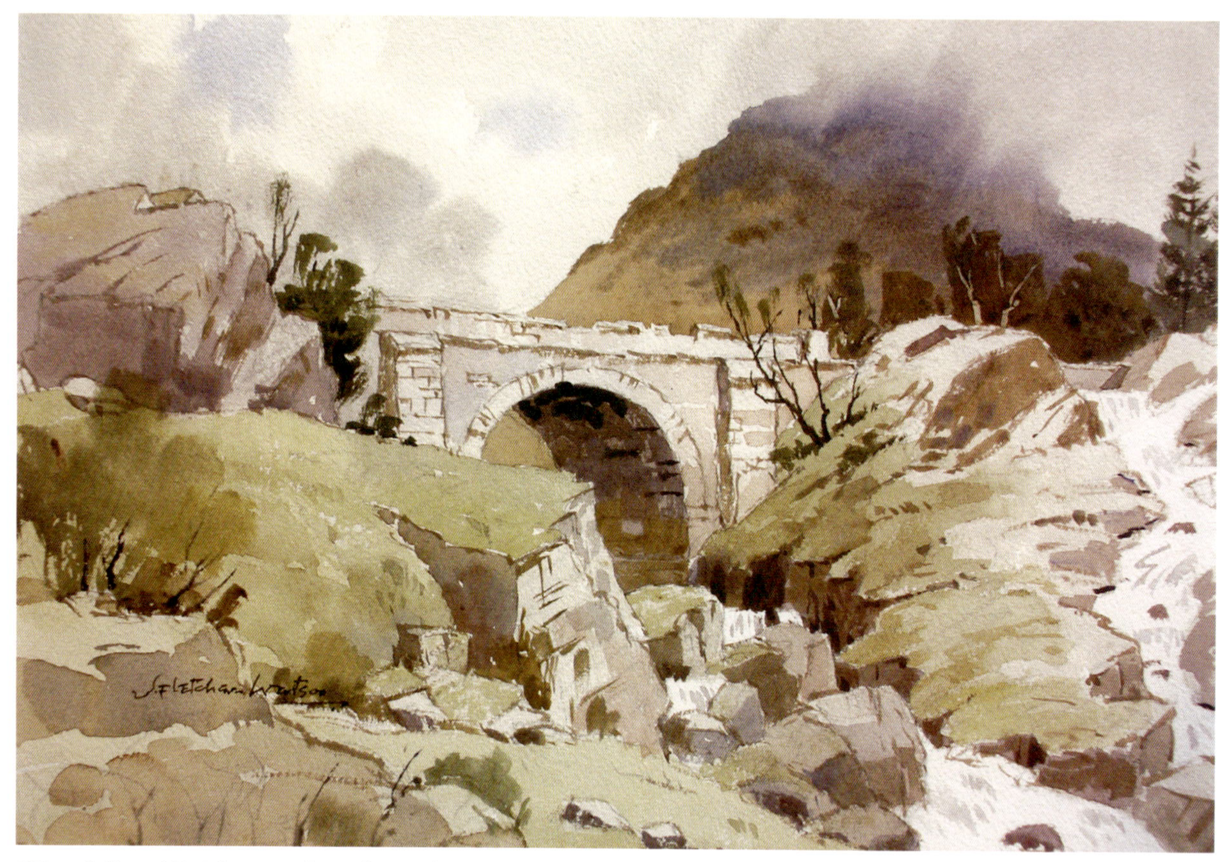

*Waterfall and Bridge, North Wales   16 x 12 inches*

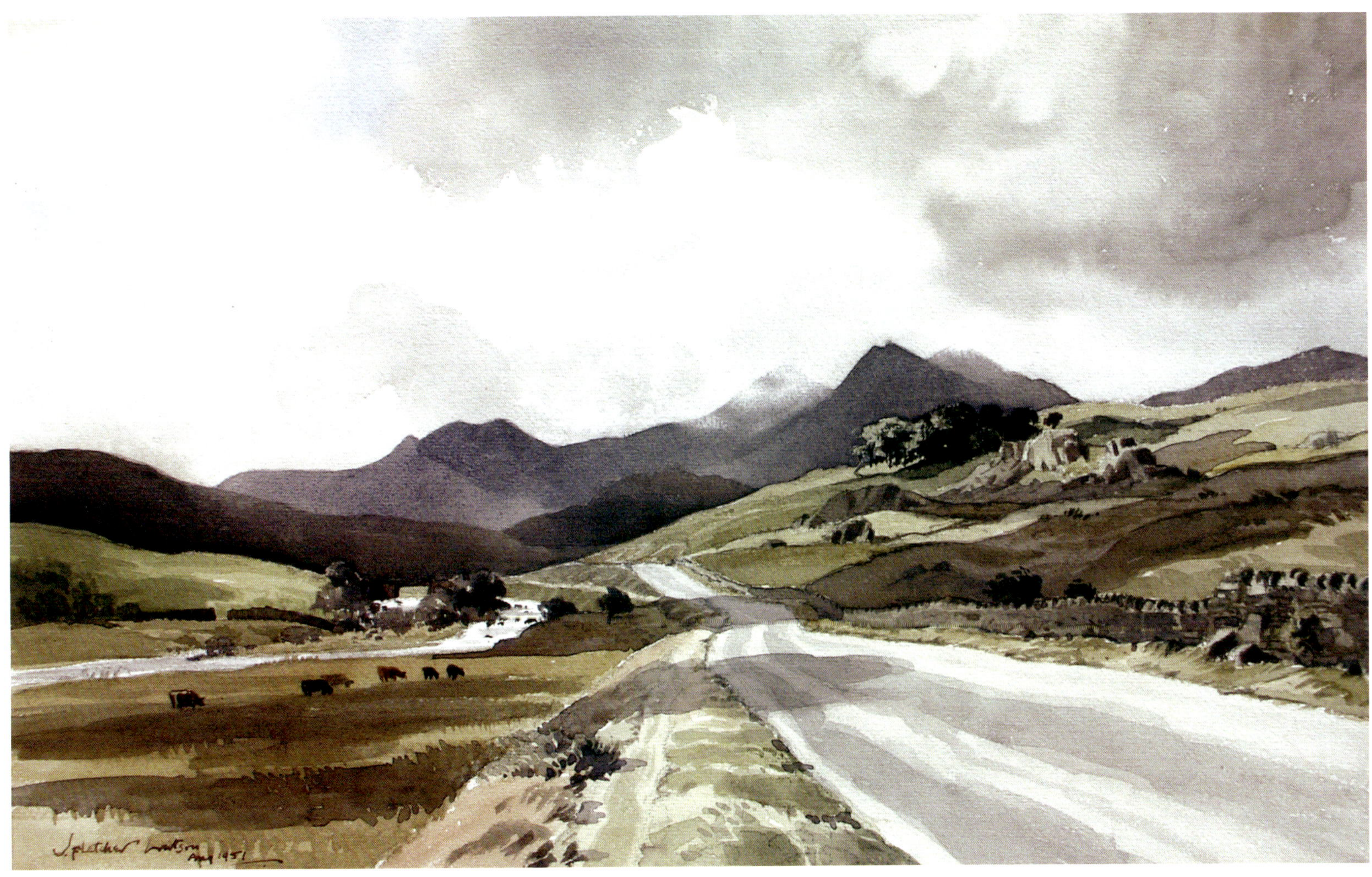

*Road to the Mountains, Scotland  18.5 x 12.5 inches*

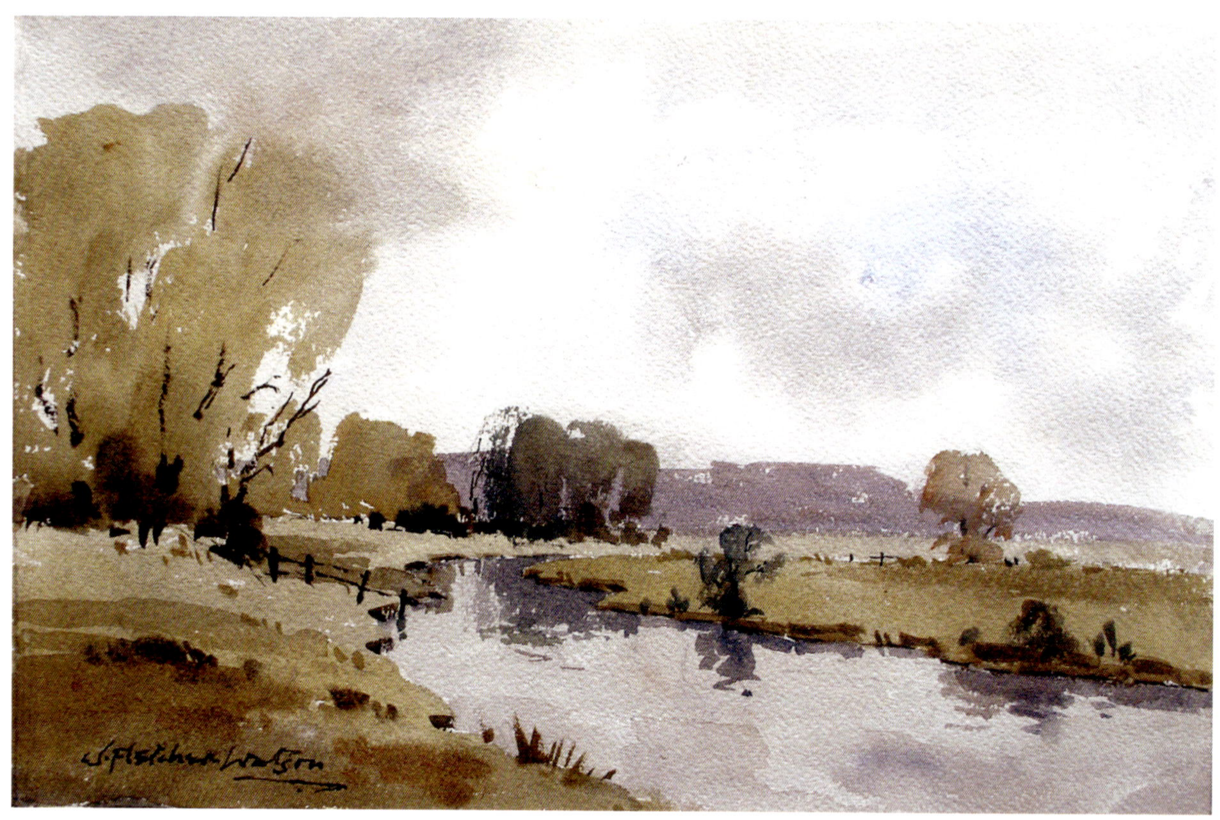

*River Windrush*  *14.5 x 9.5 inches*

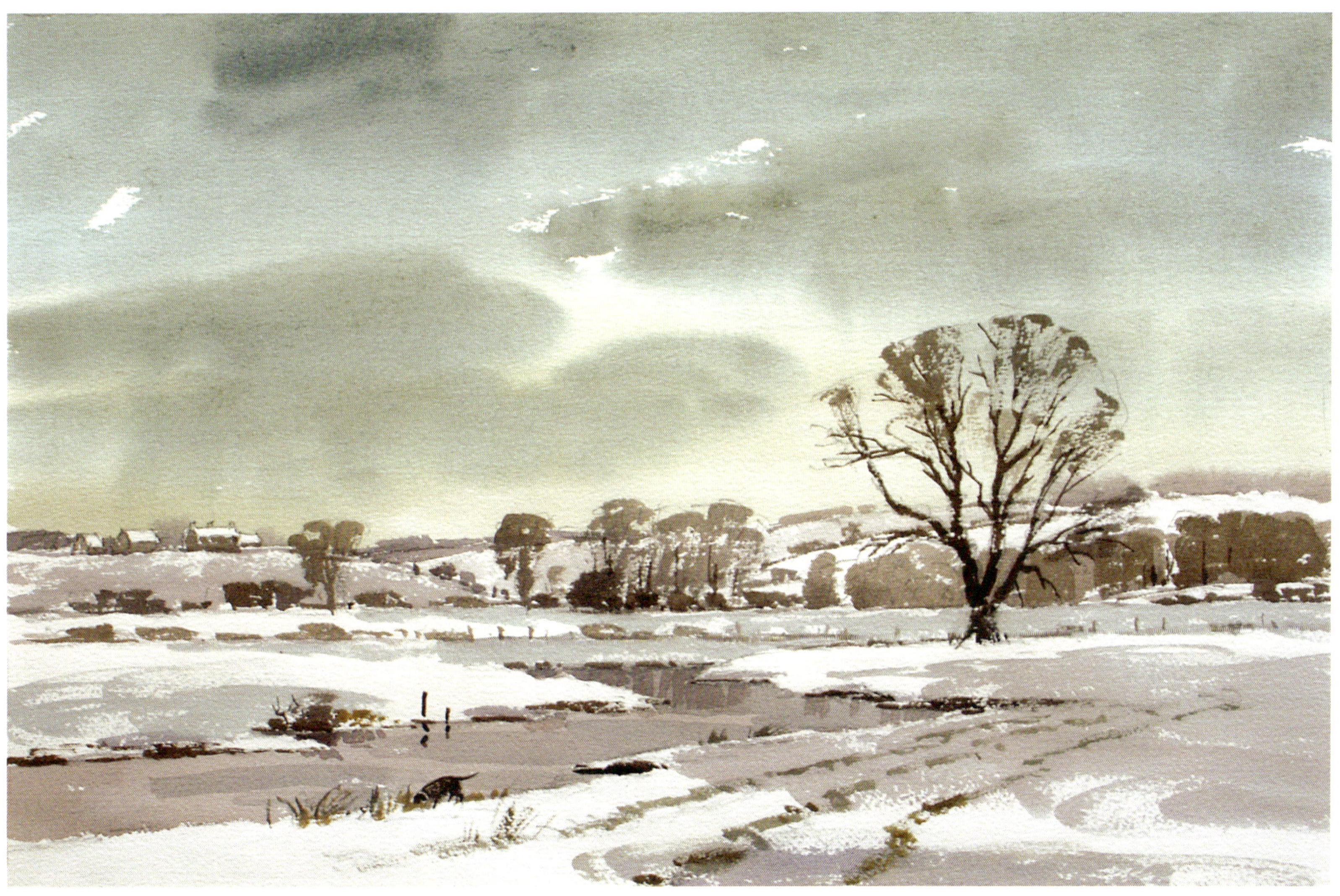

*Snow on the Windrush   18.5 x 12.5 inches*

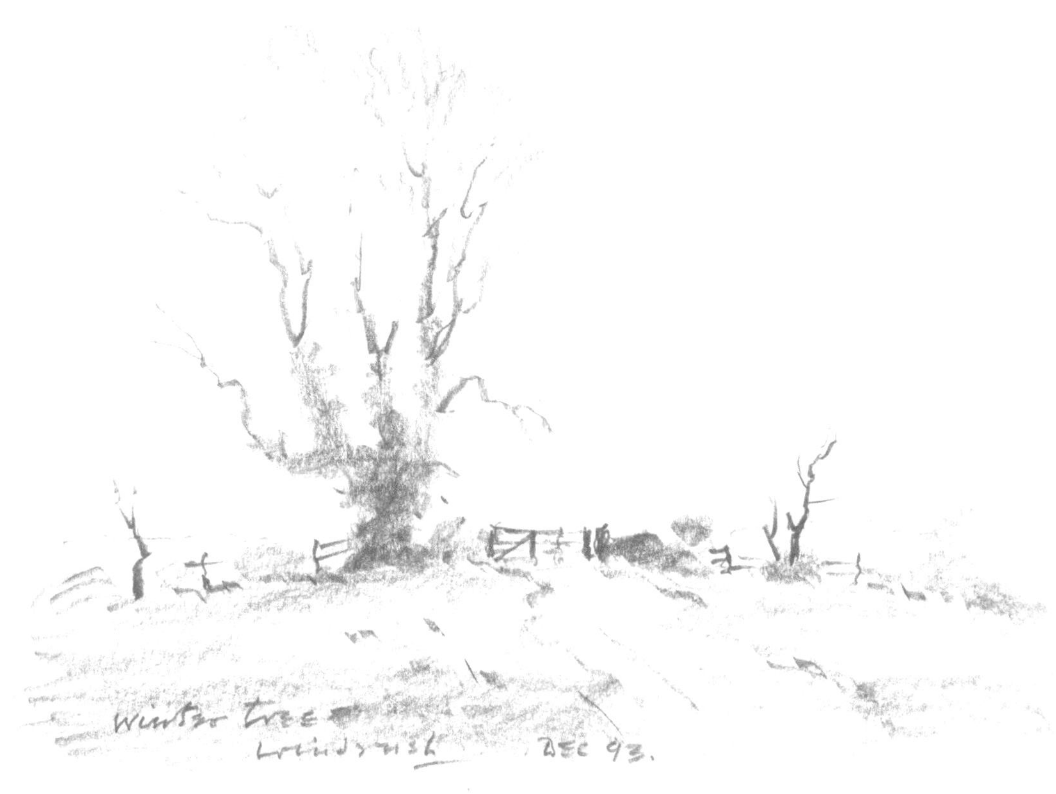

*'James would tell us to mix experience, patience and
a lot of practice and when you get the balance right
then you will paint your perfect tree.'*

One of James's students

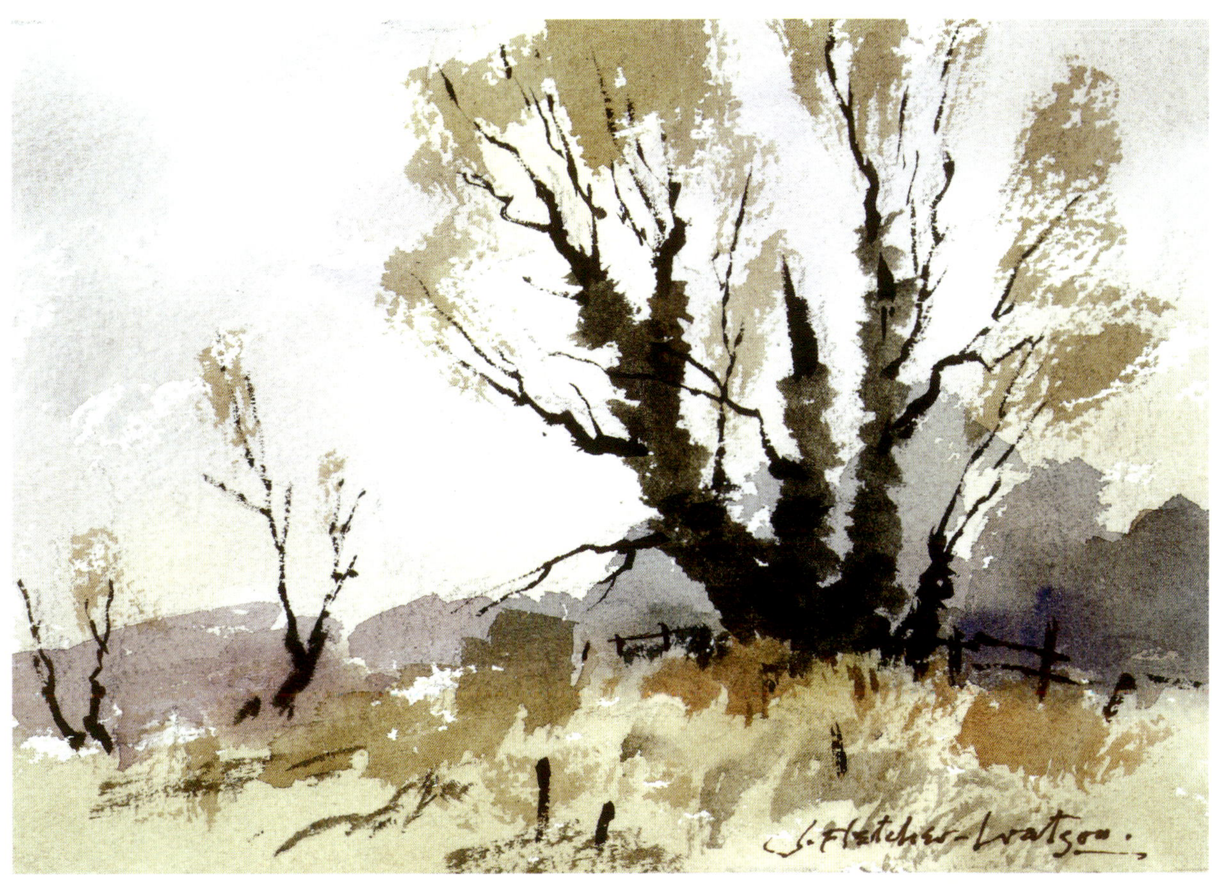

*Trees with Ivy  14 x 9.5 inches*

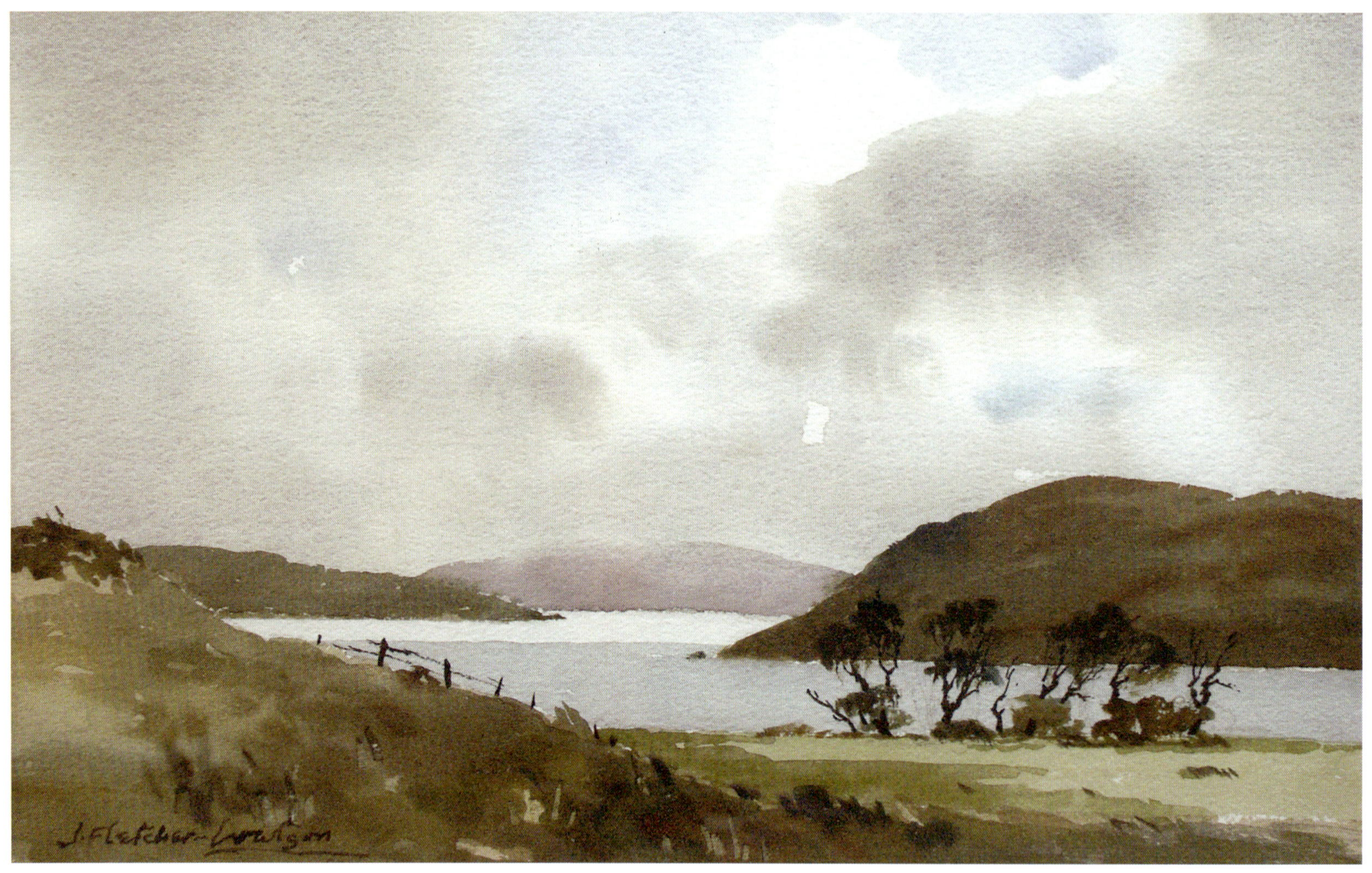

*Loch Harport, Skye   14 x 9.5 inches*

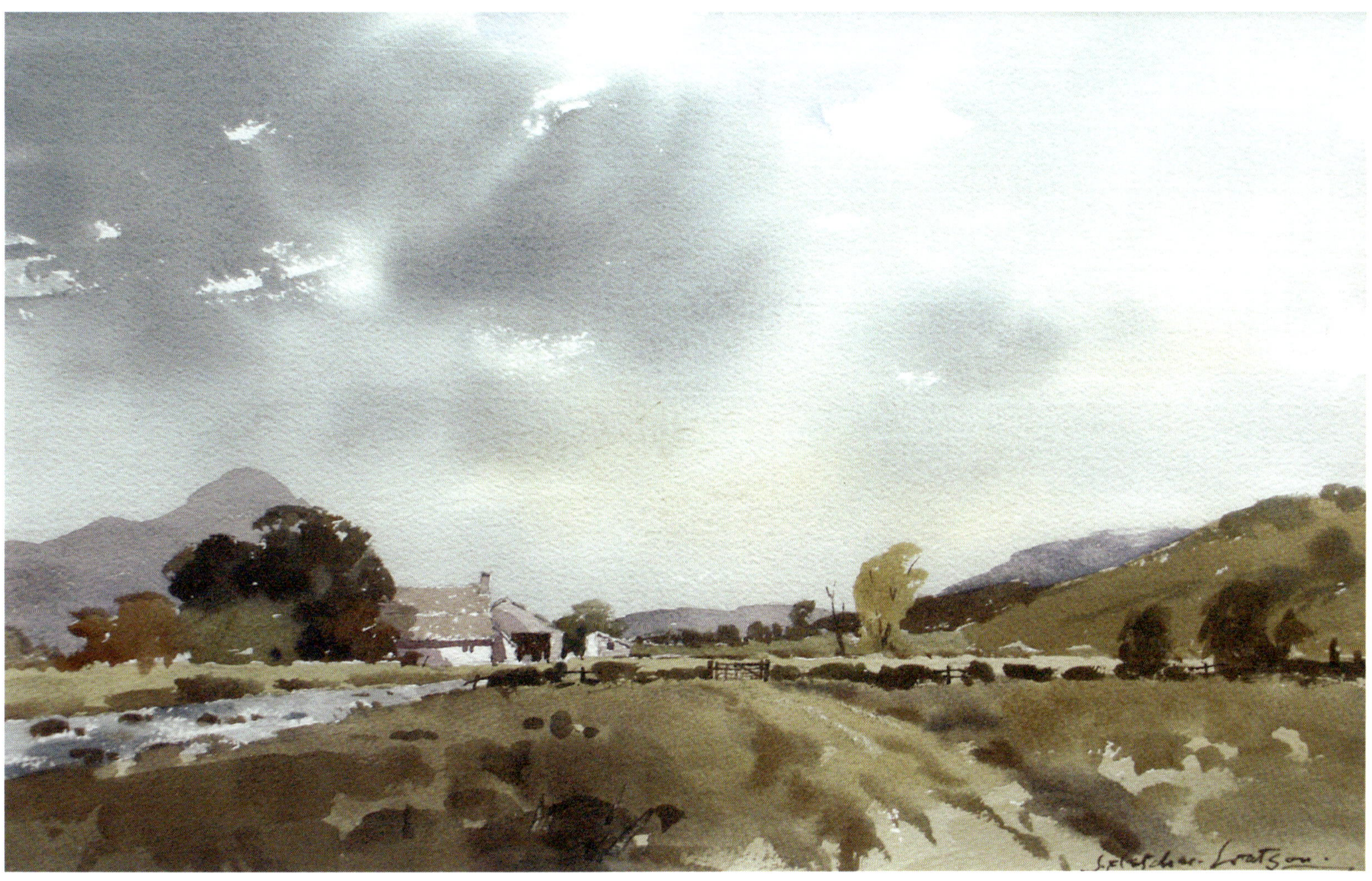

*Welsh Cottage   18.5 x 12.5 inches*

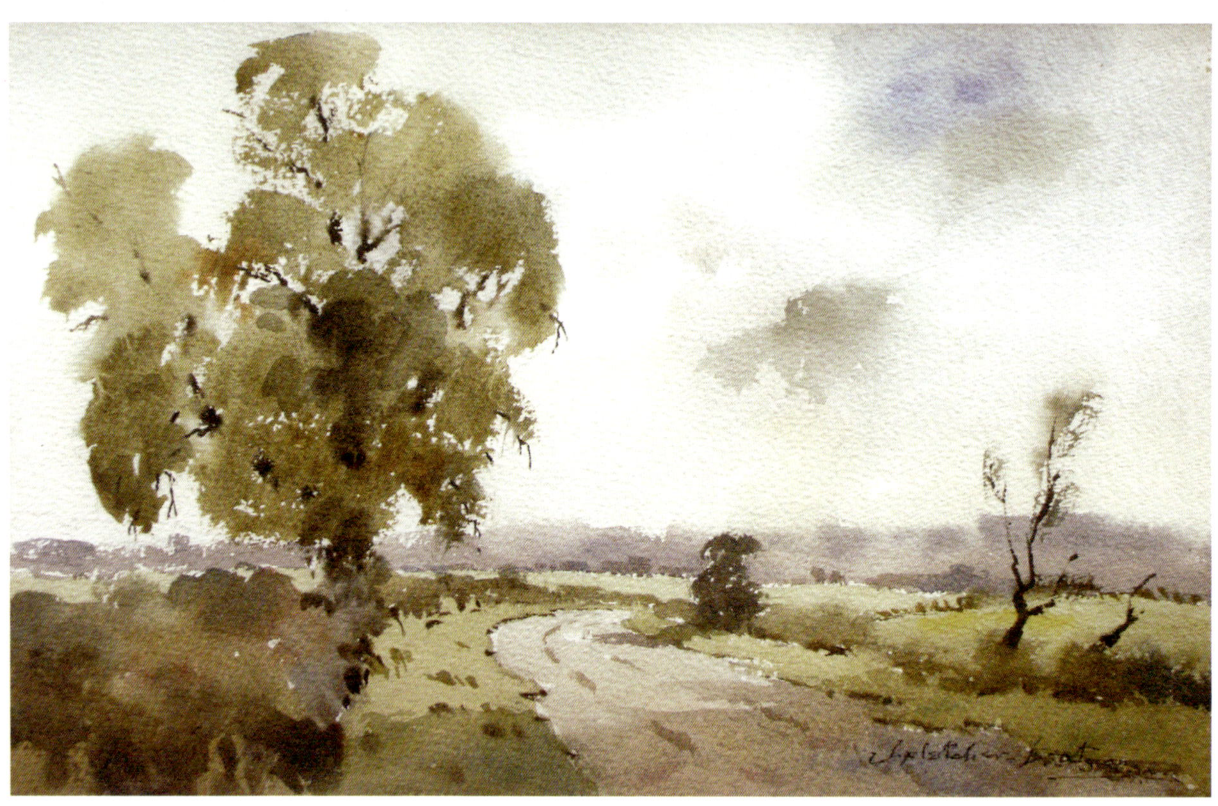

*The Road to Sherborne, Gloucestershire   12 x 9.5 inches*

# PAINTING ABROAD

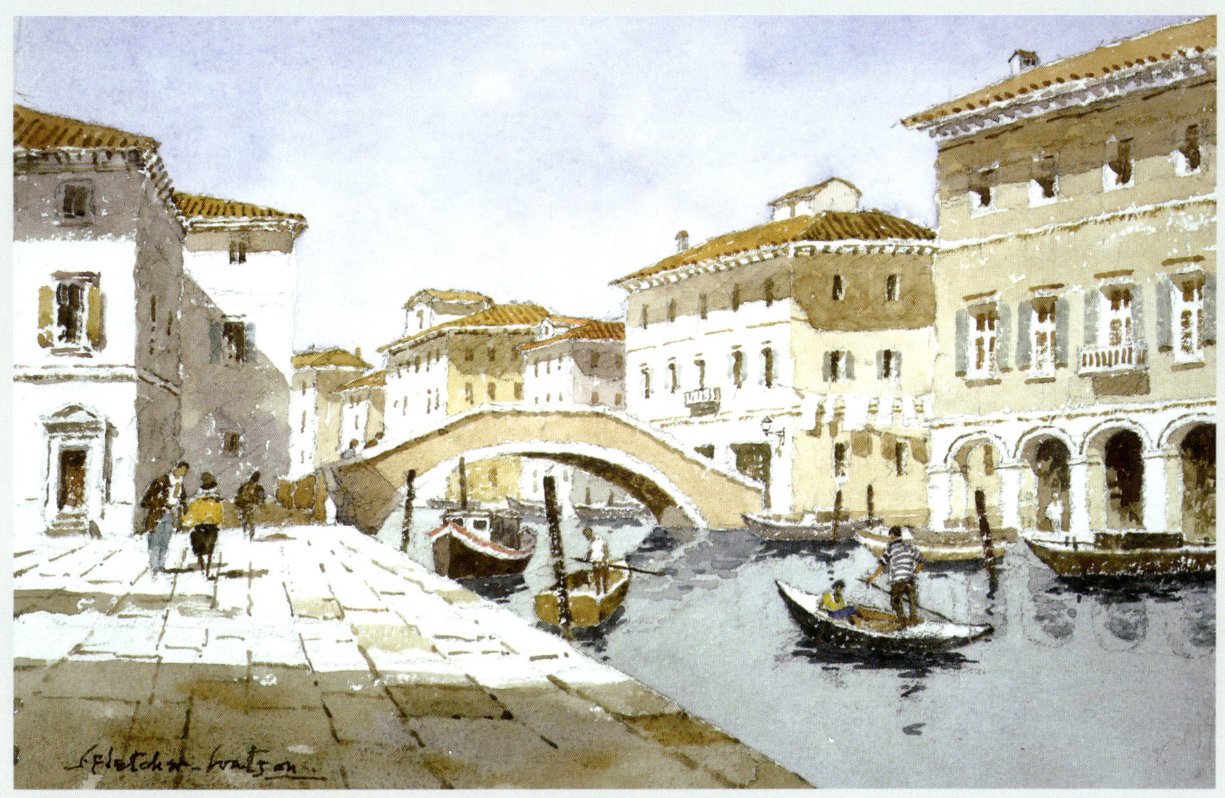

*Venetian Canal*

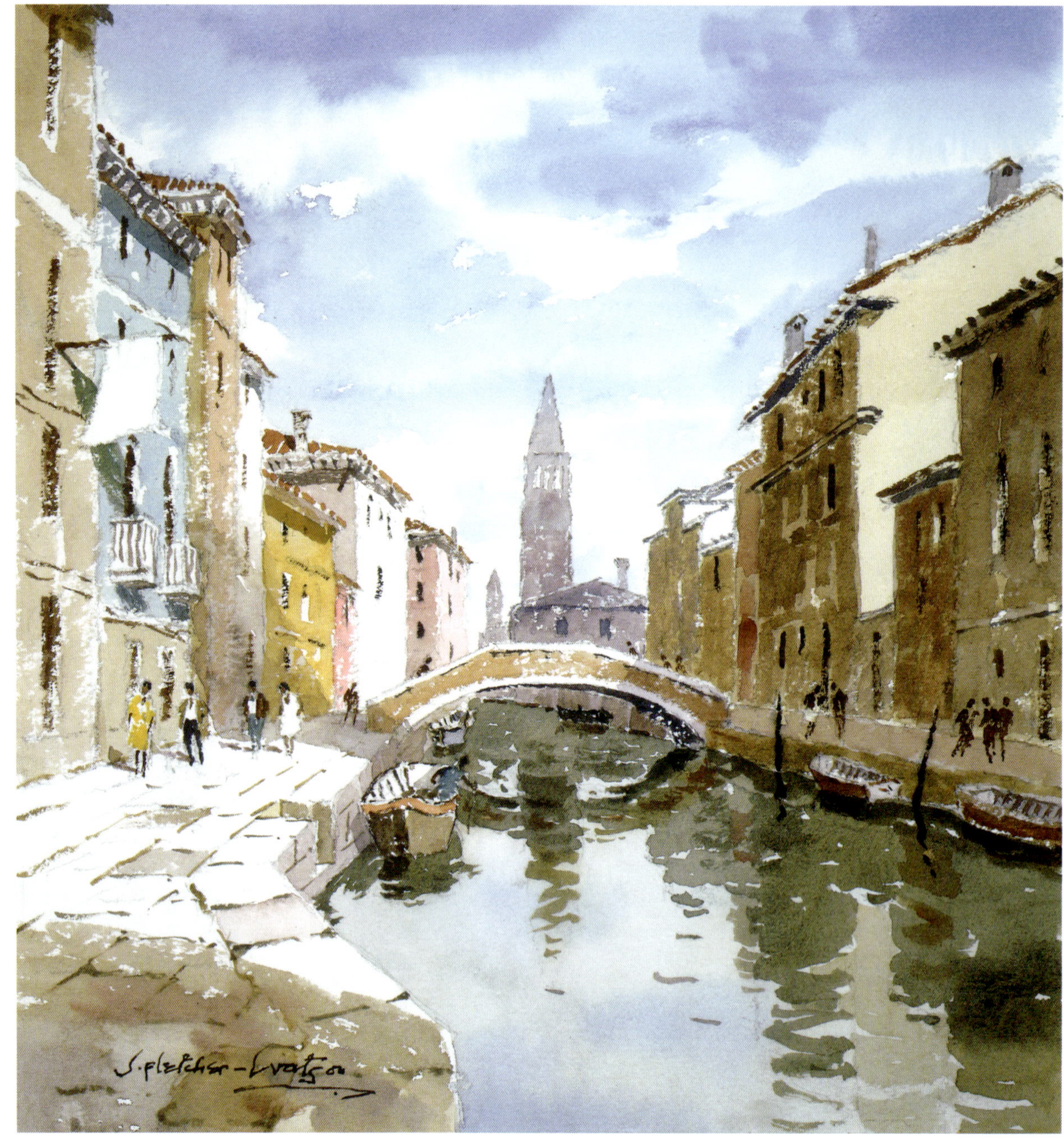

*Rio di St Barnaba, Venice   12.5 x 14.5 inches*

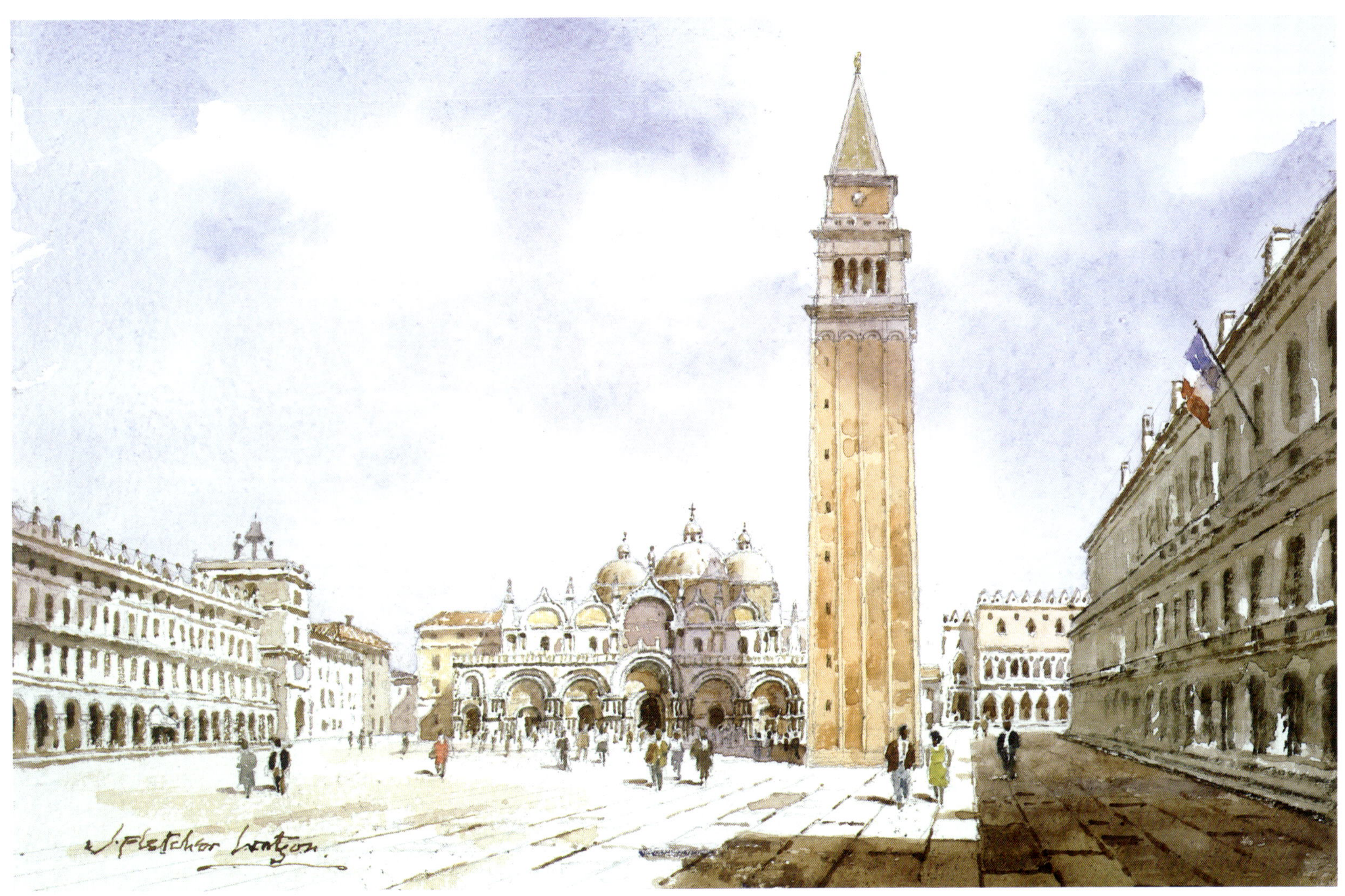

*St Mark's Square  18.5 x 12.5 inches*

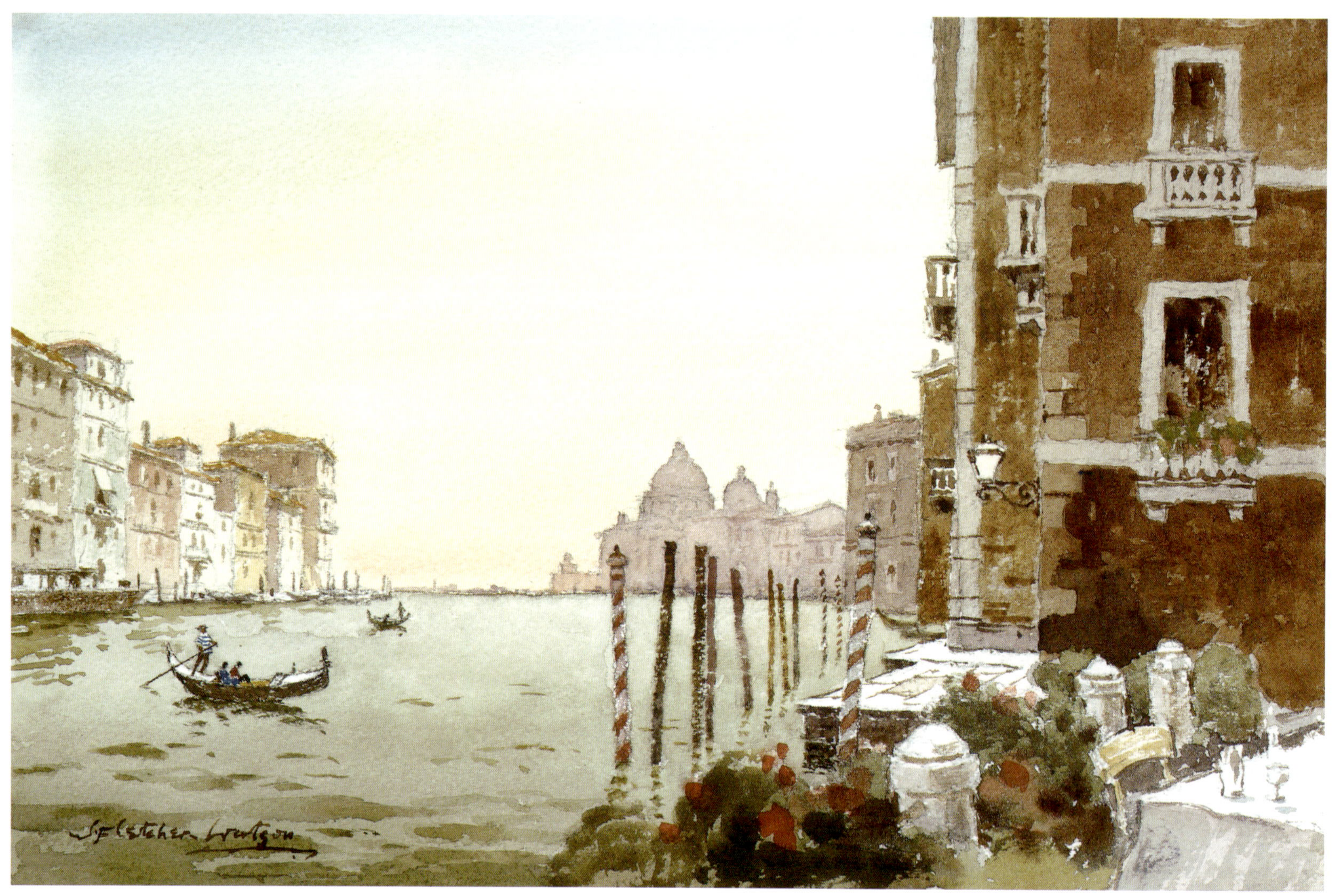

*Grand Canal, Venice   18.5 x 12.5 inches*

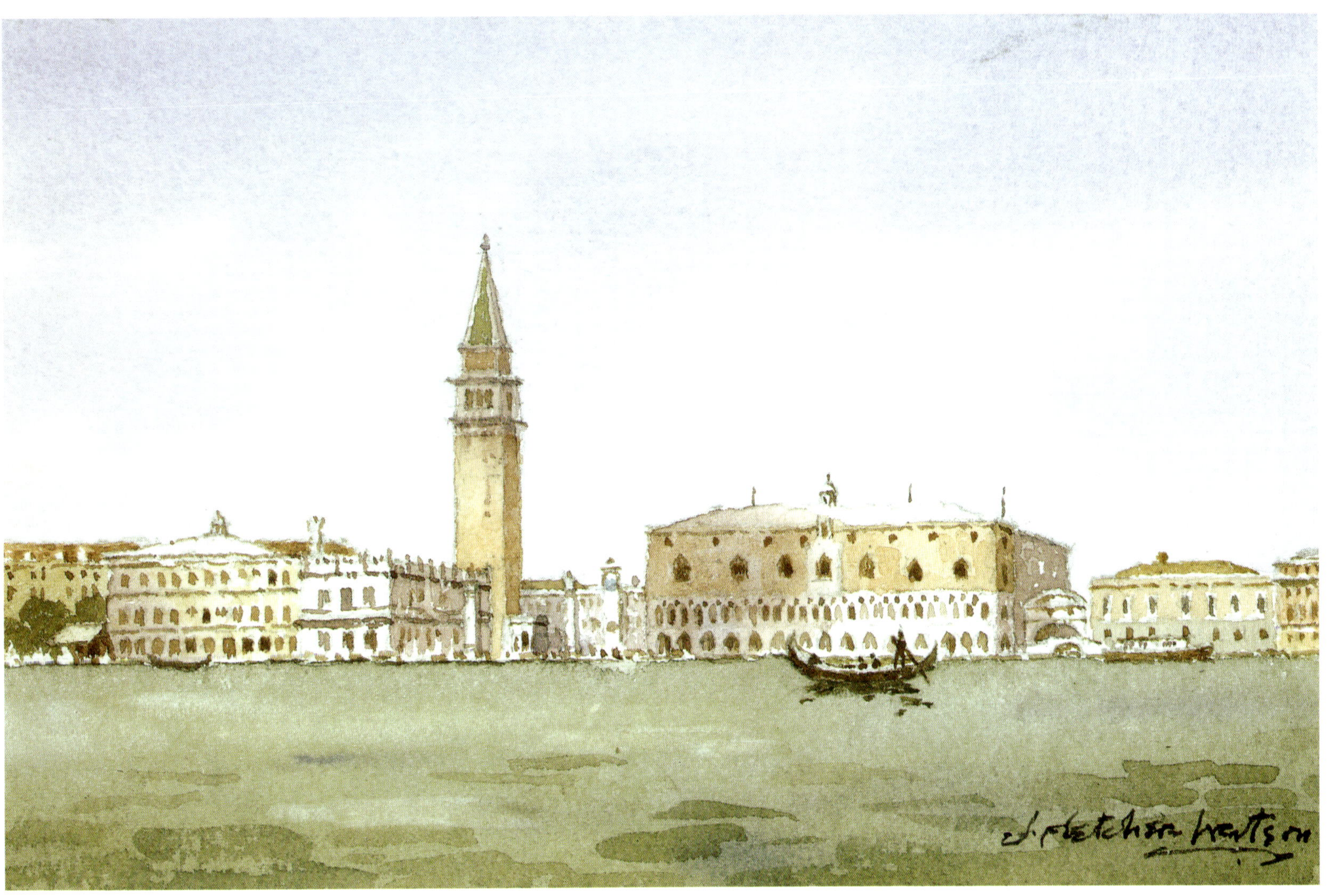

*Venice, view from the Guidecca   18.5 x 12.5 inches*

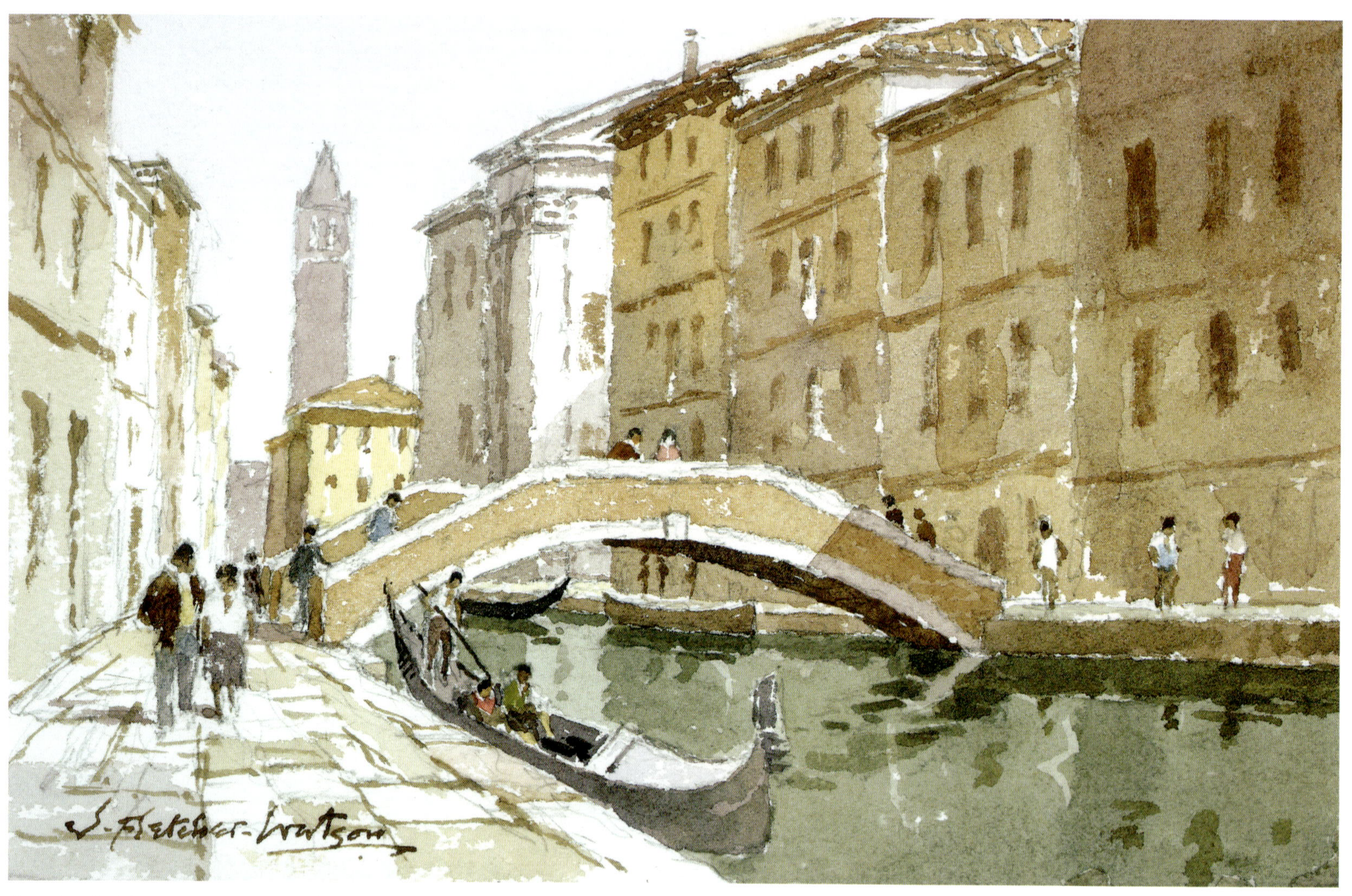

*Venetian Bridge   18.5 x 12.5 inches*

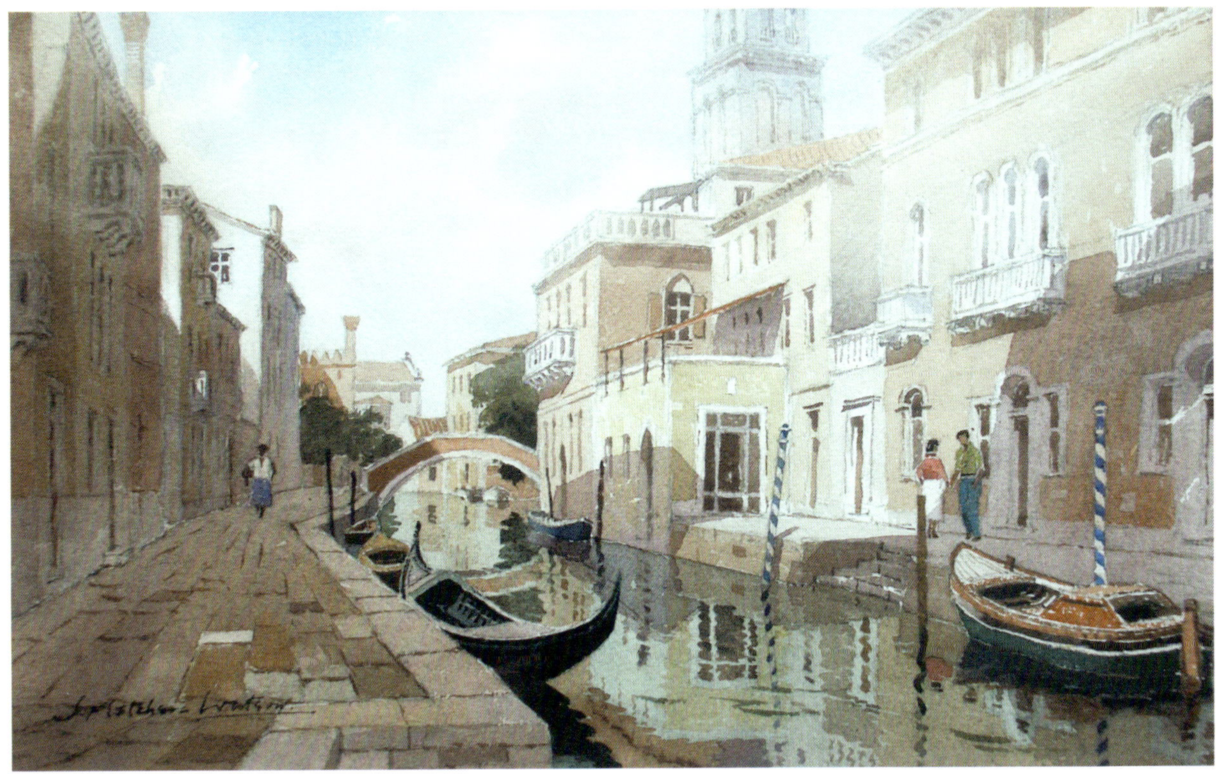

*Side canal, Venice   18.5 x 12.5 inches*

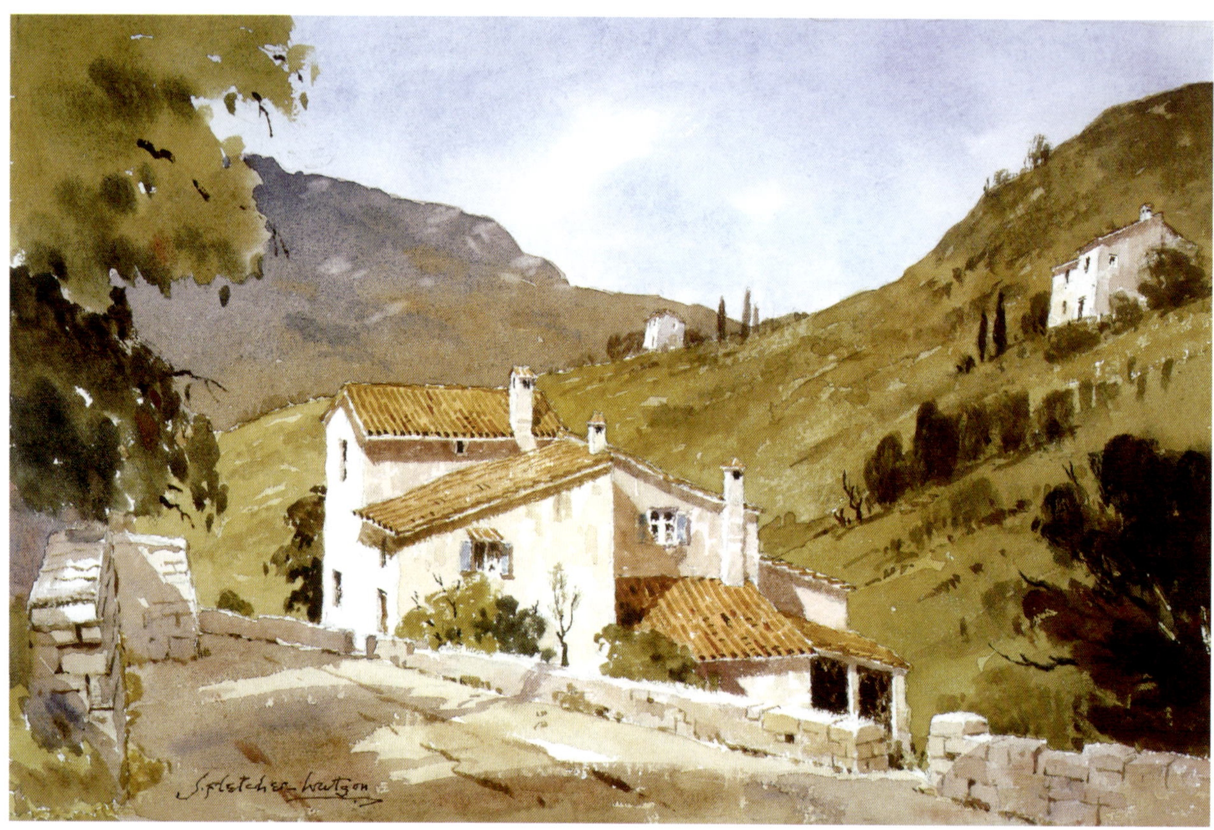

*Deia, Majorca   18.5 x 12.5 inches*

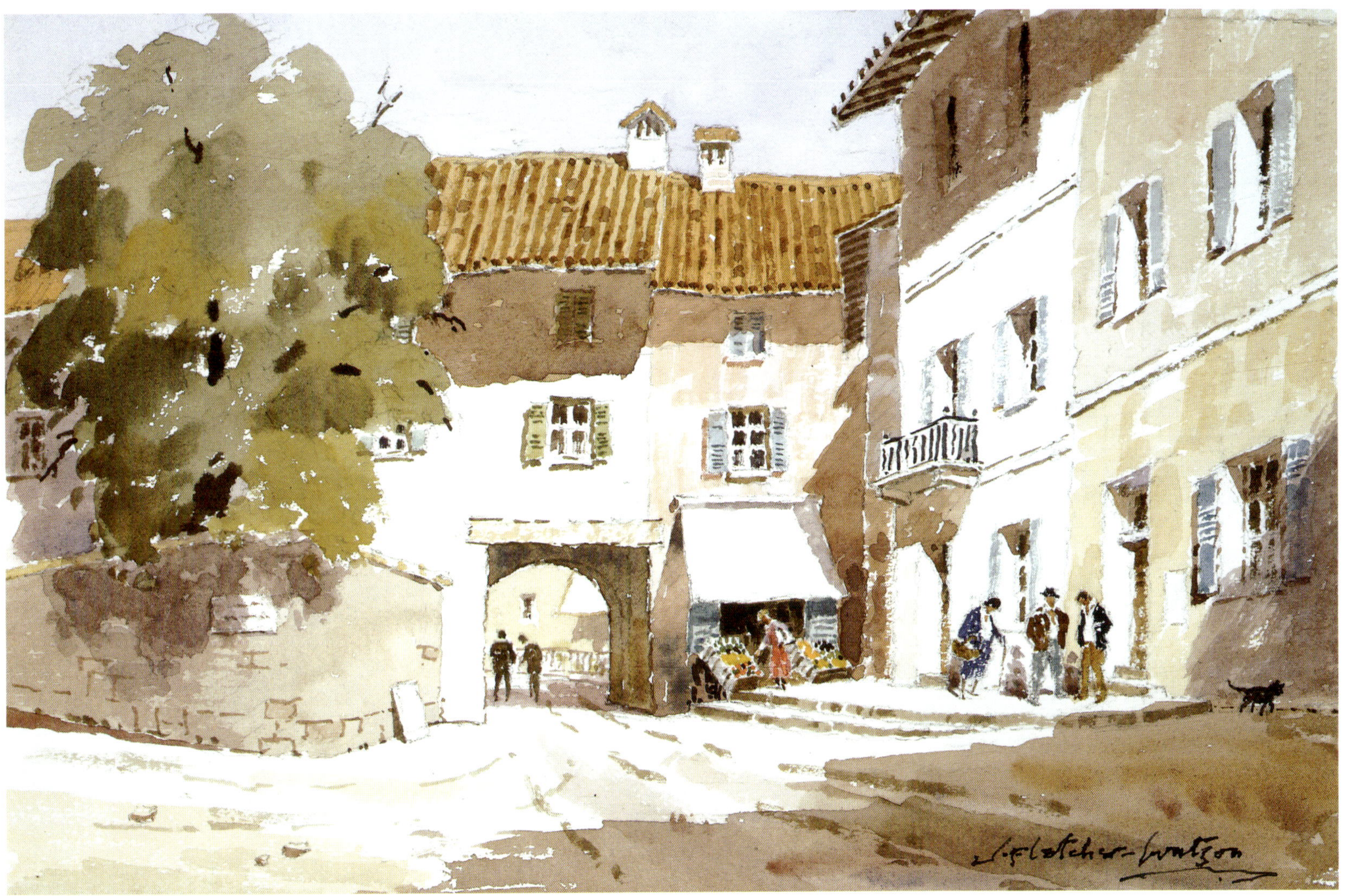

*Gavignana, Tuscany   18.5 x 12.5 inches*

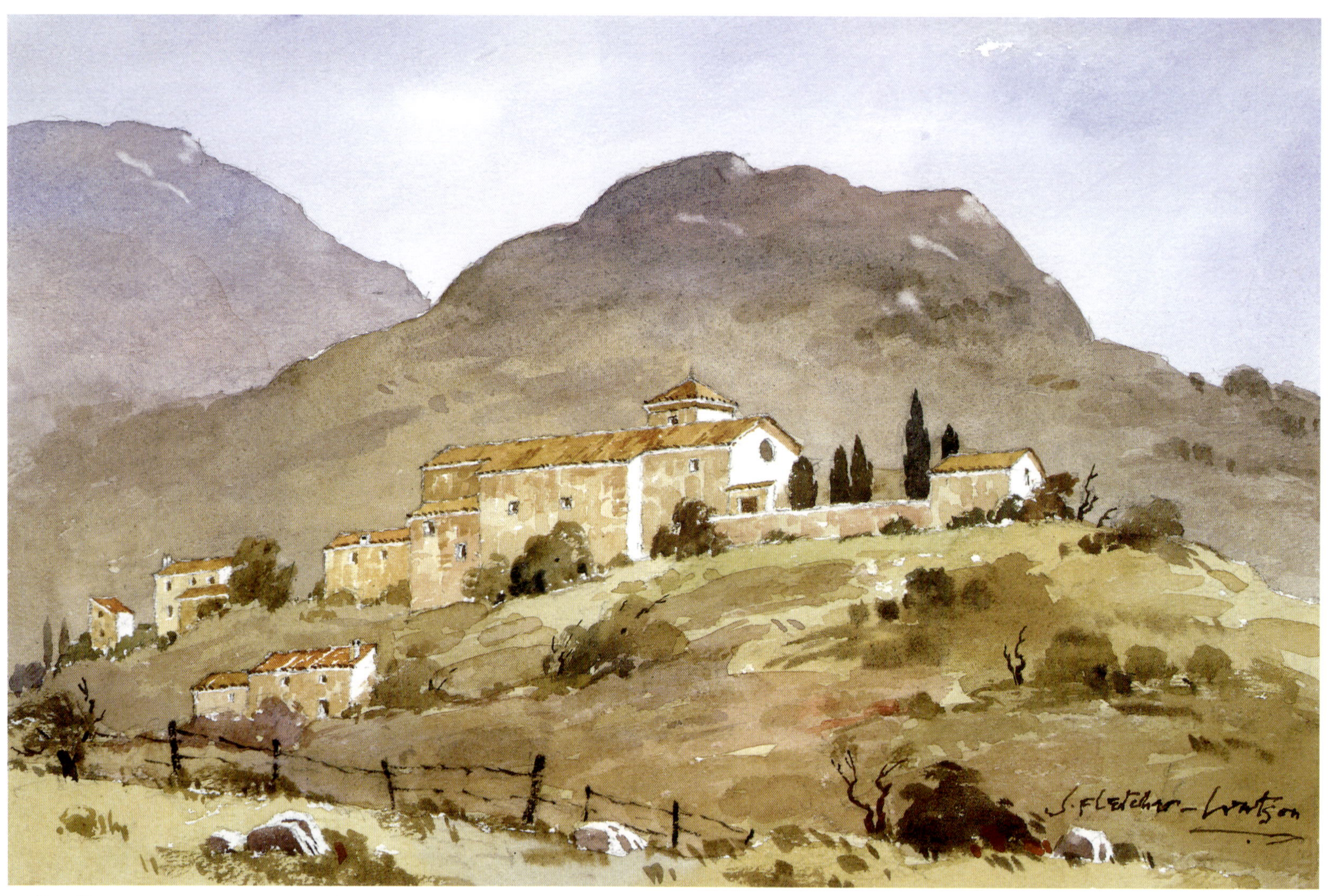

*Hill Village, Crete   18.5 x 12.5 inches*

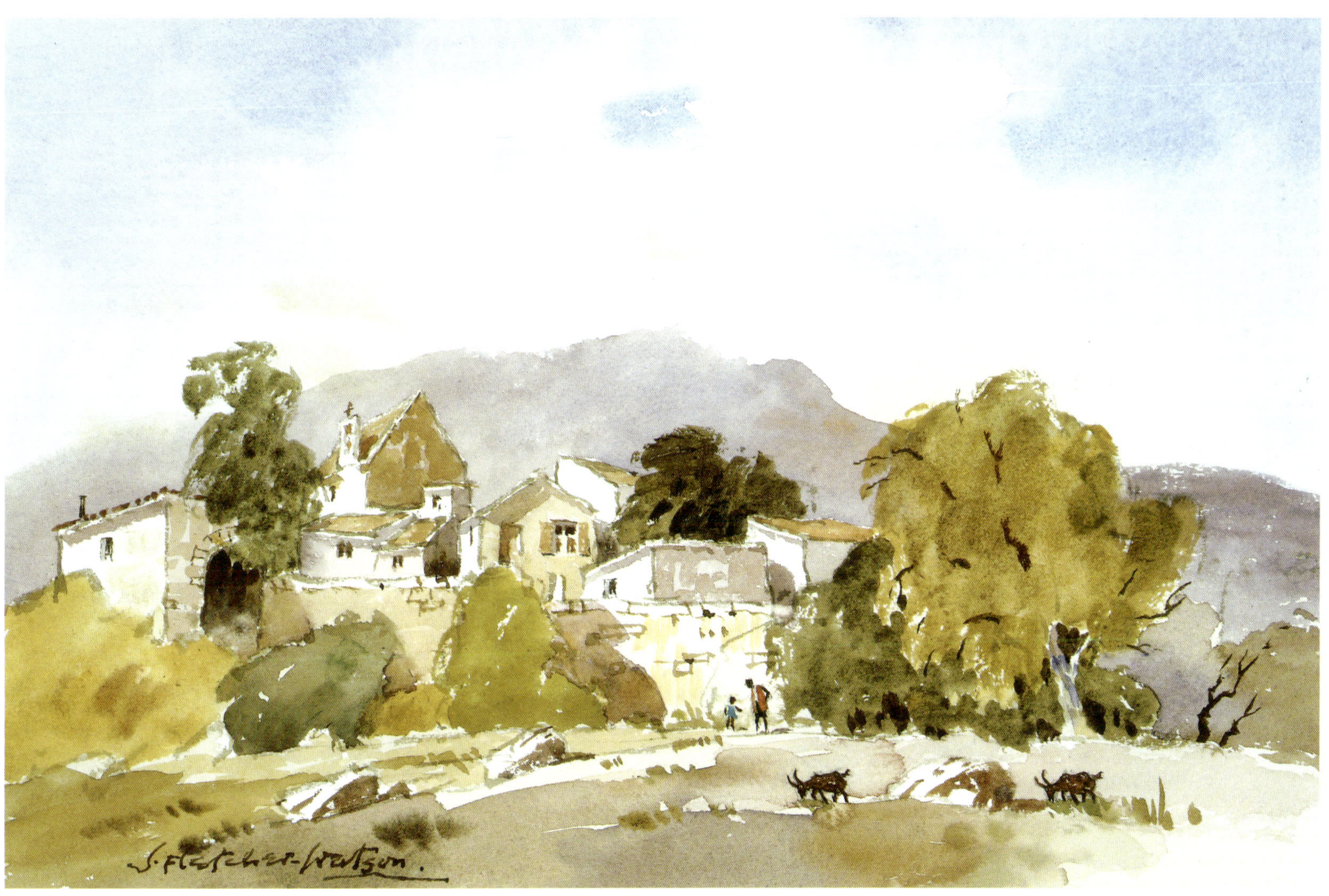

*Crete   18.5 x 12.5 inches*

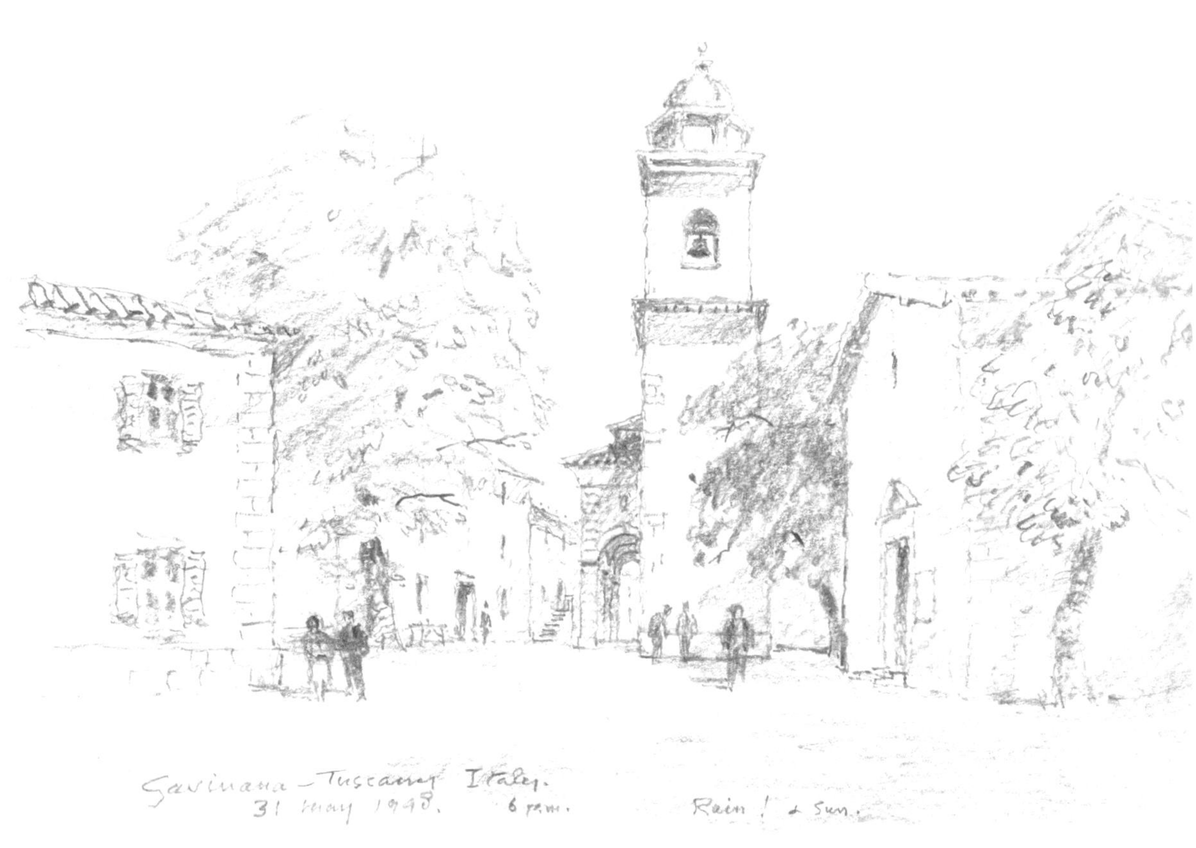
Gavinana - Tuscany, Italy.
31 May 1948.    6 p.m.    Rain! & Sun.

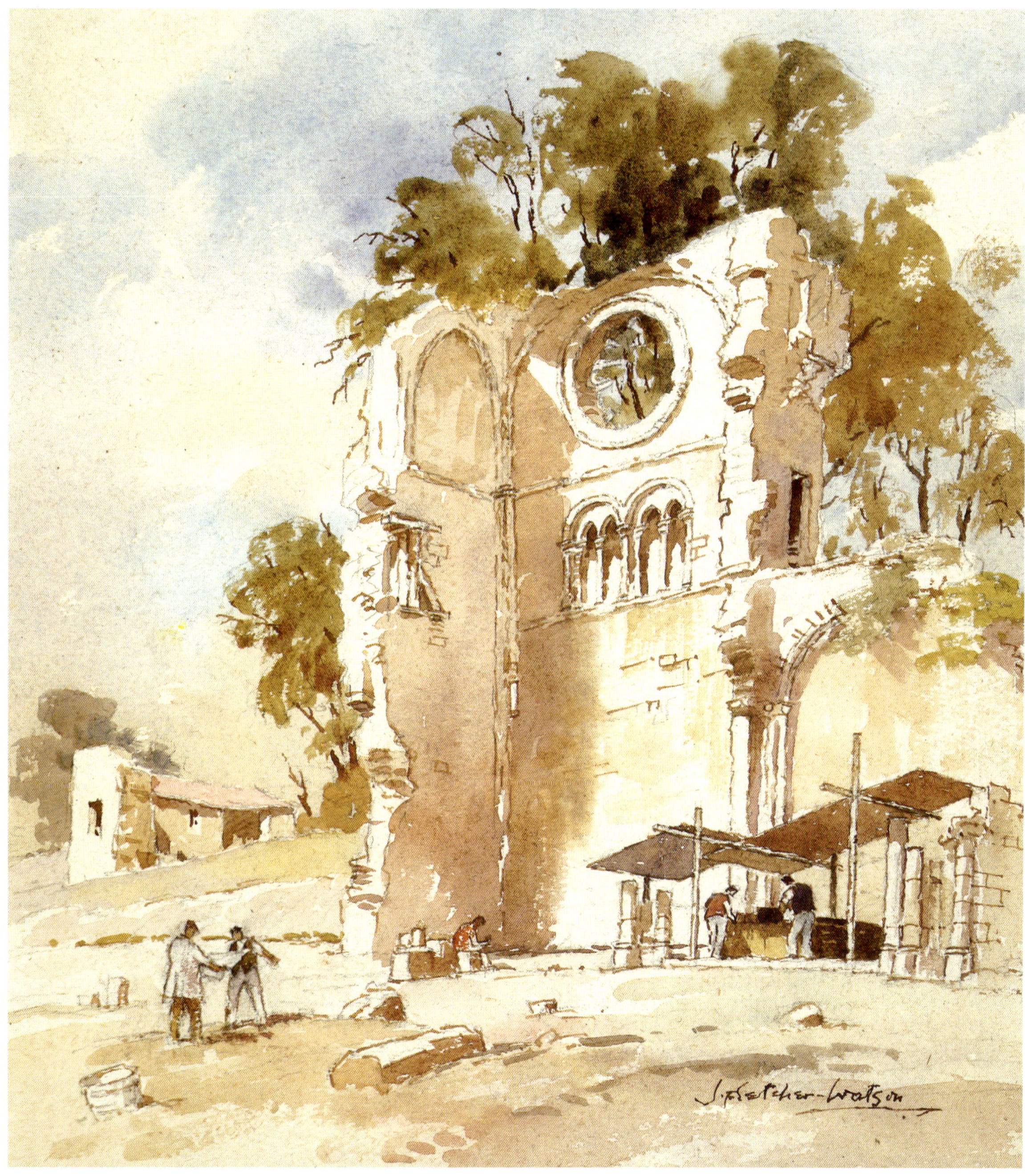

*Mortemer Abbey, Lyon le Foret, Normandy, on David Cox paper (50 years old)   12.5 x 14.5 inches*

Maison Maugis (Farm House!)
Nr Boissy Maugis – Normandy.
25th Aug 1993.    on way back after pic nic Lunch in
Belleme.
(Big wood doors in Arch way were closed before we left.!)
Plough.
5.30 pm
Brown Roofs
Cream walls
Gray soil
ploughed

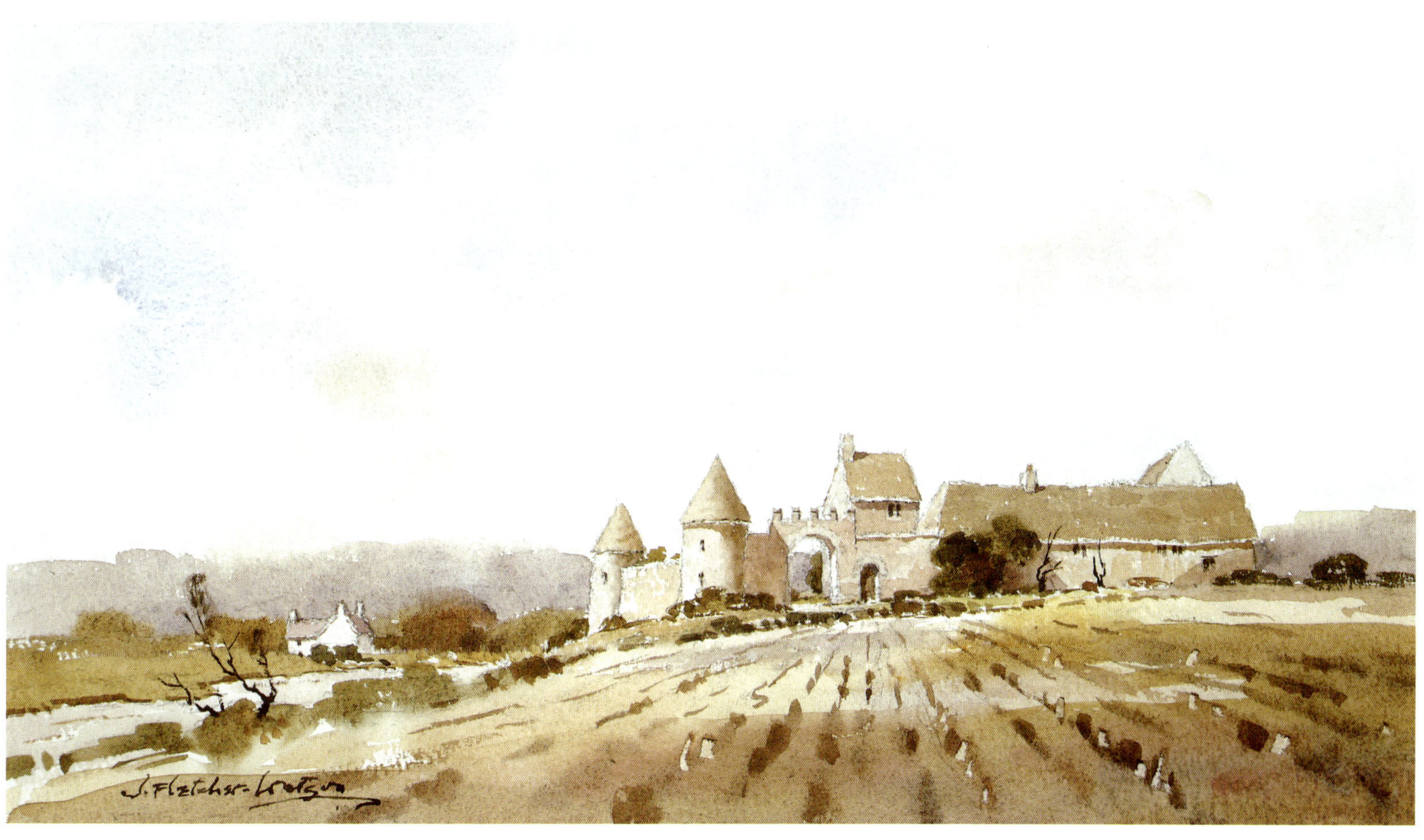

*Fortified Farm, Normandy*   *18.5 x 12.5 inches*

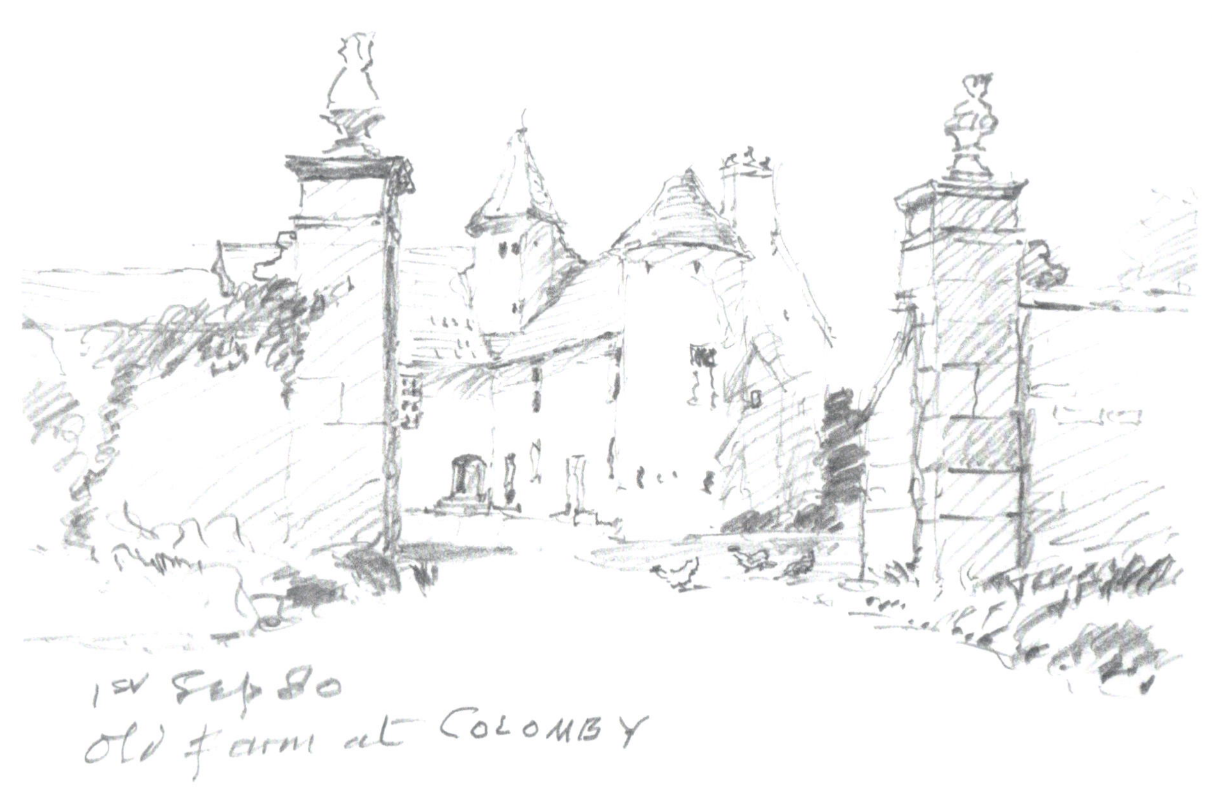



Driving through small French towns, James would suddenly shout,
'This is sheer Bonnington,' or 'Pure Callow'. An evening in the little
medieval town of Belleme produced this delightful picture (opposite).  I wonder
if the church clock still stands at ten to three!

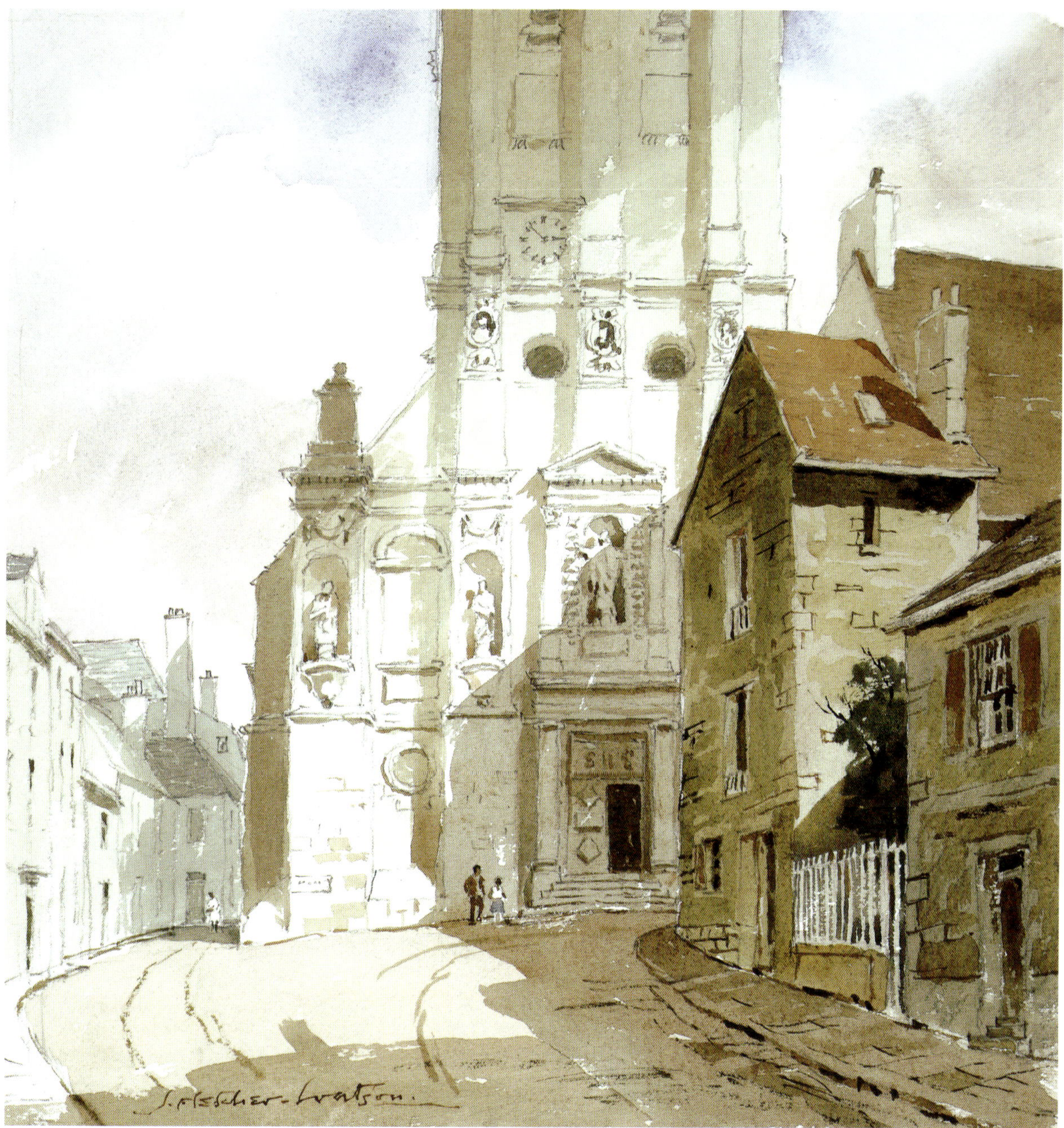

*Belleme, France   12.5 x 14.5 inches*

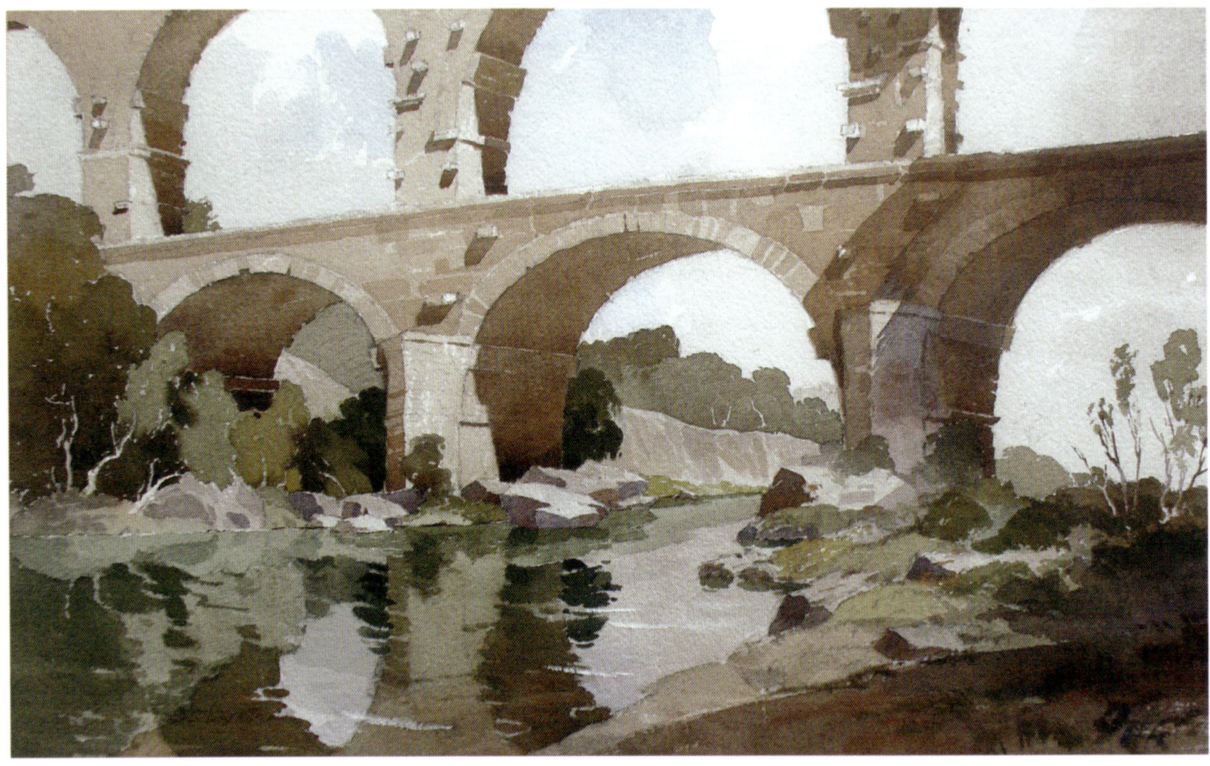

*Pont du Gard, Provence   18.5 x 12.5 inches*
*James's first view of the Pont du Gard thrilled him.  One of the greatest feats of Roman engineering, constructed in 2000BC.  He thought at first it would be a distant view, but then felt a closer view was so much more intriguing and made an exciting composition.*

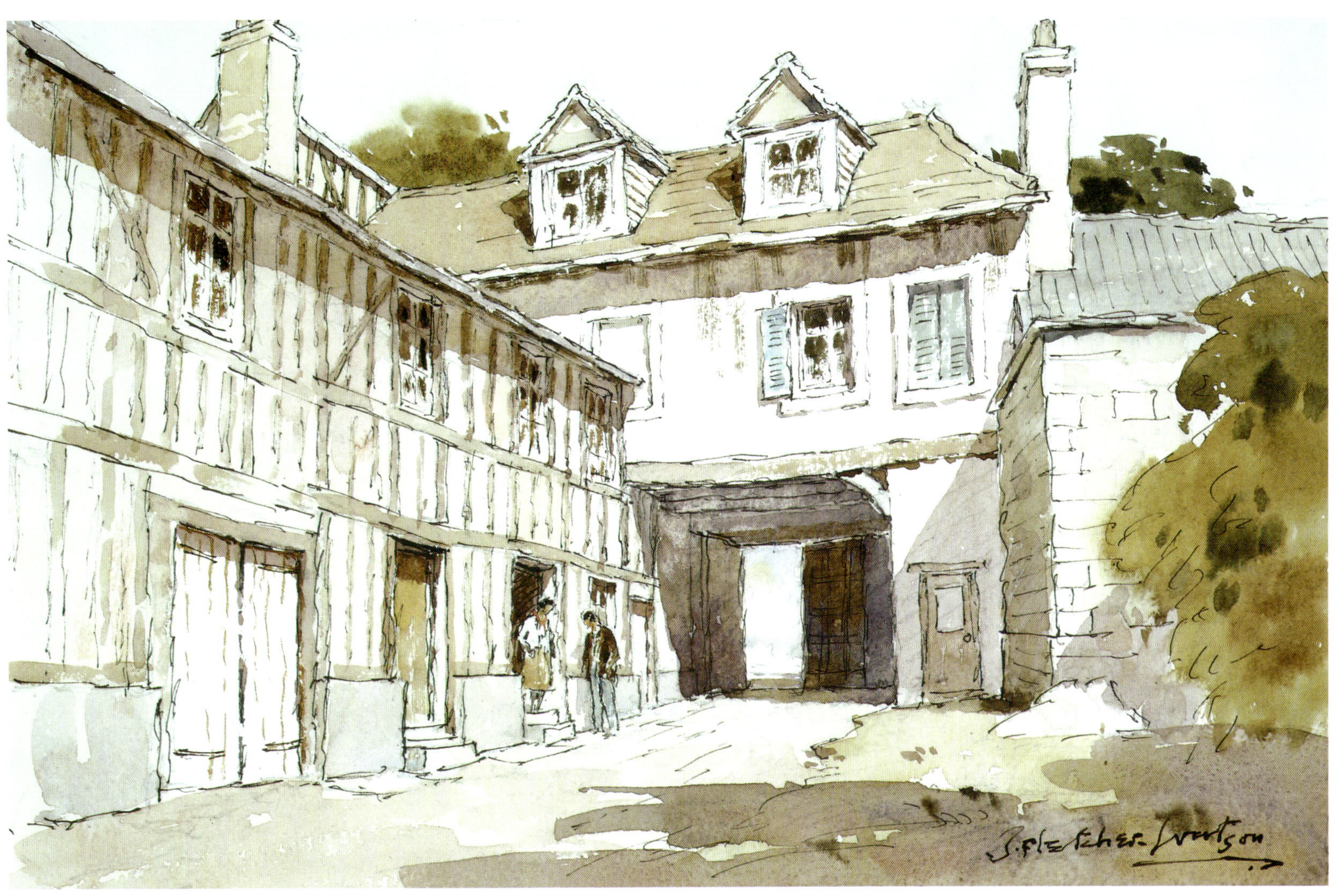

*Backyard, Normandy   14 x 10 inches*

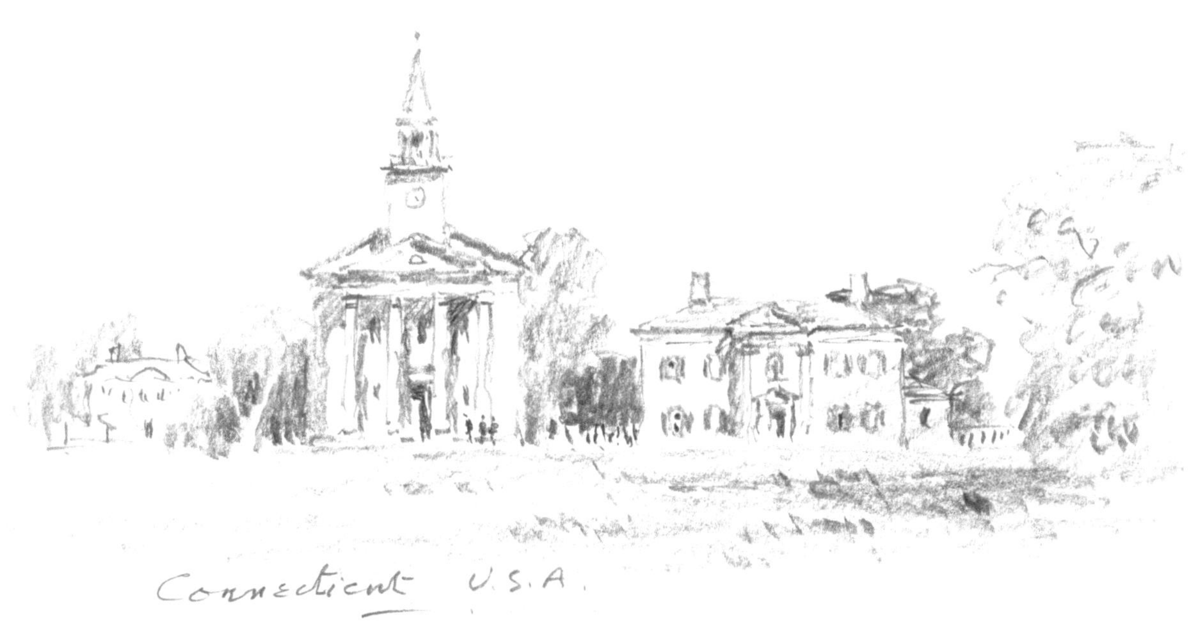

Connecticut U.S.A.

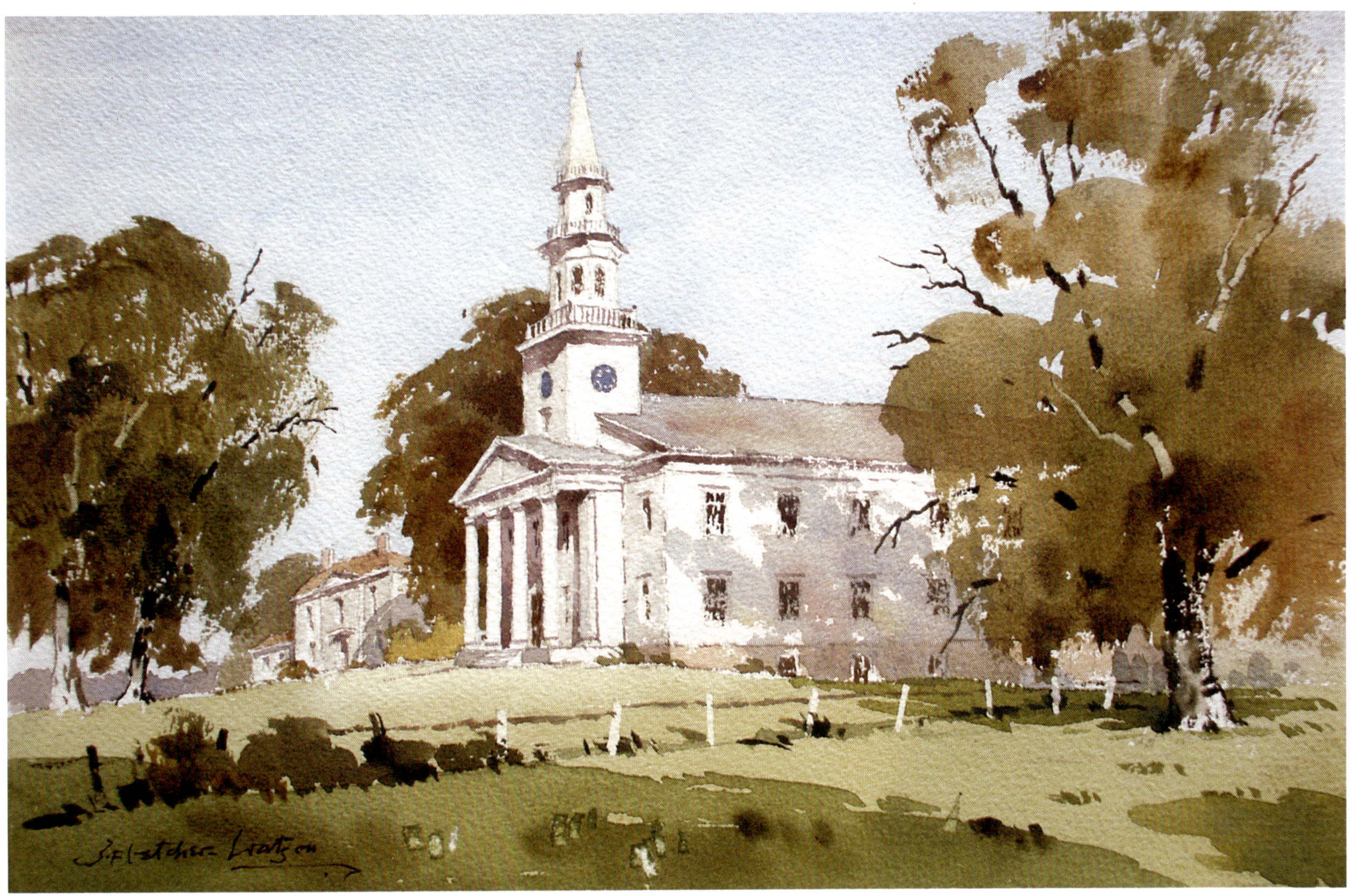

*Connecticut, USA   18.5 x 12.5 inches*

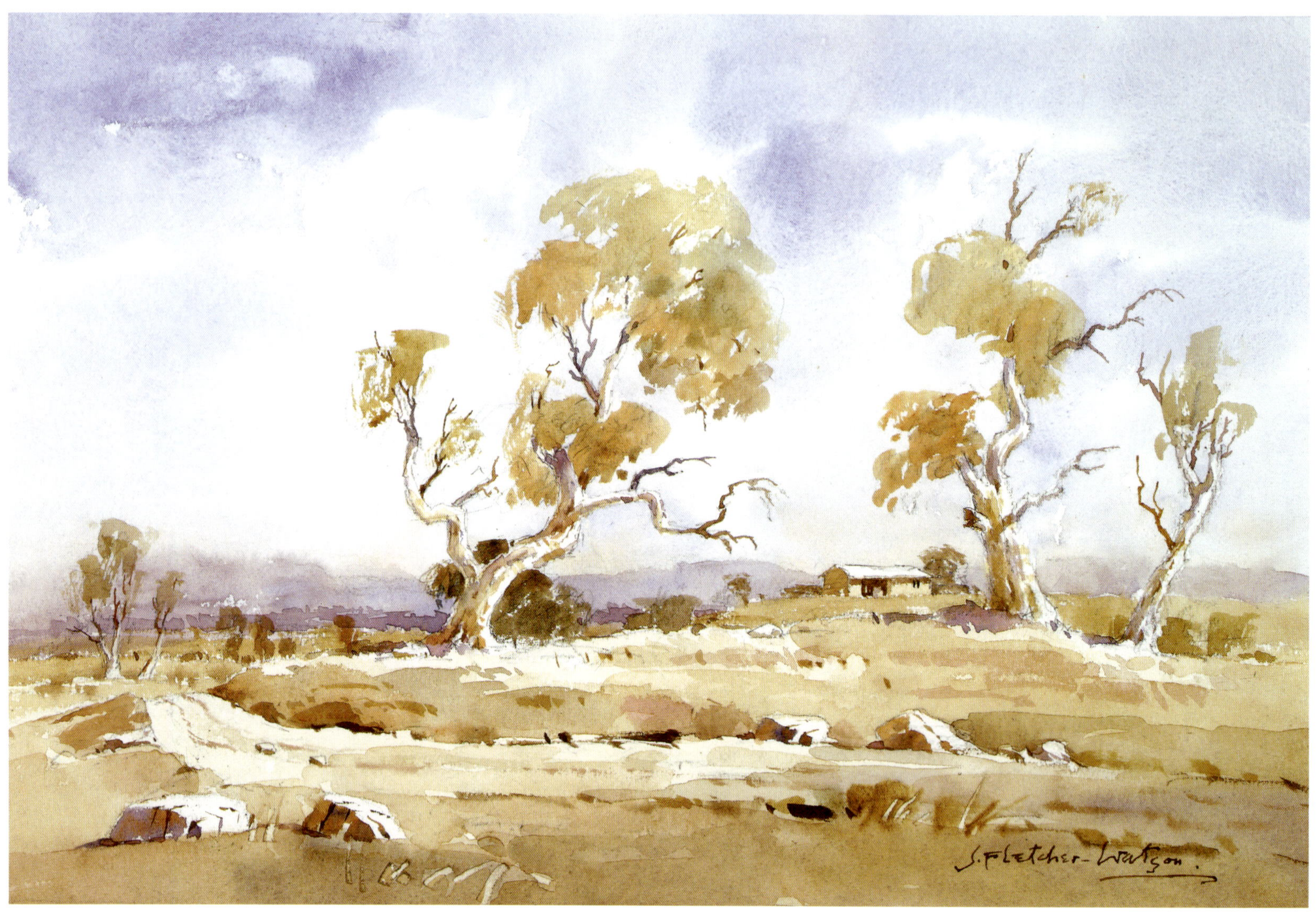

*Gum Trees, Australia    18.5 x 12.5 inches*

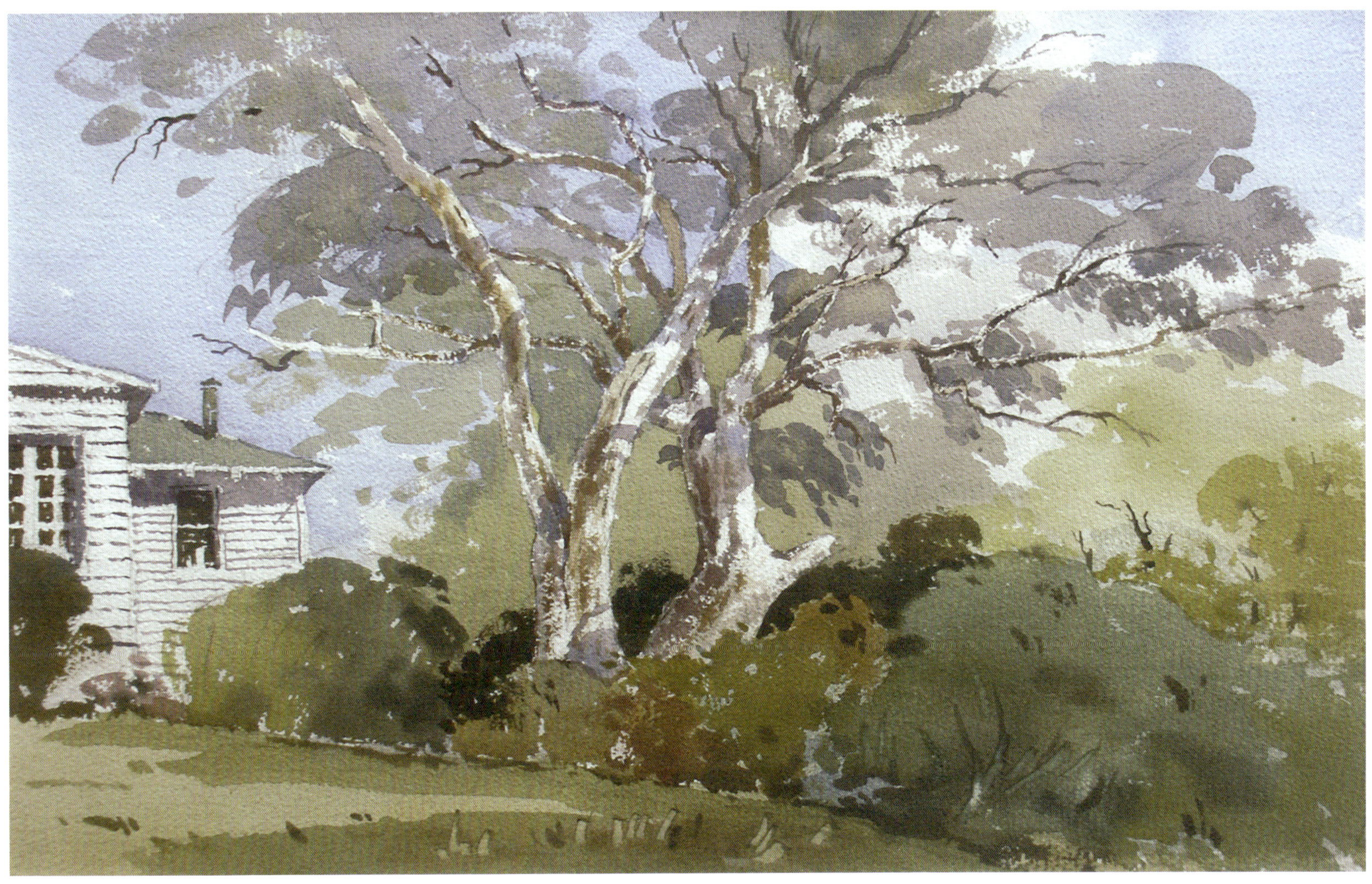

*New South Wales, Australia  18.5 x 12.5 inches*

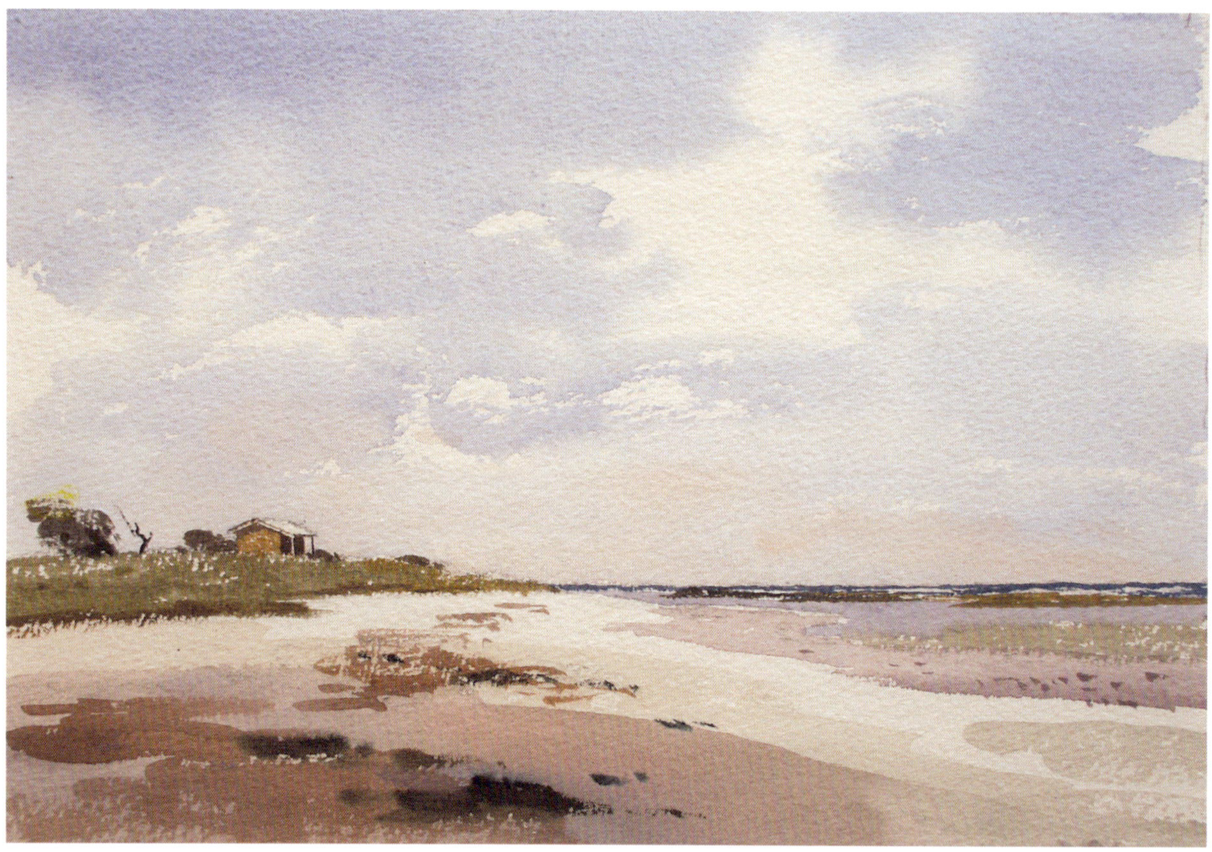

*Flinders, NSW, Australia  14 x 10 inches*

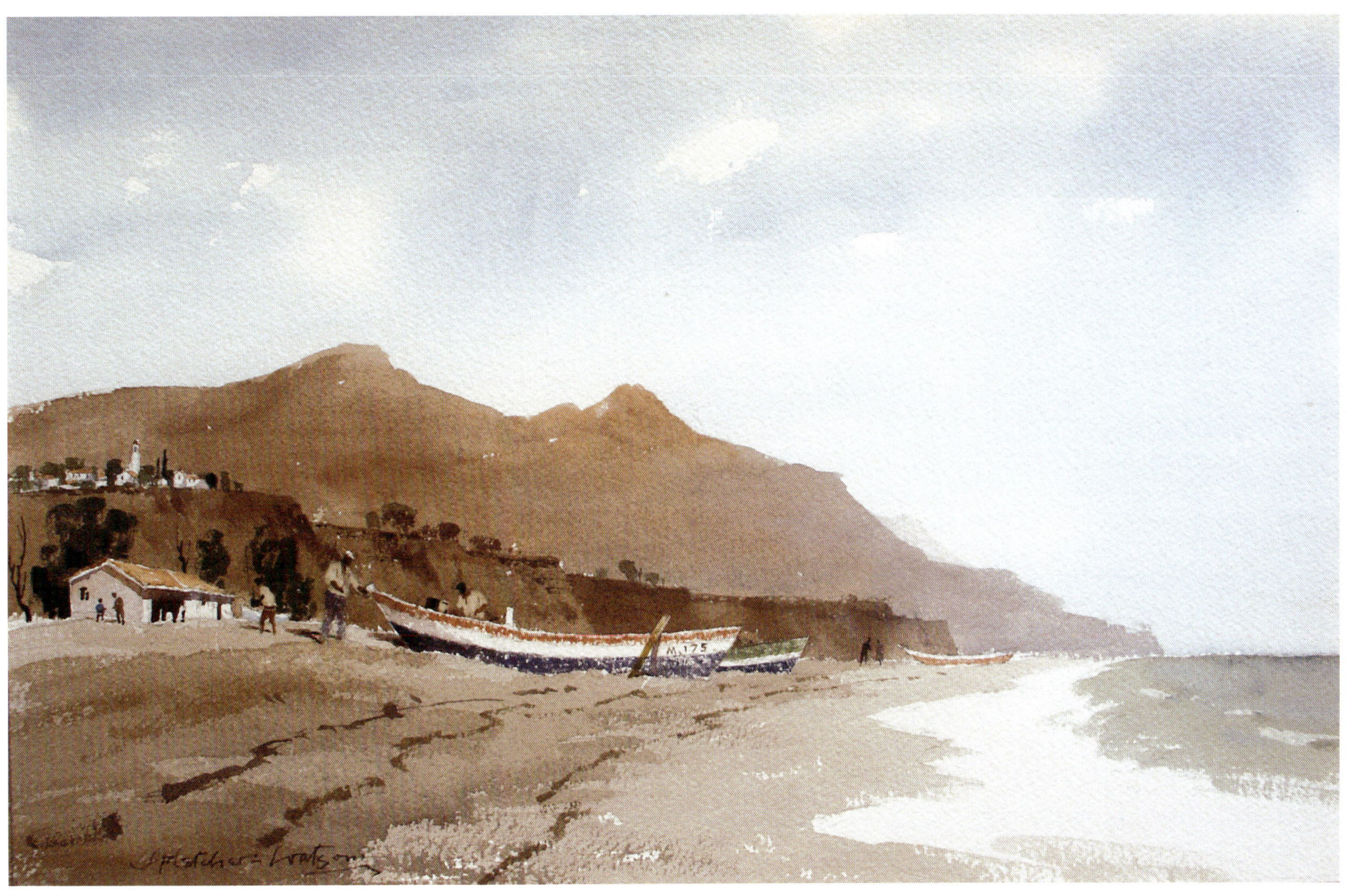

*Fishing Boats, Spain   18.5 x 12.5 inches*

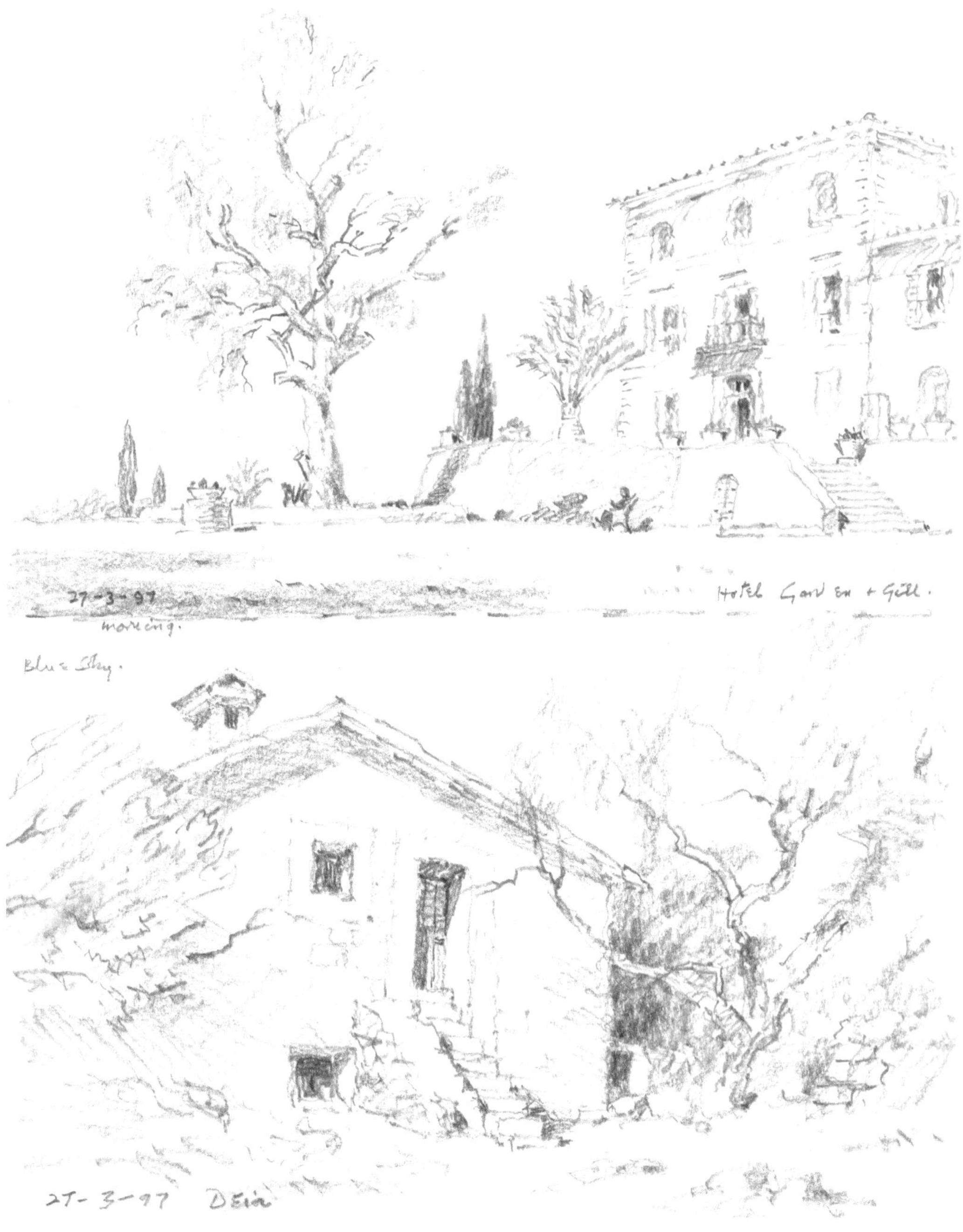
27-3-97
morning.
Blue Sky.
Hotel Garden + Grill.
27-3-97 Dein

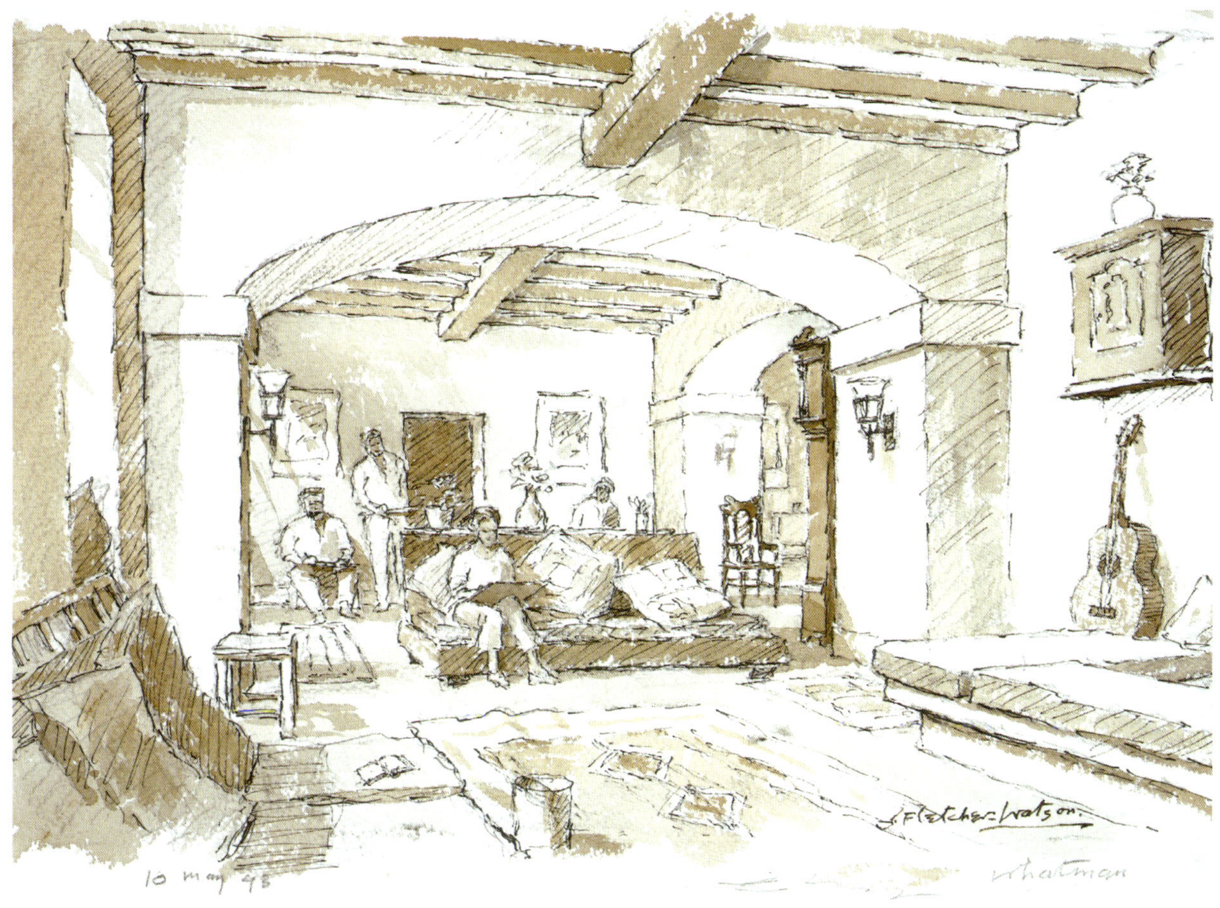

*Interior, Majorca   18.5 x 12.5 inches*
*This painting group was studying perspective, having been driven inside by rain.*

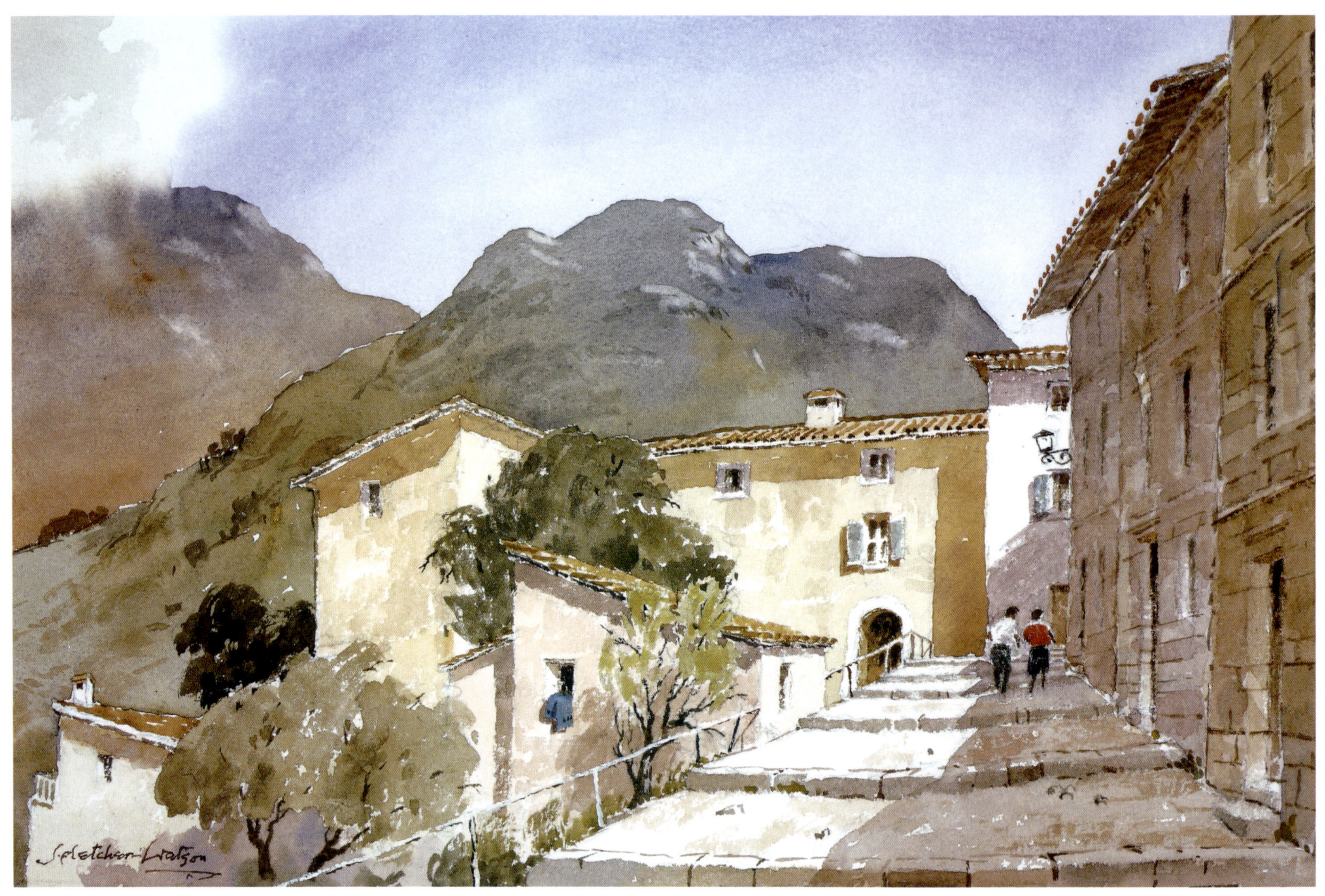

*Deia village street, Majorca   18.5 x 12.5 inches*

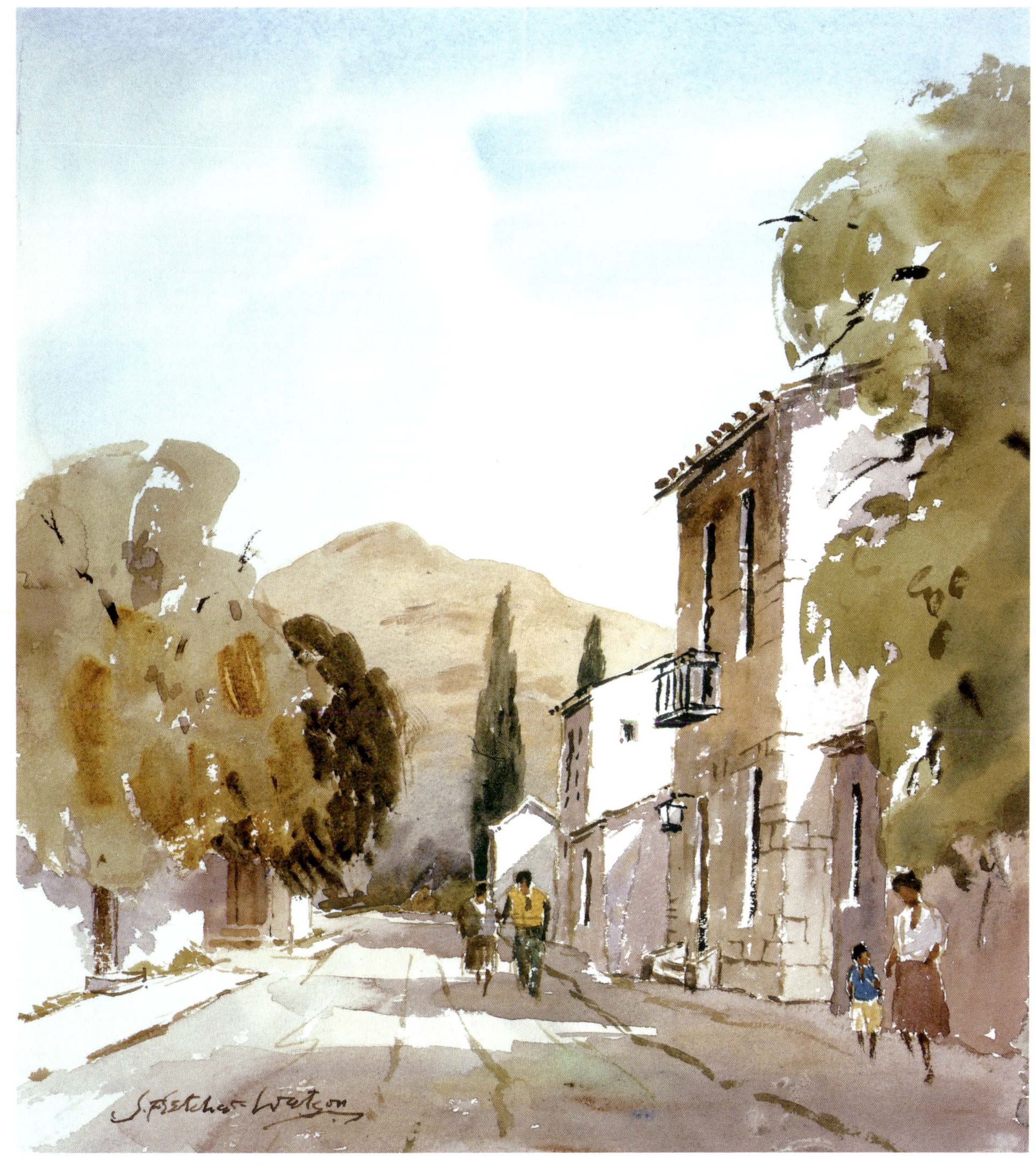

*Nerja, Southern Spain   12.5 x 14.5 inches*

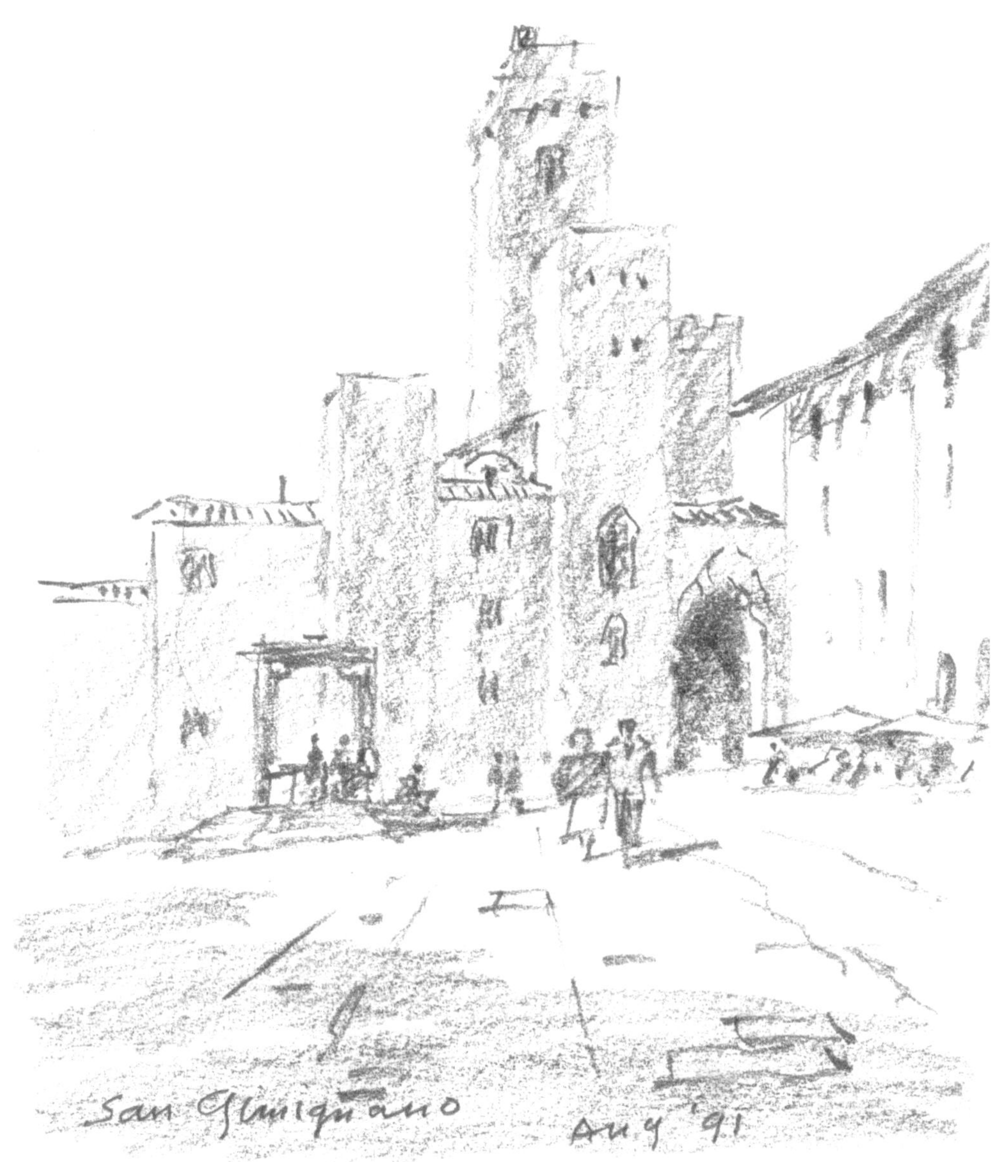
San Gimignano
Aug '91

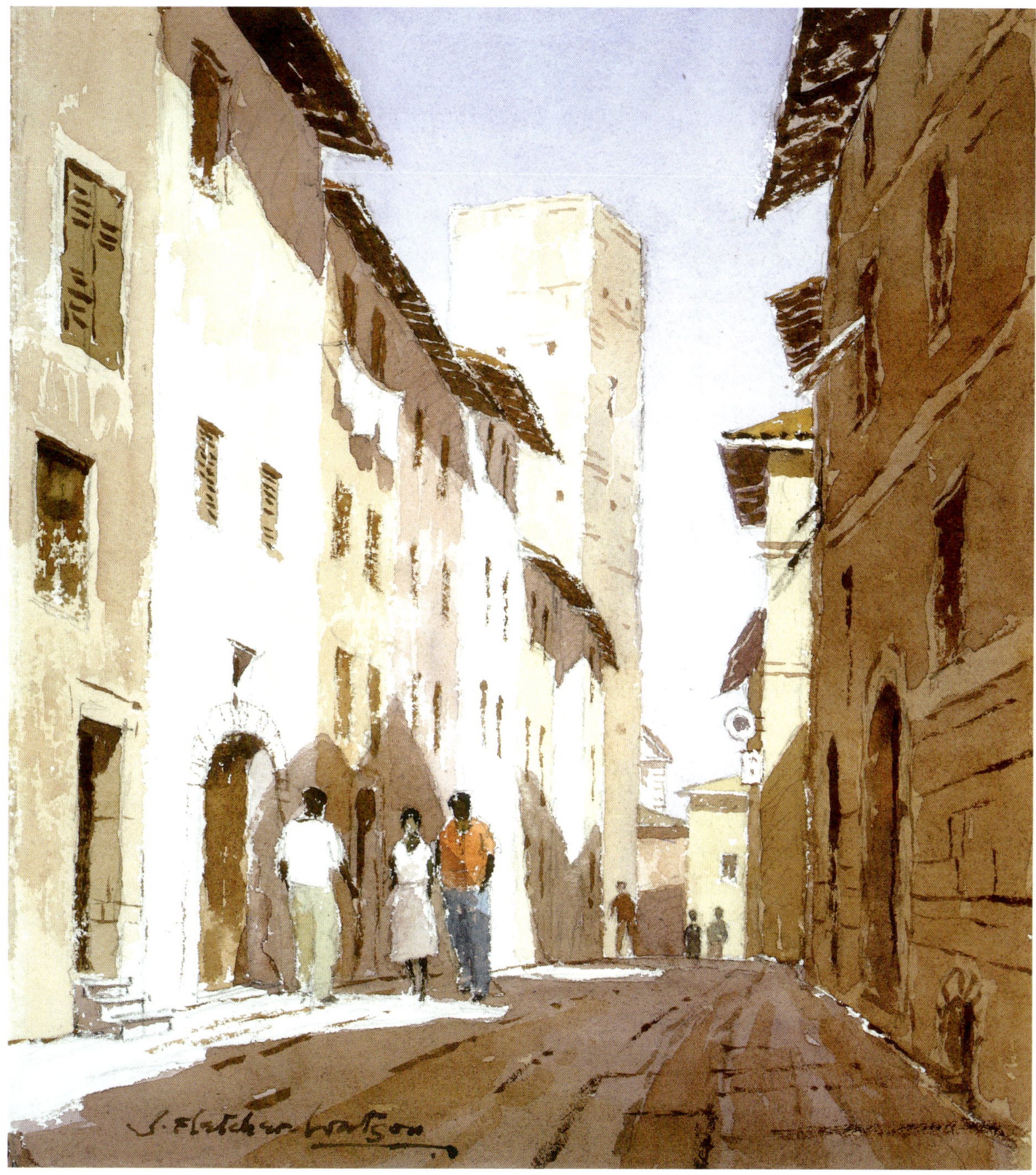

*San Gimignano, Tuscany   12.5 x 14.5 inches*

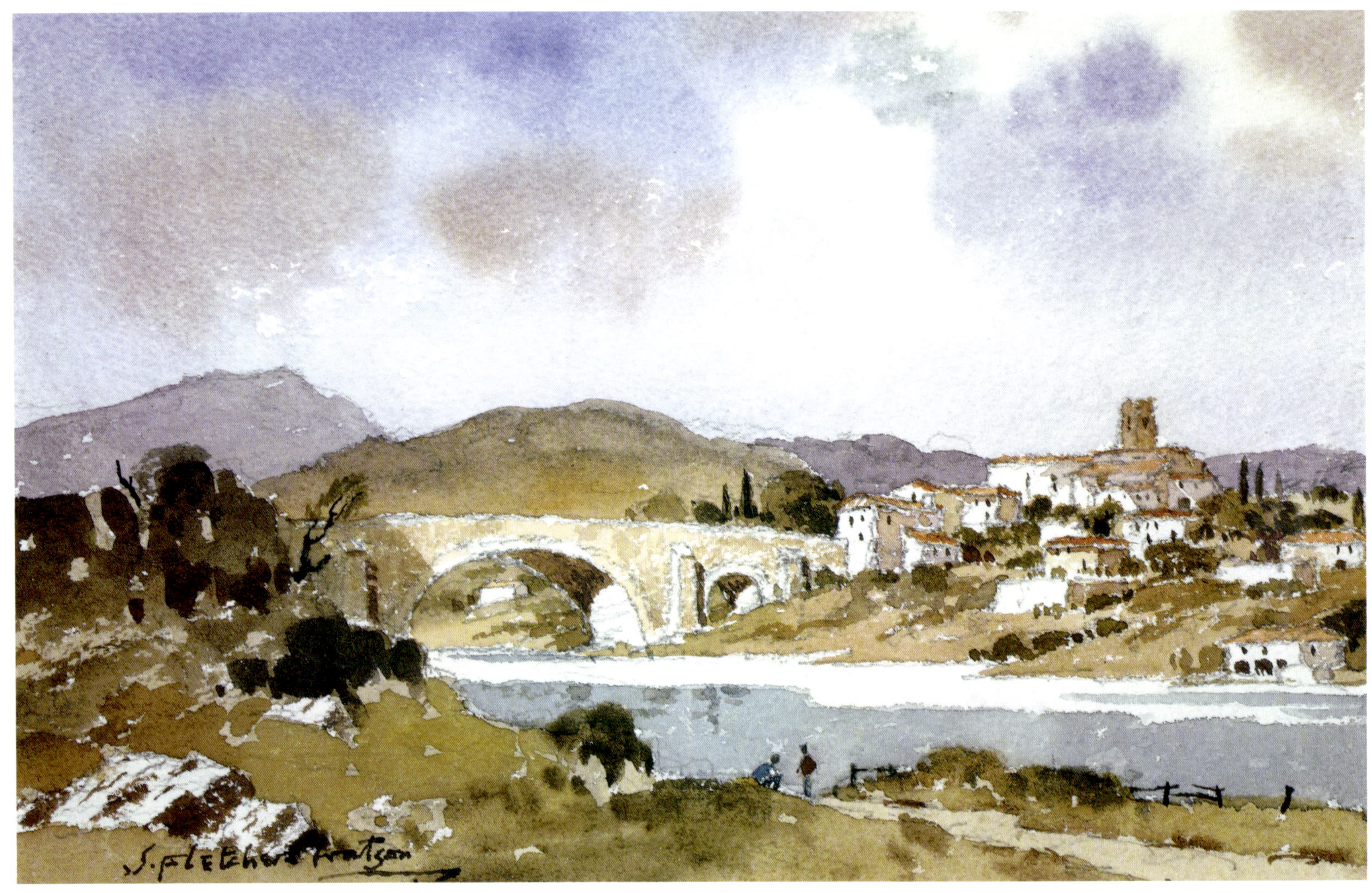

*Bridge and hill village, Spain   18.5 x 12.5 inches*
*James did the sketch for this painting from the window of a bus travelling at speed between Madrid and Burgos.*

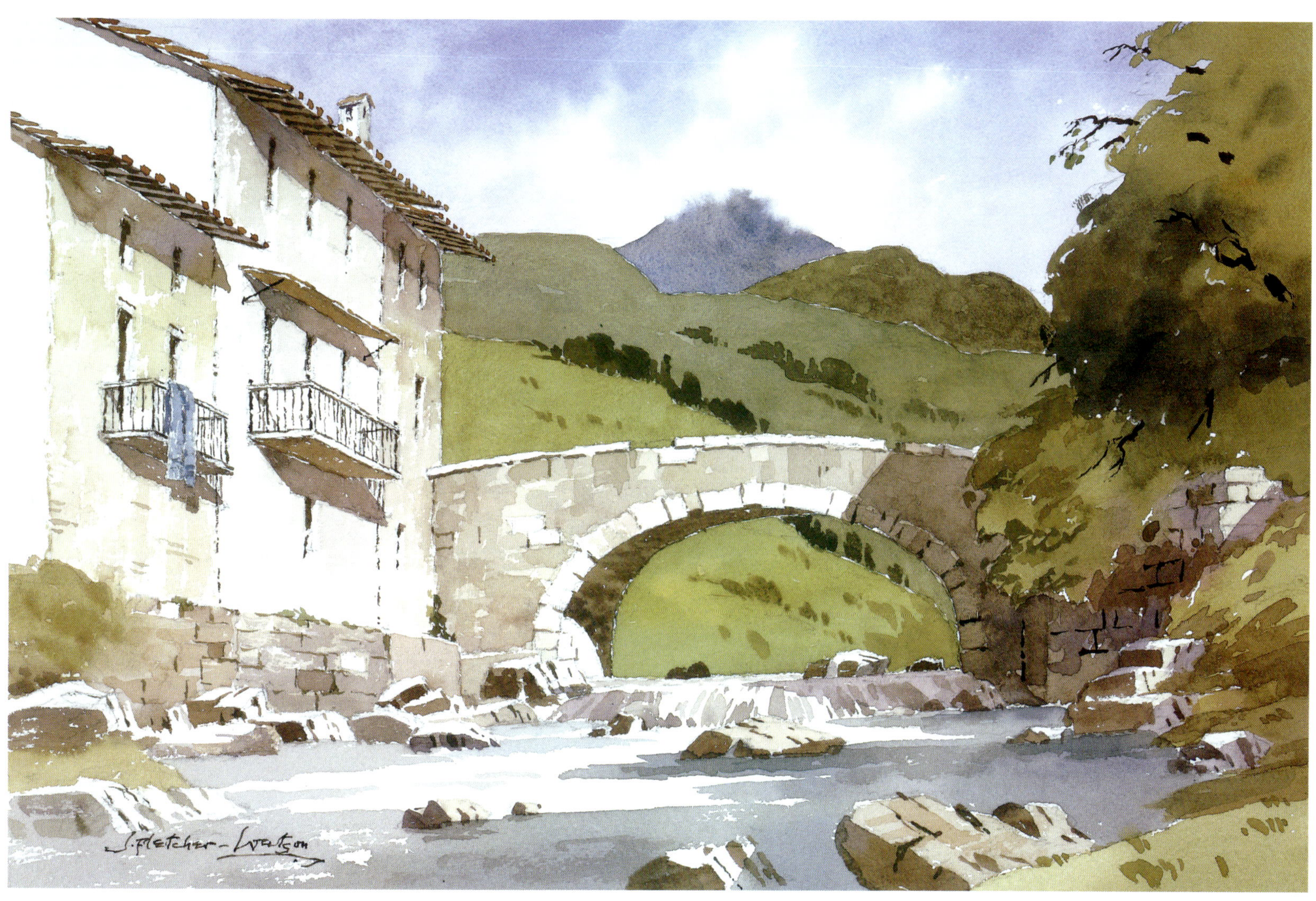

*Bridge, Regello, Tuscany   18.5 x 12.5 inches*
*The perfect subject is not always the perfect place.  The village drains were overpowering!*

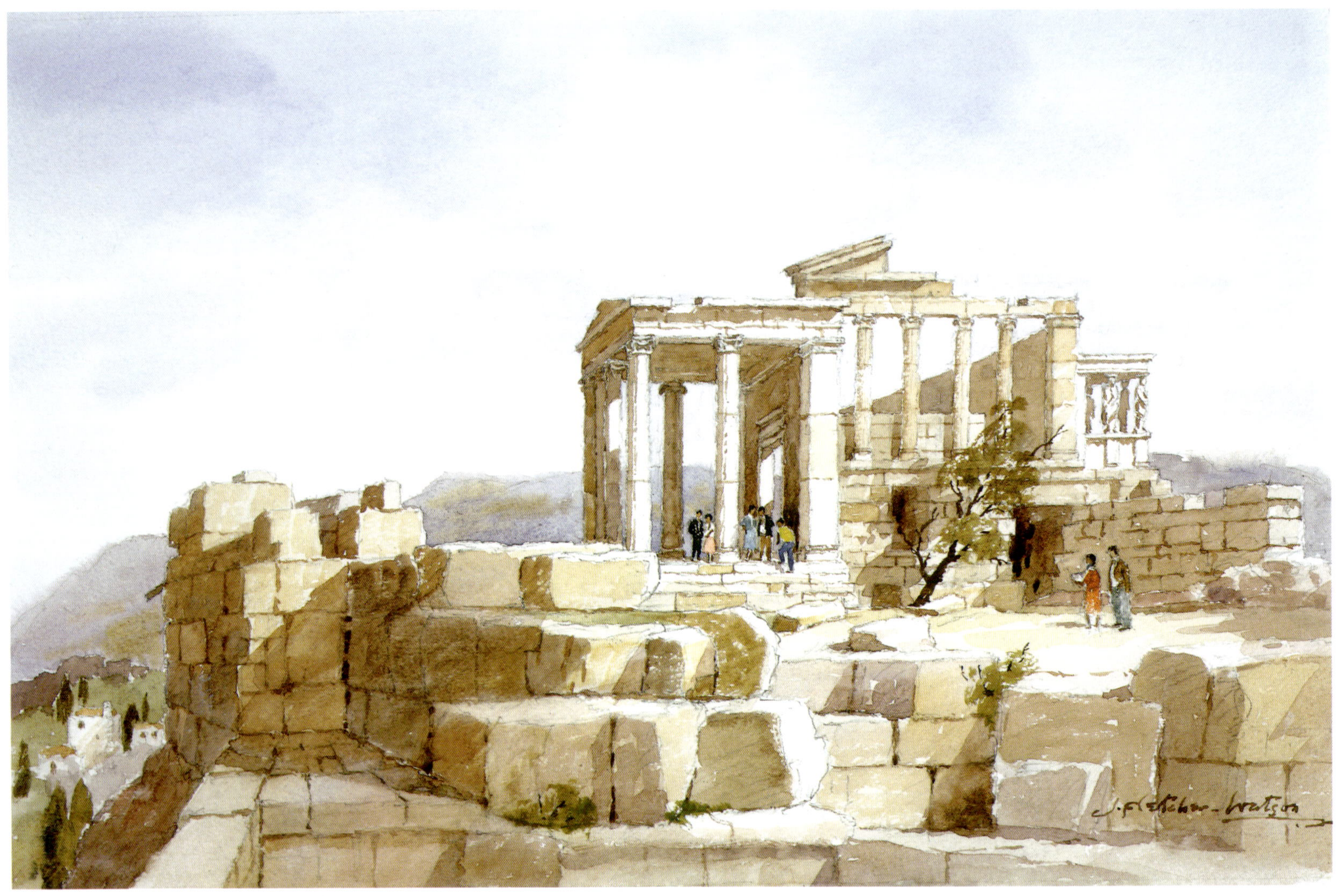

*Acropolis, Greece   18.5 x 12.5 inches*
*Painted in 1963, when there were few tourists and one could climb up to, and walk through, the Acropolis.*